ORGANIZATIONAL VALUES
IN AMERICA

ORGANIZATIONAL VALUES IN AMERICA

William G. Scott
David K. Hart

Transaction Publishers
New Brunswick (U.S.A.) and London (U.K.)

Third printing 1991
Copyright (c) 1989 by Transaction Publishers
New Brunswick, New Jersey 08903

Library of Congress Catalog Number: 88-34023
ISBN: 0-888738-279-7 (cloth);
0-88738-795-0 (paper)
Printed in the United States of America

Library of Congress Cataloging-in-Publication Data
Scott, William G.
    Organizational Values in America / William G. Scott, David K. Hart
        p. cm.
    Includes index.
    ISBN 0-88738-279-7 (cloth)
    ISBN 08-88738-795-0 (paper)
    1. Organization. 2. Organizational change--United States.
3. Social structure. 4. Social values. 5. Elite (Social sciences)--
United States. I. Hart, David K., 1933-- . II. Title.
HM131.S39   1989   88-34023
302.3'5--dc19   CIP

To our fathers
George E. Scott
and
David F. Hart

Contents

Preface   ix

1. The Surge and Decline of Organizational America   1
2. Organizational America: The Dissolution of the
   American Tradition   13
3. The Organizational Imperative   27
4. The Organizational Imperative Realized   43
5. Organizational Roles   65
6. The Insignificant People: The Strategy of Mass
   Domination   77
7. The Insignificant People: The Tactics of Mass
   Domination   97
8. The Professional People   111
9. The Significant People   129
10. The Probable Future   145
11. The Organizations of the Individual Imperative   159

Epilogue: The Requisite Conditions for a Worthy Life—
   A Dialogue   181
Index   193

Democracy has long been not only the form of government for the people of America, but a faith and an ideal, a romantic vision. This has been peculiarly our form of patriotism, our form of spiritual imperialism. The "mission of America," whether stated in religious terms or not, has been conceived as witnessing Democracy before mankind, bearing democracy's ideals of freedom and equality, and its material blessings, to the nations of the world. Belief in this mission perhaps has become less widely and intensively held during the past fifty years. Nevertheless, the romantic vision of democracy has been dimmed remarkably little by our continued experience with "realistic democracy" and realpolitik. *Of the general influence of the democratic ideal there can be no doubt.*

—Dwight Waldo,
The Administrative State (1948)

Preface

Writing a book critical of the values and ethics of American organizations is a somewhat chancy proposition when one is a professor in a management department at a university. Because all Americans are living out our lives within organizations, and because our prosperity is almost dependent upon their success, to criticize something as fundamental as their values is cutting close to the nerve. Furthermore, when one's audience consists mainly of the managerial elite who have—or soon will have—the responsibility for the care and feeding of those organizations, such criticism is about as well received as that of guests who criticize the way their hosts are raising their children. Feelings and opinions do run deep, and the way of the critic is filled with inherent risks. Nevertheless, we believe the subject is so important that we have spent two decades collaborating upon the ideas presented herein.

Those ideas first appeared in their entirety in our previous book. *Organizational America* (Boston: Houghton Mifflin, 1979). Nearly a decade later, we decided to do a new edition of the book, because both our ideas and our society had changed in very significant ways. During that interim, both of us had become more deeply involved with moral philosophy and the ethical issues of the modern organization. As we began our discussons, we quickly realized that we had to do more than revise the first book. *Organizational Values in America* emerged as a new book, the sequel to *Organizational America*.

The decision to call this book a sequel raised some ethical issues for us, because there is some carryover of material from the first book. But this is a substantially different book from the first: new chapters have been written, and much of the remaining content has been significantly changed. Moreover, the tone of this book is different. It is more of one cloth than the first volume, and it reflects a somewhat more optimistic view about the future of our nation. After nearly ten years of reflecting about "organizational America," we have come to the belief that it is possible for individuals to transcend the imperatives of the modern organization, and that totalitarianism is not our inevitable destination.

It has been a most interesting journey. Our collaboration first began in the late 1960s with a continuing series of conversations about the kind of nation that would be appropriate for Americans in the last part of the twentieth century. There was a real urgency to those discussions, conducted as they were against the backdrop of Vietnam, campus riots, and urban violence. It seemed to many that the national fabric was unraveling, and that drastic, even draconian, measures might have to be employed to reverse the process. However, since we were then professors in the School of Business Administration at the University of Washington in Seattle, it was not surprising that our attention was not riveted upon the politicians, generals, and students who occupied center stage. Rather, in those tumultuous times, our attention kept returning to the managers of the large organizaitons, both public and private. We were concerned with the essential role they would play in ushering us all into the twenty-first century.

The discussions led to numerous conference papers, articles and, eventually, to the book, *Organizational America*. From our academic work and our practical experience, in both business and politics, it was clear to us that modern organizational theory and practice was based upon *implicit* values that were optimal for organizational maintenance, but that contradicted the *explicit* values upon which the nation was predicated. Because we believed those explicit values—the Founding values—were essentially correct, the resulting confusion blighted individual growth and development. Thus, our book was quite pessimistic.

By the time that volume was published in late 1979, the turmoil of the days of Vietnam and Watergate were rapidly becoming ancient history. The 1980s have separated us even further from the raw emotions of those turbulent years of dissent and confrontation. It is now hard to recall how we all felt. The Vietnam War is so far behind us that it has become both respectable and very profitable to produce novels, television series, and movies about it.

Furthermore, the passionate, young, radical superstars of the earlier era have now faded into middle age: some into high society; a few into religion; while the rest have simply disappeared into the bowels of modern organizations. Their causes have been largely forgotten, while they themselves have been replaced by a new generation of conservative, ahistorical, money-oriented young people who seek their rewards and salvations within the organizations of contemporary America. These passings have confirmed what we argued: *the years of dissent served primarily to increase the hold of the modern organization upon us all.*

America has undergone a profound transformation since those radical days of the late 1960s and early 1970s, but in ways that few anticipated and for reasons that had little to do with the pressing issues of those times. During those dramatic years of dazzling surface changes, one institution remained stable, provided continuity, and in so doing grew even more powerful—the modern organization. The major fact of American life in the 1980s has been the continued consolidation of the power of the modern organization. Even more disturbing, as the power of the managerial elite has grown, their ethical standards have steadily declined. Granted, there are many honorable men and women who are in positions of leadership, but too many of the others regularly and depressingly violate even minimal standards of trust, decency, and stewardship.

This continued growth of the modern organization in America, along with the steady erosion of our national ethics, became the subject of most of our public presentations, classes, and published work during the 1980s. In particular, we concentrated more upon the quality of moral life within modern organizations, developing our ideas of what constituted a "worthy life" in organizational America. Many of the notions in the first book—among them the insensitivity of management to value questions and the pivotal concept of "the organizational imperative" were debated, refined, and redeveloped. As this new phase of our collaboration progressed, it became increasingly obvious that the central problem in contemporary American is *the replacement of the Founding values by the values of the modern organization*. Dealing with this problem led to the birth of the present book.

The most destructive ethical problem in America today is not insider trading, or influence peddling—it is the corrosive influence of managerial power upon all those who work in organizations, whether in the private or the public sectors. There is an irony here. Successful organizational leaders publicly attest to the sanctity of the ennabling documents, from the Declaration of Independence to the Constitution. They praise the Founders for their defence of liberty and justice in the face of tyranny and recommend the Founding value to all peoples. They do so, for the most part, in good faith.

Yet many of those same leaders preside over organizations that are, bluntly, tyrannical, with hierarchical power structures and nary a sign of democracy in internal operations. If employees object, they are told to ship out: freedom apparently means only the right to leave. No one seems particularly concerned with the huge gap between the professions of allegiance to the Founding values and the standard operating procedures of our organizations. Apparently those values are only relevant in off-hours. That is not what the Founders had in mind.

Conventional wisdom has it that management is all about human *behavior*, which leaves the values of the individual untouched. To the contrary, we argue that organizational theory and practice is intentionally aimed at controlling organizational personnel, most particularly the managers, through controlling their *values*. The premise is: if you control the values, the behavior will follow. We refer to the moral justification of this process as "the organizational imperative" and argue that it undermines both the Founding values and the essential pluralism of our nation. We contend that the organizational imperative has become the dominant influence upon American values. The result is the increasing homogenization of the American people, which facilitates organizational control through an interlocking system of elite managers.

Sadly, most of the managerial elite are guided by no principles more noble than maintaining the health of their organizations. And if, perchance, the

Founding values should get in the way of the organizational status quo, then they will be dumped as quickly as an insubordinate employee. The evidence is all around us. As this preface is being written, the world is in a furor caused by the Ayatollah Khomeini's contract on the life of the British novelist, Salman Rushdie. The lethal pot was even sweetened with a few million dollars in bounty money. Rushdie's sin: a satirical novel, *The Satanic Verses*, which the Ayatollah decided was blasphemous.

The response to this outrage by the political leaders of the free world was feckless, of course: moral courage has fallen out of favor in out time. But it was the response of the heads of three of the largest American bookstore chains that caught our attention: they immediately pulled the books from their shelves. In simple terms, they censored Rushdie. They offered excuses, of course. The major one was the protection of their customers and their employees, but that really didn't wash. At about the same time, terrorists had bombed an air liner and were threatening more attacks. Of course, the airlines did not stop flying. It would be nice to think that moral courage motivated the decision, but it was more likely brute economics. They increased security, and kept on flying.

The point with the bookstore chains is that their leadership had no apparent compunction about this form of book burning. Evidently, nowhere in their training did they learn that there was a sacred obligation in their profession: that freedom of speech and press is the sine qua non of democracy. As booksellers, they should have been aware of that obligation, which was contained in the books they sold: from Marcus Aurelius's appreciation of Severus for acquainting him "with the conception of a community based on equality and freedom of speech for all . . . ," to Thomas Jefferson's criticism of the British king, made "with that freedom of language and sentiment which becomes a free people claiming their rights, as derived from the laws of nature, and not as the gift of their chief magistrate." To choose to sell books is to assume the moral obligation, in all instances, of defending the right to freedom of expression.

But all that was apparently fluffy stuff, found only in books, which no longer meant anything to those who had chosen to sell books. Books are products, no more, no less. As the leaders of bookselling businesses, their primary moral imperative was to maintain the health of their organizations and show a profit. Later, some of the book chains recanted, but evidently not upon principle. In the media accounts, they cited that their customers seemed to want the books. And so it was revealed that the profession of bookseller had no unique moral obligation because it was not different from any other business selling any other product. We can think of no recent example that more clearly demonstrates our thesis that the organizational imperative has triumphed over the Founding values.

But there are glimmers of hope, here and there. While we still hold to the central premises of the earlier argument, we have been profoundly impressed with the possibilities of individual action based upon commitment to humane values. *Organizational America* was both pessimistic and deterministic; our reappraisal is less deterministic, which makes it much more optimistic. We believe that key executives, acting as autonomous moral agents, can beat the organizational imperative. Our previous mistake was to argue that the organizational imperative was virtually the sole motivation for managerial action. This was an oversimplification, even though most managers serve that imperative most of the time. The irony of our re-evaluation is that it was the influence of miscreant managers that brought to our attention the power of individual action, in confrontation with the seemingly implacable force of the organizational imperative. If the individual can defy the organization for ill, then the individual can also defy it for good. In spite of all the pressures to the contrary, the worthy life can be achieved within modern organizations.

As we wrote preliminary drafts, and argued with each other—often with considerable intensity—about the nature of the worthy life, we became more confident that our assessment is correct. Although we are not overly optimistic about the future of our nation, we do not believe that we are caught in an inescapable vortex pulling us down into a predetermined totalitarian society. To that end, this book emphasizes the importance of the moral character of managers and the extreme importance of managerial moral heroism.

While some of our more enthusiastic critics have placed us at the extremes of an ideological continuum, from crypto-fascists to neo-Marxists, neither identification is correct. It is our most fundamental belief that nothing is worthwhile in this world that does not enhance the moral character and autonomy of individuals. Anything less than a free and open society, which makes such moral enhancement possible, is unacceptable. Furthermore, we believe that such a society is still possible if we honor, in belief and practice, the Founding values upon which this nation is predicated. While we cannot expect all of our readers to agree with us, it is our hope that the book will make clearer the lethal dangers that come from muddling along with the status quo.

At this point, we will step away from the argument to acknowledge some important debts. Our collaboration has always been based upon close friendship, shared humor and a willingness to disagree with each other. Our backgrounds are different, and so we drew upon a wide and varied literature as we hammered out our ideas. Our appreciations were many in the first book, and we still thank those individuals and organizations. But we have also incurred new debts that we happily acknowledge here. We greatly appreciate the constant support of Professor Dwight Waldo. Long before us, he wrote about the significance of organizational and administrative values as they pertain to the essential questions of who should rule, and what constitutes the worthy life in

America. Also, Professor H. George Frederickson, the Edwin O. Stene Professor of Public Administration, University of Kansas, has provided constant friendship and intellectual challenge.

Many other friends have been most helpful. In particular, Bill Scott would like to thank Terence R. Mitchell, the Edward Carlson Professor of Management, Graduate School of Business Administration, University of Washington. Kirk Hart would like to thank Menlo Smith, for his great generosity; J. David Billeter, for his constant support of the ethics program; N. Dale Wright, for walking miles beyond the second; and James D. Hart, who prevents things from going supernova with reminders of an actual world. Both of us wish to thank the people at Transaction Books: Irving Louis Horowitz, Mary Curtis, and Esther Luckett, in particular, have been extremely helpful and supportive.

There are some special associations that enhanced this sequel. First, Ms Krista West, of the Institute of Public Management at Brigham Young University and the Virginia Polytechnic Institute, has been the voice of sanity and organization. She has been research assistant, editor, colleague, and friend. Her contributions have been "massive." Had we the money, Krista, we would equip your car with a computer that would find any airport in the country.

Second, Cary D. Wasden, of the Institute of Public Management at Brigham Young University, has worked long and hard on computers and duplicating machines, getting the manuscript ready to go. In the final revision, a computer "virus" struck through the electrons and consumed huge chunks of each chapter (salvation lies in the backup disks!). Cary isolated and defeated the villain, and then carried the manuscript through to completion.

Finally, in the first book, the epilogue was entitled "The Requisite Conditions for Human Happiness." In the sequel, it is entitled "The Requisite Conditions for a Worthy Life." The larger problem we now address is how individuals can live virtuously and freely within modern organizations. Our friendship with Professor David L. Norton, Department of Philosophy, University of Delaware, has sharpened our ideas on these matters. His brilliant book, *Personal Destinies* (Princeton: Princeton University Press, 1976), has been a major source for our understanding of the individual imperative, as it is manifested in the development of moral character and moral autonomy.

Last of all, we concluded the preface in the first book with the comment: "Thank you, Mary Poppins, wherever you are." That still holds, but now a question must be raised: "Why Deer Lodge, Ashley Wilkes?"

W.G.S.
D.K.H.

1

The Surge and Decline of Organizational America

> *The clash between the individual and contrived social systems is permanent and inevitable.*
>
> —A. G. Ramos,
> *The New Science of Organization*

The Rise of the American Juggernaut

The twentieth century has been rightfully termed "the American Century." It has been shaped in form and substance by the boisterous successes of the United States. America has crashed through traditional customs like a bright and glittering juggernaut. Following the van—loud, rambunctious, and arrogant—Americans have swept over the globe like a triumphant army and the world has changed accordingly. In response, all nations, even those that hate us, have struggled to emulate our material achievements. This is understandable, for the conditions of those successes are also the conditions for real national power.

The centuries have seen many nations surge to international dominance. But the American rise has been significantly different, because it came from organizational ability rather than from force of arms. Even more important has been the desire of most American leaders to use their power to improve the material lot of the ordinary citizens of the nation. In that they have been largely successful, perhaps even too successful. As de Tocqueville observed so many years ago: "The love of well-being has now become the predominant taste of the nation; the great current of human passions runs in that channel and sweeps everything along in its course."[1]

Granted, our claims of triumph must be tempered, for our present station has not been attained unsullied. Too often we have forgotten the ideals of our founding and have been guilty of terrible mistakes, inexcusable oversights,

1

and even gross injustices. Thus, we have given those whose vision is constricted by their hatred of all things American reason to use the phrase "the American Century" as an epithet. But they are wrong, for arguably more good than ill has been achieved by the American endeavor: unmatched political freedoms, unimagined opportunities for personal development, and a global generosity unparalleled in human history. For all its faults, the United States has set a worthy example for the peoples of the world.

This has been recognized by most fair-minded people. In his final, poignant essay, the South African novelist, Alan Paton, reminisced about an electrifying moment in a seminar with Reinhold Niebuhr. Niebuhr deplored the lost appreciation of the moral obligations of freedom, particularly in the United States. He then took his audience off-guard:

> He did this with a kind of somber gravity that certainly subdued his audience, and then inflicted on them a heavy blow by saying fiercely of American society, "It's a mess." We were silent, feeling that the world was beyond redemption, when—after a pause—he suddenly said to us with equal emphasis, "But I like it." It brought down the house, and we felt that there was hope for the world after all.[2]

It was an appropriate evaluation.

Scholars the world around have tried to account for the American Century, but even the most ardent of the watchers failed to grasp the primary reason for the triumph. The main instrument of our successes in this century has been neither our military prowess nor our wealth, but our most successful social invention: the modern organization. In short, we managed our way to the top. Thus, while other nations have often borrowed our technology, they have not had comparable success, for the simple reason that they failed to borrow the managerial theory and practice that put it all into motion. The nations that understood the preeminence of management and organization in their national life are those that now competitively challenge us.

Some will argue with our claim that the modern organization is a new invention. After all, were there not organizations in advanced societies, from ancient China to contemporary America? In a minor sense, those critics are correct, for organizations of a sort have always been with us. But they fail to see that the modern organization is sui generis—a form unique in human history. By "modern organization" we mean a great deal more than simply large institutions in the modern age. *Modern organizations are managerial systems, using universal behavioral techniques and communication technologies, to integrate individuals and groups into mutually reinforcing, cooperative relationships.* These relationships are designed by management to increase the effectiveness of organizations in achieving their goals in harmony with advancing technology.

At the center of the definition is the phrase "universal behavioral techniques"; these are *the techniques, drawn from the behavioral sciences and instructed by humanistic psychology, used to obtain obedience to managerial instruction.* This means that modern organization is as modern as the behavioral sciences, which arose in the latter nineteenth century. These sciences were not adapted to management purposes until well into the twentieth century; but when they were they added a dimension to the power of managers that previous rulers had not enjoyed.

Three points, then, need to be emphasized. First, these techniques are universal because they are based upon behavioral characteristics common to all human beings. Thus, they cut across organizational boundaries, making management in the public sector comparable to management in the private sector. Second, the techniques are a means of power because they are used to obtain obedience. Third, these techniques are aimed — ultimately — at altering the values of individuals and the cultures of organizations, on the premise that if the values can be controlled, the desired behaviors will follow, almost automatically.

We must add another term, identifying those who wield this new power: "the national managerial system." Modern organizations are run by a class of professional managers, all schooled in the same organizational values. *The national managerial system is a vast complex of interlocking organizations, managed by people sharing a common set of values, that provide institutional order and stability in our national life.* It does not matter whether the systems are public or private; by now they are so interdependent that these traditional boundaries are irrelevant.

Finally, there is an underlying ultimate value that justifies the exercise of managerial power. We have termed it "the organizational imperative," the premise that *whatever is good for the individual can only come from the modern organization.* Once that premise is accepted, then managers are justified in extending managerial control into all aspects of human life, for the welfare of the people.

Thus, the American Century was organized and managed into being, and the dominant people in this process were the managers. The successes and failures of modern organization are the results of this historically unprecedented class of professional managers. The distinguished public administration scholar Dwight Waldo pointed out that their class was a "historic mutation," arising from a "self-awareness" of its unique qualities as a group apart, practicing a discipline that could be studied, communicated, taught, and improved.[3] But beyond this disciplinary base is the normative premise that raised managerial class consciousness. It is that managers believe that they have the power to create important social changes that could improve the material well-being of the nation. In other words, they are bonded by a cause, a moral justification for what they do.

Management's foremost apologist, Peter Drucker, captured the spirit of the professional managerial age when he wrote, in 1954:

> The emergence of management as an essential, a distinct and a leading institution is a pivotal event in social history. Rarely, if ever, has a new basic institution, a new leading group, emerged as fast as has management since the turn of the century. Rarely in human history has a new institution proven so indispensable so quickly; and even less often has a new institution arrived with so little opposition, so little disturbance, so little controversy.... Management, which is the organ of society specifically charged with making resources productive, that is, with the responsibility for organized economic advance, therefore reflects that basic spirit of the modern age. It is in fact indispensable—and this explains why once begotten, it grew so fast, and with so little opposition.[4]

Drucker is correct. In the thirty years following World War II, management has been the essential human activity within modern organizations. It was taken as gospel that those interlocked and well-managed organizations would inexorably lead America to unending material prosperity and unquestioned world power. Therefore, the orthodox moral justification for the managerial endeavor appeared to be quite democratic: managers executed the will of the people. They actively and benevolently shaped organizations to respond both to public and private needs, which was communicated to management through a representative government and a free market.

But beneath that ostensible nobility of purpose lay two facts that no one— except for a few cranky intellectuals—wanted to confront. The first was that the organization of America was killing individualism, pluralism, and community. The second was that, in our society, power accrues to those who control the major organizations. So Americans have moved into the final years of the twentieth century with only the slightest awareness that the modern organization, with its accoutrements of managerial power and control, has become the dominant force in our lives, shaping and changing our traditional values, and even our personalities, to suit its requirements. Modern organizations have influenced us profoundly, but so quietly that we are scarcely aware that they are our major agencies of social control. We take them for granted in much the same way we accept television commercials, the "two-minute warning," and Muzak.

It should not be surprising, therefore, that the serious value issues resulting from the dominance of modern organizations have not been of major concern to most Americans. Certainly, all of us have had occasional twinges of doubt about the organizations in our lives, but they have seemed only minor irritations compared to the wretchedness of so many nations on this earth. Besides, it seems almost sacrilegious to tamper with a system that has proven itself capable of delivering so much to so many. However, there is such undeniable evidence of present discontent and future peril that we must look critically at our society and ask what is going wrong.

The Juggernaut Falters

Something happened to our expectations that the American juggernaut would roll on unimpeded. We found ourselves dependent upon other nations for many of the resources necessary for our continued affluence, and those nations were demanding larger shares of our national wealth. Even more significantly, other nations, led by Japan and Germany, caught on to the central role of management and began to out-manage us. Suddenly, "Detroit" was synonymous, no longer, with automotive excellence, but with automotive obsolescence and managerial stagnation. Managerial shortsightedness and complacency also caused our financial systems to wobble, and sent innovative research and development off to Asia and Europe.

Painfully, we became aware that our national leadership in all fields began to fail us badly. Too many abandoned principle for profit and celebrity, and it seemed as if wisdom and honor were lost virtues. Whether we agreed with them or not, the titans were no more: Franklin Roosevelt and Harry Truman in the presidency, Richard Russell and Sam Rayburn in Congress, Dean Acheson and John Foster Dulles in the public service, Thomas Watson and William Allen in business, or George C. Marshall and Chester Nimitz in the military. Was it any wonder that the American people became restive, knowing something was greatly amiss in the land? People began to ask why America was faltering.

Did the reasons for our decline lay with the reasons for our success? As management professors, we asked that question in the late 1970s. Our answer then was that modern organizations, driven by a unique set of values, had deflected America from the ennobling goals envisioned by the Founders of the Republic. As we described the situation, Americans, with little or no control over their destinies, were caught in a vortex of organizational determinism, being swept inexorably downward into totalitarianism. We placed the primary blame for this grim state of affairs upon the imperatives of the modern organization. While we still believe there is truth in this assessment, it now requires some modification and elaboration.

By the mid-1970s, some perceptive scholars were arguing that bureaucracy, both public and private, had become a more powerful reality in American life than family, community, religion, or politics. We agree. The managerial elite had become unaccountable to the public they ostensibly served.[5] In short, there were few popular controls over the managerial elite, who exercised enormous power. But those affected by that power could not get at their controllers.

Thus, the role of professional managers, in these interlocking networks of power, had to be reinterpreted. It was obvious that they were not just the intermediaries between their organizations and the mass of producing-consuming citizens, translating public desires into products and services. Instead, managers began to legitimize their real power by arguing that their *primary* responsibility was the maintenance of their organizations. Once their organizations were secure, then their efficient use of resources allowed for a "just" distribution of organizationally created benefits. A two-step legitimacy began to develop: first, secure the organization and then, second, serve the organization's constituents. But the security of the organization came first.

Managerial priorities began to change, as — more often than not — managers served their organizations more faithfully than their constituent stakeholders. This priority became their imperative — the organizational imperative — that is, by now, the very soul of American management. Belief in it compels managers to give virtually all of their attention to the maintenance of their organizations, even though such behavior incurs broader social costs too vast to calculate.

As modern organizations grew in size, complexity, and power, they also took on the appearance of an inexorable force on their own, akin to a force of nature. In concert, management theory and practice assumed deterministic overtones that suggested that although the organizational imperative might be marginally influenced and strategically adapted to, there was not much that anyone, including managers, could do about it. All were trapped in an organizational determinism that followed its own logic — a logic that defied human influence.

This line of reasoning was not new. Early in the twentieth century, the sociologist Max Weber argued the inevitability of bureaucracy and the political scientist Robert Michels described the "iron law of oligarchy." But the rise of the modern organization gave new life to the concept of organizational determinism and this approach to complex organizations became — and still is — influential in management thought and practice.

Moral Intentionality versus Organizational Determinism

While we are sympathetic to some of the arguments for organizational determinism, we do not view them as absolute. Determinism operates only if individuals allow it to operate. In saying this, we are arguing for a genuine power of individual moral intentionality. Granted, some people are caught in organizational systems so restrictive that they cannot get out. But most people are trapped by ignorance, laziness, inertia, or the absence of belief that they can change their condition. Thus, unless individuals act intentionally to alter their condition, they will indeed be carried along by the momentum of the organization.

There is, we contend, an organizational imperative and it is a force in contemporary America. But there is also a counterforce in the moral character of individuals who work for organizations. For that reason, we are more concerned with the moral dimensions of organizational life than with the instrumental and structural dimensions. Our assessment will be from the standpoint of that most venerable of subjects, moral philosophy. There is good reason for this approach, because all that is important in a society depends upon the values that the society holds sacred. The very words of moral discourse define those values—words such as right and wrong, truth and falsehood, love and hate, courage and cowardice, liberty and justice. They express our most important thoughts and emotions, identify our most meaningful actions, and exemplify our societies. Even the pragmatist philosopher John Dewey held that all things essential, including the common, are controlled by one's values.[6]

Thus, the moral principles derived from such values influence every life-choice, both within and without organizations. This means that every managerial act is a moral act. Because managerial actions involve the exercise of power, the lives of others are affected. For that reason, there are considerable moral obligations that go along with the job, and managers must be aware of the moral ramifications of what they do. Some managers understand that their actions are value laden and some even understand the origins of their moral choices. But most managers seldom consider the values upon which their actions and decisions are based.

But if values are so important, why have not more managers become philosophers, in the manner of the scholar-executive Chester I. Barnard? There are compelling reasons why most managers want nothing to do with moral philosophy. For one thing, it presumes prior knowledge of a very complex subject. To ask one to follow a moral philosophy without some learning is as reasonable as asking one to do accountancy without prior training. More important, however, is that asking questions about organizational values is unsettling, because such questions may raise doubts about the values upon which the organizations themselves are based, which might lead individuals to distrust both organizational leaders and practices. But, mainly, moral thought and discussion demands an intellectual, spiritual, and active boldness that is antithetical to the organizational imperative's demand for unquestioning faith in its precepts.

Suffice it to say, no issues—past, present, or future—are more important than the value issues. In our time, organizational values have become predominant in our totally organized society. These values have elevated the needs of the organization over the needs of the individual and have given moral justification to a new and imperious power elite of managers. The values of the modern organization have been substituted for the traditional Founding Values.

Voices of Dissent and Despair

None of this should surprise us, for we have had ample warning. The impact of modern organizations on American values began to receive significant attention in the 1950s, a decade wrongly criticized for complacency and Babbittry. Yet during that decade, a number of impressive books were written about the extraordinary effect the modern organization was having upon personal and social values. Among the leading organizational critics of that period were William H. Whyte, Jr., Jacques Ellul, Hannah Arendt, Robert Nisbet, David Riesman, Sheldon S. Wolin, and Dwight Waldo.

Their concern about the modern organization was summarized, ironically, by the supposed personification of complacency, Dwight D. Eisenhower. The president, in his farewell address, warned the nation of the dangers of a "military-industrial complex." That phrase received widespread publicity, but what is less well remembered is that he went on to warn against allowing public policy to become "the captive of a scientific-technological elite."[7] Unfortunately, his warning was misinterpreted as just another admonition to be on the lookout for high-level shenanigans between business and government executives, for the sake of personal gain. Eisenhower understood that the real danger lay in the unprecedented fusion of the public and private sectors that had its tentative origins in the years following World War I.

However, the warnings of the 1950s were largely ignored and the extremely important discussion about the pervasive growth of modern organizations did not mature. Why? For one reason, 1961 ushered in a decade of distractions — wars, assassinations, riots, demonstrations, and dramatic attempts to radicalize public and private institutions. While these alarums and excursions certainly captured public attention, they also exhausted public emotion. While we as a nation debated these highly visible attacks on the status quo, we had the impression that we were facing the important issues of the moment and, to a limited extent, we were.

What we failed to understand was that behind all the publicized turmoil, modern organizations continued to grow, consolidate, and, eventually, to encompass all aspects of American life within their values. It does not minimize the importance of the struggles of the 1960s to say that, in the end, they worked to strengthen modern organizations. For the most part, the remedies for injustice and anguish were sought in improved organizations that embodied and advanced the liberal and humane ideals expressed during this decade. But there was a fundamental irony in all of this, for the solution to social injustice was sought in more effective organizations.

During the 1970s modern organizations appeared to go on autopilot and to move with an inertia all their own. The majority of Americans were seen as trapped within mammoth governments or corporations or universities — powerless either to affect or escape them. To survive in such an environment, people had no choice but to conform to the requirements of the modern organization, laid down as rules by the national managerial system. The determinism seemed complete.

The intellectual mood of the 1970s was poignantly demonstrated in a small conference of influential public administration scholars held late in 1977 at Charlottesville, Virginia. Some of the participants had been at a similar conference in 1968. The hallmark of the 1968 gathering had been an optimism that a new public administration could shatter the established organizational patterns that had so exacerbated so many of the problems that troubled that most troubled decade. The participants believed they could reshape government, at all levels, to become more personal, humane, and responsive.[8]

In contrast, the mood of the 1977 conference was pessimistic, arising from a sense of powerlessness. The optimism, as well as the outrage, of the 1960s had evaporated. Instead, there was the feeling among most that no one in government, business, education, or politics could reduce the dominance of modern organizations. For some, this was acceptable, for they saw nothing essentially wrong with those modern organizations. For others, the attitude seemed to be "if you can't lick them, join them," which was translated into support for management conducted safely within the orthodox theoretical and practical boundaries. For a small segment, however, the situation provoked bleak despair.

It is difficult to decide which attitude is worse: the helplessness expressed by some about their inability to change organizations, or the insensitive belief among others that all is well in the organizational firmament. But, either way, it was as obvious then as it is obvious now that the United States languishes in a moral confusion about whether organizational values are conducive to living a worthy life.

Some recent critics of American culture argue that those organizational requirements are antithetical to the requirements for worthy living, especially as envisioned by the Founding Fathers. For instance, the sociologist Robert Nisbet argues that the over organization of America has come at the expense of pluralism, voluntarism, localism, and kinship associations. That, in turn, is eroding the legitimacy of our key institutions, producing a "twilight of authority."[9] Freedom is being replaced with centralized planning and diversity with homogeneity. In a parallel critique, the historian Christopher Lasch examined the cultural consequences of organizations that rely upon a morality of self-interest and a society "that has reduced reason to mere calculation," in which "reason can impose no limits on the pursuit of pleasure."[10] Thus, our self-absorption, aggressive accumulation of material goods, and calculated rejection of social consequences have resulted in a narcissistic cultural anarchy. As we will argue in later chapters, this has created a society that is at significant variance with traditional American values.

The Vulnerability of the Organizational Imperative

The experiences of the 1980s have generally confirmed these dour predictions. On the whole, the 1980s will be remembered for the mediocrity of our national leaders, along with a fast-buck sleaziness and an appalling moral slackness. Leaders, in high places and low, assaulted the national sense of moral propriety. The widely reported excursions into the moral swamps by business, governmental, and military leaders; public administrators; evangelical ministers; academics; and political candidates continued the decline in public confidence in the leadership of American organizations. Perhaps the most dismaying spectacle of all, however, was that of the President of the United States, Ronald Reagan, who could not comprehend that moral integrity was more important than cronyism.

Moral failure, in all its forms, made the nation aware of what moral sloth can produce. But something unanticipated happened at the same time: moral ugliness has also affirmed, in a backhanded way, the singular importance of the moral agency of individuals, especially as they work within organizations. We have relearned what we had forgotten, that individual moral character makes a difference in how organizations work. Ironically, it was the rogues that made the lesson clear, for they brought sharply to our attention that individuals can beat the organizational imperative, even though for morally objectionable personal ends. Therefore, if an individual can beat the system for immoral purposes, then it is clear that the system can be beaten for moral purposes. The higher individuals rise in their organizations, the more this leverage increases. The problem is that it takes a person of extraordinary moral character to resist the allure of power and privilege that accompanies high organizational positions.

Furthermore, the American people began to sense that organizational leaders have higher moral obligations than fidelity to the organizational imperative. It is not without a certain warranted confidence that some moral philosophers—such as David L. Norton, Alasdair MacIntyre, Edmond Pincoffs, and Konstantin Kolenda—are refocusing our attention on both the importance and the possibilities of ethical individualism and moral autonomy in organizational life.[11] Their arguments in defense of individual moral autonomy stress the importance of the development of moral character. David Norton observes:

> The worthy person fulfills his social responsibility initially and foremost by living his own life justly. But he is in himself the expression of truths that ... are elsewhere only implicit, and as such he bears his measure of responsibility for achieving and maintaining the conditions that promote their emergence. In his measure he is responsible for the installation of these truths in the institutions of society, foremost among them the institutions of education, division of labor, the law and the penal system.[12]

We believe, with these moral philosophers, that moral tradition, moral community, education, and kinship are indispensable to enhancing moral growth. What is most important is that moral character is recognized as the most important factor in judging the worth of all individuals, including managers. But the stakes are higher for managers because of their power. They must be held accountable for their individual acts. They cannot evade such accountability by claiming that the organizational imperative made them do it.

In conclusion, we have altered the point of view expressed in our first book. Individuals in organizations do count, and the organizational imperative is less powerful than we previously supposed it to be. As it has been overcome by acts of moral villainy, so it can be transcended by acts of moral heroism. We agree with William H. Whyte, Jr., in his influential book *The Organization Man*[13], that the individual, as an autonomous moral agent, will be in conflict with the organization. There should be no resolution of this conflict, because it represents an important aspect of the American identity: the continual tension between the individual and the collective.

This dialectical tension has been a major theme in our national ethos and its resultant American character. It has brought out the best and the worst in us, but the result has been, on the balance, a comparatively free and just society. *We hold that the danger to America is not, as Chester I. Barnard argued, either unbridled freedom or vast systems of regimentation, but rather the end of the dialectic.*[14] This is the danger that the organizational imperative presents and the reason why it poses the greatest threat to the Founding Values. The end of the American dialectic means drift into an American totalitarianism. This destination, however, is not inevitable.

Notes

1. Alexis de Tocqueville, *Democracy in America*, ed. P. Bradley from the Reeve text (New York: Knopf, 1945), 2:130.
2. Alan Paton, "A Literary Remembrance," *Time*, 25 April 1988, 106.

3. Dwight Waldo, *The Enterprise of Public Administration* (Novato, CA: Chandler and Sharp, 1980), 11-12.
4. Peter Drucker, *The Practice of Management* (New York: Harper & Row, 1954), 3-4.
5. See, for instance, Robert Nisbet, *Twilight of Authority* (New York: Oxford University Press, 1975).
6. John Dewey, *Theory of Valuation* (Chicago: University of Chicago Press, 1939), 2.
7. Herbert S. Parmet, *Eisenhower and the American Crusades* (New York: Macmillan, 1972), 572.
8. The conclusions of the conference are contained in Frank Marini, (ed.), *Toward a New Public Administration: The Minnowbrook Perspective* (Scranton, PA.: Chandler, 1971).
9. Robert Nisbet, *Twilight of Authority* (New York: Oxford University Press, 1975).
10. Christopher Lasch, *The Culture of Narcissism* (New York: Norton, 1978), 69.
11. David L. Norton, *Personal Destinies* (Princeton: Princeton University Press, 1976); Alasdair MacIntyre, *After Virtue* (Notre Dame: University of Notre Dame Press, 1981); Edmond L. Pincoffs, *Quandaries and Virtues* (Lawrence: University of Kansas Press, 1986); Konstantin Kolenda (ed.), *Organizations and Ethical Individualism* (New York: Greenwood-Praeger, 1988).
12. Norton, 309.
13. William H. Whyte, Jr., *The Organization Man* (Garden City, NY: Doubleday, 1956).
14. Chester I. Barnard, *The Functions of the Executive* (Cambridge: Harvard University Press, 1938), 294-295.

2

Organizational America:
The Dissolution of the American Tradition

> *Some of the owner men were kind because they hated what they had to do, and some of them were angry because they hated to be cruel, and some of them were cold because they had long ago found that one could not be an owner unless one were cold. And all of them were caught in something larger than themselves. Some of them hated the mathematics that drove them, and some were afraid, and some worshipped the mathematics because it provided a refuge from thought and from feeling.*
>
> —John Steinbeck, *The Grapes of Wrath*

The Fading of Traditional Confidences

The dreams of the American Century were given their most eloquent expression on 20 January 1961, a day bright and clear. The occasion was the inauguration of the thirty-fifth president of the United States. John F. Kennedy seemed the perfect embodiment of what we had tried to achieve through the years of our history. Young, handsome, articulate, confident, intelligent—he symbolized what we expected of the apex years of our century. His speech was impressive, the apotheosis of the American tradition of accomplishment. In one magnificent passage he fused past and future:

> We dare not forget today that we are the heirs of that first revolution. Let the word go forth from this time and place, to friend and foe alike, that the torch has been passed to a new generation of Americans—born in this century, tempered by war, disciplined by a hard and bitter peace, proud of our ancient heritage—and unwilling to witness or permit the slow undoing of those human rights to which this Nation has always been committed, and to which we are committed today at home and around the world.[1]

And so it seemed that the tradition was secured in the confident abilities of a new generation of the best and brightest. President Kennedy went on to express what most Americans believed: that we could accomplish it all. From racial justice and extensive economic security to world peace and the mastery of space—there was nothing Americans could not do, for surely the world and its anguishes would yield to our decent intentions. They were heady days, those days of Camelot.

But in less than three years, those expectations were shattered in Dallas. The years following the killing of the president were marked by further assassinations, the slaughter in Vietnam, festering domestic inequalities, government venality, crime and riot and decay in our cities, an economic inflation that seemed to have no end—all of which contributed to a growing national malaise. But as dispiriting as the 1960s were, there was worse to come.

By the 1970s, the days of Camelot seemed as far removed from us as the Jazz Age. We had believed that our leaders—in every area—would dominate events through honor, intelligence, and new technologies, thus ensuring that our collective future would be an improvement upon our present. But two shameful failures brought the loss of our innocence, demonstrating the inadequacies of our leaders. In spite of ample warnings, in the fall of 1973 the oil industry was mousetrapped by the OPEC cartel's boycott with vast repercussions for the quality of life in America. In the public sector, the Watergate scandal presented us with the specter of a president, consumed by personal insecurities, who loosed morally insensitive aides into the political arena. And so we learned that we were not led by those with the character of Thomas Jefferson or a Abraham Lincoln, but rather by those with the character of Georgie Babbitt or Sammy Glick.

The theme of the 1970s turned out to be the use of organizational power to maintain the leadership status quo. Leaders, who had the ability neither to understand nor to control events, held on to their positions by intensifying their commitment to the organizational imperative. Steinbeck caught the mood in his description of the "owner men" in the epigraph of this chapter. Even worse, in spite of their obvious inabilities, these leaders demanded that the people believe their stewardship was inspired. But the disparity between their management claims and the realities of the organizational results was all too evident. For instance, Detroit crumbled for the simple reason that foreign-made automobiles were better than the shoddy wares of the obsolescent American automotive industry.

As the 1980s spun themselves out, economic woes, social injustices, and moral contradictions continued to diminish our confidence in the future.[2] Little came as a clean success. Political leaders proclaimed the conquest of inflation, but ignored the price paid for it: a national debt that was beyond comprehension. A domestic war was declared on drugs, but we continued to strike vile deals with the political despots that protected the drug trade. Endless contradictions confront America and probably always will. The tragedy of America in the 1980s was not the seemingly irreconcilable tensions of national life, but the failure of leadership, across all American institutions, to inspire a moral vision of the future that would restore the confidence of the people.

So the vision was lost and the people leaderless. In response Americans turned inward, settling into the mind-numbing routines of the preservation of an affluent, but essentially unsatisfactory, status quo. Our dreams are no more, our glories are of the past, and hedonism prevails—and with the loss of those dreams comes a hurtful, drifting determinism.

But the drift masks the fact that we are being dislocated by a social revolution, and while it is altering all our lives in fundamental ways, we neither understand it, although we could, nor control it, although we should. We have fallen back upon the security of familiar tasks and tried to ignore the pain. But we cannot avoid the questions: Why, with all of our notable successes, are we not a more peaceful, a happier people? Why, with all of our marvelous inventions, does the future look so perilous? The American Century was to open out into a utopian twenty-first century, but the future seems anything but ideal now. Organizational America is not working out that well, and our confidence in the future is being sorely tried.

The Assault on American Confidence

If one examines the many interpretations of our national character, four themes of confidence emerge as constant: a confidence in the generosity of the environment, a confidence in the benevolence of time, a confidence in American know-how, and a confidence in the rewards that come from diligent personal effort. No small part of the obvious national trauma in organizational America results from our increasing doubts about the validity of these confidences.

A Dun from the Environment

Our unquestioning confidence in the endless abundance of the environment produced a historically unprecedented optimism that the future would allow for all American ambitions. Granted, the record contains horrifying accounts of the trials endured by our forebears—from droughts, floods, and starvation to communal strife, plagues, depressions, and wars. But such problems were seen as temporary and correctable situations. The presumption has been that environmental intransigencies would be mastered, and there would be sufficient land, resources, and capital to realize our individual and national aspirations. This optimism was historically warranted, as Robert Heilbroner has argued in his book, *The Future as History.*[3]

Our history bears constant witness to the fact that the environment was generous, once its puzzles were solved. There was little reason to expect it to dun us for an overdue bill we could not pay. Environmental Jeremiahs have been around for a long time, but their dire forecasts were always deferred by technological breakthroughs or fortuitous wars. But now the environment is collecting and we seem unable to pay our overdue bills. One reason is that the environmental dun has become both global and interconnected: there are too many people, not enough resources, not enough space, and not enough time for all nations to realize their material ambitions.

In the face of this global situation, some Americans still believed that we could go it alone. In the past, America was one of the few nations that came close to realizing the geopolitical possibility of national self-sufficiency. However, the modern argument that we should avoid foreign entanglements and live independently in "Fortress America" is passé.

For better or worse, we are inextricably entangled in a global society that is so interdependent there is no foreseeable way for nations to get free from one another. There are many reasons for global interdependency, and most are so familiar that we shrug them off. But that will not do. All nations are now interdependent on each other for both renewable and nonrenewable resources. The fact is that the United States uses more of those resources than any other nation, for domestic consumption.[4] This means that our standard of living is dependent upon the supply of resources provided by the nations with whom we trade. It does not take a geopolitician to realize that unless we reduce our standard of living, we will increase our political and economic vulnerability.

This has nowhere been more evident than with oil. Because we are an energy-intensive nation and because our known domestic oil reserves are dwindling, we must find alternatives to oil, increase exploration for domestic reserves, or rely upon oil-rich nations.[5] The oil surpluses of the 1980s led to the abandonment of research into alternatives for fossil fuels. Those who warn that the world situation could change at any moment are usually ignored, but change it will.[6] All nations are under sentence of a diminishing supply of easily accessible oil, and the oil-rich nations are using oil for political leverage. The economy of the United States is at present linked to the politics of the Middle East—one of the most volatile regions of the world.

With oil added to the multitude of other environmental problems, the American confidence in the generosity of the environment has been badly shaken. In the late 1980s a host of other problems surged to the fore, from acid rain and the deforestation of the planet, to holes in the ozone layer and the greenhouse effect. These are not minor conditions that will respond to quick fixes.

The situation is even more complex when one looks at the global economic interdependencies. The world's financial markets are linked by global communication networks that make world-wide transactions almost instantaneous. Multinational manufacturing corporations and international marketing confederations spill over national boundaries, and they often mime the behavior of sovereign political states. America must not delude itself with a fortress mentality or by an illusion of self-sufficiency: we are as much a part of the global environmental and economic network as any other major industrial nation.

The real dun from our environment, however, has come primarily because America has pillaged and despoiled its own physical environment to satisfy its commercial interests, both domestically and globally. It is beside the point that nearly all other nations are behaving in a like manner. American leadership in business and government is responsible for our dun from the environment, because it is too committed to organizational survival and an ethic of personal advantage.

Traitorous Time

America's history has given us an unquestioning confidence that time would never be wicked to us. We were occasionally caught unprepared, but we could always count upon a stalwart few—from Great Britain to Bataan— to stand fast and purchase whatever extra time was needed for us to gear up for the new challenge. Time has been our kindly friend and staunch ally.

But lately has come the shocking realization that time has turned traitor and works against us. We are faced with a host of time-related difficulties, the paradoxical anguish of which was eloquently stated by David Easton: "The agony of the present social crisis is this contrast between our desperate condition and our visible promise, if we but had the time."[7] He has summarized the irony of the time crunch: problems could be mastered, if time will just give us a break. But the fact is that we now must work within narrowing time spans, and this is having a decisive effect upon the means we select to satisfy various economic, social, and political demands.

We are rapidly abandoning our more leisurely, pluralistic ways of decision making to rest our national survival upon the national managerial system. Given the constraints of time, centralized control of the political economy seems more effective than our pluralist tradition. The key here is speed, for the managerial elite contends that by centralization it can quickly reconcile the relationships between commercial, financial, and industrial strength on the one hand and political and military power on the other.[8] If their contentions are valid, then individual interests and autonomy must be subordinated to the single purpose of national welfare. This view is clearly at variance with the economic and political models of competition, free trade, and pluralism in which we had such confidence in the past.

The Frustration of Practicality

The real significance of practicality to Americans was that it relieved an individual of dependence upon others for the necessities of life. Our language is filled with approving expressions for those who are able to solve practical problems ingeniously: from "Yankee know-how" to the motto of the Seabees, "Can do." It has been axiomatic that there are no practical problems, particularly technological ones, that we cannot eventually solve. Thus, Americans could laugh at the amateur-loving British, or the emotional Italians, or the tradition-burdened Chinese, and then proceed to solve problems with confidence in their technical skills and managerial expertise.

But this confidence in our practicality, and hence in our independence, has sagged, for two reasons. First, we are learning that we do not have a monopoly on solutions to practical problems. Our industrial and technological know-how is not quite the prime export commodity it once was. We have been astonished and chagrined at the ability of other nations to match and surpass us, product for product and process for process, in areas of management and technology in which we once excelled. Second, our lives are arranged by organizations too complex for an individual to comprehend, and these organizations are in turn served by machines that often perform beyond human capabilities. The confidence Americans had, that they could be useful in the world and could effect that world to their advantage through personal efforts, is being tried. As individuals, we stand increasingly helpless before machines and organizations. We are proficient at doing things that really do not matter much at all and that have meaning only in terms of their relationship to organizations.

The incongruity between our professed belief in individual practicality and our undeniable dependence, both as individuals and as a nation, has led to public frustration. Other countries can now ignore our demands because they realize we need them as much as they need us. On the plane of personal feelings, the effects of dependency are even more acute, since they reflect the utter reliance of even the most practical Americans upon impersonal, and too often ineffective, delivery systems for goods and services. Our frustration stems from this pervasive personal sense of our own powerlessness.

The Erosion of Expectations

No small part of American confidence was the expectation that the future would be better than the past—if not for the present generation, then for the next one. This confidence was, in many respects, a summation of the others: given an abundant environment and adequate time, the individual, with proper diligence and ingenuity, would be able to achieve economic security and a reasonably comfortable life. Further, there was the confidence that such personal efforts would put one's children at a better starting point for their own lives.

By most standards, these expectations have been met for the majority of Americans, and therefore it seems unreasonable to talk about austerity, especially when our stores are piled high with a prodigious variety of goods. However, the important issue is what people believe about their future, for people will endure enormous hardships if their dreams of the future remain intact. By that criterion, the trouble is evident. In their analysis of polls from 1968 to 1986, Lipset and Schneider described a growing "confidence gap" in the public's perception of its organizational leadership.[9]

To illustrate, the *New York Times* reported in February of 1988 that, for the first time during the Reagan administration, Americans did not have rising expectations for the future of the nation.[10] That poll reaffirmed the Lipset and Schneider findings and suggested that Americans had real doubts that their leaders would fulfill their expectations for a better life. The 1980s revealed that Americans, in spite of occasional fluctuations, did not believe that the future would be better than the present, no matter how hard we tried. Such pessimism comes not entirely from our concern for the problems of the environment, or the pressures of time. Rather, we began to experience the frustration of expectations more directly.

American productivity, research, and world competitiveness slumped. Our financial system wobbled as record numbers of commercial and savings banks failed. The stock market became wildly erratic, marked by the unanticipated crash of 19 October 1987. Jobs were downgraded, as workers moved from traditional basic industries to lower paying service industries requiring less skills. Two-person incomes became a necessity for those American couples who wanted even the ordinary trappings of a middle-class economic status. Public and private debt soared, mortgaging the welfare of future generations. The trade deficits that had propped up the prosperity of the early Reagan years eventually led to the sale of American capital assets.

Compounding the economic tribulations were the palpable threats to public health posed by such things as the AIDS epidemic and toxic waste pollution. Drug abuse ran rampant and struck devastatingly at our children. The old specter of racial tension and violence reappeared, most disturbingly on the campuses of our colleges and universities, where tolerance and the acceptance of diversity is supposed to be supreme. Mass entertainment alternated between puerility and abnormal psychology, while the incessant clamor of mass marketing numbed the mind. There was a virtual disappearance of service in the alleged service industries. A trip to the devastated downtowns of American cities brought to mind more and more a visit to Calcutta—the major difference being that Calcutta is not as dangerous. Suffice it to say, the quality of life for the average American—regardless of the measures used—took a decidedly tacky turn. If some Americans are still optimistic about the future, they have little reason to be, for the cards are stacked against that possibility.

However, the members of the managerial elite—whose power, perquisites, and security are dependent upon the status quo—have shown no inclination to change the order of things. Their utter contempt for the moral obligations of high position, entailed by the Founding values, is most clearly demonstrated by their golden parachutes, their guarantee to themselves that they will never have to suffer from their failures. Their major goal is to construct a new legitimacy. To that end, they smother the ordinary citizens with superlatives about how much better off they are. But this is not the case and the majority of Americans—subject to the indignities of modern life—know it. This new legitimacy is being constructed by increasing organizational domination and by managing the decline in the quality of life of the masses.

The Reconstruction of Legitimacy

As the traditional American confidences are being undone, the leaders of organizational America are confronted with the critical problem of creating a new legitimacy. No society can long exist unless the public acknowledges the right of the prevailing elites—social, economic, and political—to govern.[11] The new managerial elite must establish its right to rule.

The articulation of this new legitimacy actually began in the 1920s. The argument was introduced that the leaders of the great national organizations were both the actual and the rightful governors of this country. This leadership now is an elite composed of the top people in the private corporations, government agencies and commissions, labor unions, private philanthropic foundations, the mass media, and the premier universities (both administrators and academics). As a result, this elite brought the principles and practices of the modern organization into every part of American life. This solution to the question of national rule has been understood for years and by more writers than we can mention here; however, the works of Robert Michels, James Burnham, and Jacques Ellul are especially noteworthy.[12]

Robert Michels is not very fashionable these days, but his ideas are accurate and unsettling. The essence of his argument is that in spite of the most idealistic intentions of leaders, the democratic waves in history "break ever on the same shoal": the immutable needs of organization that create the "tyranny of expertise" and its corollary "iron law of oligarchy."[13] Depending upon one's ideological preferences, the cycle Michels described can be judged favorably or unfavorably; either way, his analysis was essentially correct.

Two points must be emphasized. First, given the inevitable rise of organizational oligarchies, Michels believed that the "ideal government would doubtless be that of an aristocracy of persons at once morally good and technically efficient."[14] This was the ideal of the early management theorists and practitioners, which was embodied in the life and work of Chester I. Barnard.[15] Second, the people had little to say about all of this: they would be governed by an elite, like it or not, in all organizations because this was an inescapable law of nature. In other words, Michels considered the idea of the legitimacy of rule by a managerial elite to be beyond question; one does not discuss the legitimacy of a natural force.

The triumph of managerialism was spelled out by the reformed American Trotskyist James Burnham. While his book, too, has drifted into relative obscurity, most of what he predicted has come true. *The Managerial Revolution* has a distinctly old-fashioned air today, for Burnham was busy settling accounts with various Marxist factions and speculating whether capitalism could survive. But his contention that the managerial elite was winning everywhere was correct, even though their organizational techniques were then most primitive.

Burnham understood that the principal element of control inherent in modern organizations was the expertise of management, which involved both arcane knowledge and intuitive understanding. Because it took managerial skill to keep an organization alive, this led to an elitist oligarchy. This is most evident today: in modern organizations, power accrues to those who have expert knowledge in management. Those who occupy the key managerial posts constitute a governing elite.

Regardless of our democratic and humanistic intention, the inescapable admission is forced upon us: "that which *is* oppresses *that which ought to be*."[16] People still use their learning to obtain influence and power, but those prizes now lie within managerial positions. Once such positions are obtained, the power of the incumbents is used to preserve and nourish administrative oligarchies.

No one has analyzed the developing organizational culture better than Jacques Ellul. It is impossible to summarize his work—he strides through all subject matter disdainful of small thoughts and precise expression. However, he repeatedly stressed one point of enormous importance to our argument: the adoption of "technique" by the state. In 1954, he wrote

> From the political, social, and human points of view, this conjunction of state and technique is by far the most important phenomenon of history. It is astonishing to note that no one, to the best of my knowledge, has emphasized this fact. It is likewise astonishing that we still apply ourselves to the study of political theories or parties which no longer possess anything but episodic importance, yet we bypass the technical fact which explains the totality of modern political events.[17]

This situation has resulted partly from a fusing of the traditional legitimacy of the state with the modern organization. It is further compounded because we cannot readily observe the managerial elite which is commanding us. The old-time dictators were obvious, and there was little doubt about their intentions.

If anything, managerial elites in the national managerial system are even less accessible today than when Michels, Burnham, and Ellul wrote. They are shielded from public appraisal by the cloak of organizational invisibility and further insulated by the languages and practices of managerial specialties. Indeed, the symbolic jargon of management reinforces the uncanny feeling that when one deals with someone who does MIS, PPBS, CPM, and OD, one is not dealing with an ordinary person. Managers alone understand the sacred language of the new secular priesthood, and their sense of legitimacy and elitism is intensified the higher they move up through the organizational hierarchy.

But, a tough-minded person will argue, so what? Michels, Burnham, and Ellul have spelled out the facts of life, so why fight the inevitable? The national managerial system probably is a blessing, for it creates order and, through some mystical form of organizational Darwinism, the fittest managers rise to the top. Since we want to be managed by the best and the strongest, Thrasymachus has been reincarnated in a gray flannel suit. This is one of the most lethal mistakes made by the supposed tough-minded apologists. Certainly, order is imposed by the national managerial system, but neither Michels nor Burnham nor Ellul believed that the rise of managerial power also brought with it some form of winnowing by which virtue triumphed. To the contrary, they believed that managerialism encouraged organizational stagnation, the spoiling of idealism, official insensitivity, despotic repression, and the blighting of human aspirations.

A humanist will argue that one reason for the early, unfortunate effects of modern organization—as seen in the early years of the American Industrial Revolution—was that the managers were forced to use very crude techniques of management. Not much sensitivity can be expected from leaders if the primary instruments in their behavioral repertoire are autocratic command and coercive power, coupled with a raw kind of expertise in the use of influence within organizations.

In reaction to such obvious organizational barbarisms, many management scholars and practitioners have turned to other, more "humane" modes of behavior control. Considerable attention has been given to alternatives to the crudities of past management theory and practice. These alternatives are found in processes like participatory management, organizational development, and management-initiated systems of due process, which stem from the humanistic psychology of Elton Mayo, Abraham Maslow, Douglas McGregor, and others of their persuasion.

Ellul foresaw this development of humanism and discussed it in a chapter entitled "Human Techniques."[18] He observed that much of the new behavioral research would eventually be adapted to serve as rational tools for managers. This did, indeed, happen, and management practices were sanitized along humanistic lines. The significance of this cannot be overemphasized. The behavioral sciences added to management's legitimacy a previously missing dimension: a demonstrable intention of benevolence toward the people being managed. Since everyone is either a manager or is managed, humanistic practices have become important in establishing the right of the new managerial elite to rule. Legitimacy is augmented by niceness.

This new order of things, an organizational America governed by a managerial elite, has been announced and accepted as routine by such authorities as George C. Lodge and Harlan Cleveland.[19] They, among many others, believe the triumph of the modern organization has created new possibilities for America and that further social changes in this country can be effected without a falter in stride. Whatever our problems, they can be solved by making our organizations better. Their optimism is not warranted.

The Deceptive Decency of Functional Morality

There has been another important shift in emphasis in our perceptions of leadership in organizational America. In the past, the public has always expected that the individuals who ran organizations would be accountable for the morality of their acts, rather than the organizations themselves. When something went wrong, the cry went up to "kick the rascals out!" With respect to the top leadership, much of the civil ruckus in our society has been over the conduct of those at the helm of the ship of state—or the corporate galley ship, for that matter. Put in simple terms, most of us want to equate good and evil with identifiable people: evil people do evil deeds and vice versa. Obviously, once the good guys are in control, all will be well.

This is now a child's game. Does anyone honestly believe there will be no more Vietnams now that Lyndon Johnson has passed away, or no more Watergates since Richard Nixon went to his own Elba, or that Iran-Contra connections will vanish with Ronald Reagan? Obviously not. So we are again confronted with the eternal question of democracy: how can a free people guarantee that only worthy persons move into the positions of leadership in both the public and the private sectors? The answer is, they cannot. There are no guarantees. But that is the essence of democracy: that a free people must constantly search for virtue, in themselves and in their leadership.

But modern organizations cannot tolerate such uncertainty; they have too much invested to allow for the ambiguities of searching for virtue. Therefore, a belief developed in management that organizations are moral because they grew out of a voluntary, spontaneous, and informal act of cooperation by the people in them. This original, primitive expression of collective purpose was the foundation for the functional morality of modern organizations. Thus, the members of the elite who occupy high positions in these organizations become morally cauterized because they help achieve the ends of cooperation. They are merely instruments for fulfilling the will of the people. As such, the elite is virtuous because of its incumbency.[20]

Karl Popper has written that "who should rule?" is no longer the question but rather, "How can we so organize . . . institutions that bad or incompetent rulers can be prevented from doing too much damage?"[21] He contended that the strength and vitality of organizations must never be predicated on the assumption that the best people will rule, since if it turns out that such is not the case, as often happens, the survival of public and private institutions is compromised, along with our freedom, welfare, and national security. Therefore, our energies should not be consumed with the issue of virtue in professional management; rather, they should be directed toward making it accountable. Popper was not writing an apology for the modern organization; rather, he was reaffirming an almost Jeffersonian position. The difference is that the Founding Fathers wanted strong organizations which would curb the excesses of faction, but which would not intrude, at the same time, on the liberties of the individual. Modern organizations and their leaders seek strength to preserve themselves.

Management scholars and practitioners have tried to follow what Popper said, even though they misperceive the ends. They have worked from the premise that functionally moral organizations are not only effective in achieving goals, they also mold the leaders into good people. Virtue, then, lies first in organizational structures and processes and, second in individuals. The blatant contradiction in this argument is that it violates the traditional American legitimacy, in that it relieves individuals of the moral responsibility for their managerial acts—good or bad. If good is done it is because good was foreordained by managerial dedication to the functional morality of organizations.

Evil, however, is a bit more difficult to account for. If it turns up in organizations, the leaders may blame it on the faulty character of low-ranking individuals, or they may argue that circumstances outside their organizations imposed evil upon them. This was illustrated by legal actions in the infamous E. F. Hutton case of the late 1980s. The brokerage firm pleaded guilty to two thousand felony counts involving check kiting, and it paid a two-million-dollar fine and reimbursed its banks for defrauding them. But no individuals were indicted for fraud. E. F. Hutton's defense made it seem as if a morally corrupt competitive system compelled it to engage in illegal financial transactions and that individual managers had no moral choice but to go along. That is, of course, arrant nonsense.

Most of the problems that beset the nation now are a result of the substitution of the functional morality of organizations for the moral obligations of individual managers. But they have not seriously addressed the issue of the moral obligation of the individual within modern organizations in the light of moral philosophy. They have used their extensive and useful knowledge about behavior in organizations as a substitute for considering the values underlying modern organizations.

The result of this neglect is impressive, for we have allowed the modern organization to reshape the qualitative expectations we have for our lives and to reorder our moral priorities. Thus, organizational values have taken precedence over individual values, and the individual is now made for the organization, rather than the organization for the individual.

But even granting this point, is this necessarily bad? Humanist managers argue that there is no cause for alarm, for many personnel problems can be countered by the management techniques developed from the humane behavioral sciences. The contradiction within such an argument is that the problems of organizations will be resolved by techniques that owe their existence to them. Historian Loren Baritz described the ethical and political positions of industrial social scientists as "a red thread in the otherwise pallid canvas on which they have labored."[22]

This is where a major Catch-22 arises. Managers have abandoned the obligations of moral autonomy in favor of the value system of modern organizations, to which they owe their loyalty. Thus, their very definitions of "good" and "bad" are predicated upon their prior and unexamined acceptance of the values of the organizational imperative, which in itself involves a major moral decision that few recognize as such. Such slothful individual acceptance of organizational values is at the root of our contemporary malaise.

Notes

1. *Inaugural Addresses of the Presidents of the United States: From George Washington, 1789, to John F. Kennedy, 1961* (Washington, D.C.: U.S. Government Printing Office, 1961), 267. See also the account in Theodore C. Sorensen, *Kennedy* (New York: Bantam, 1965), 269-278.
2. Note, for instance: Seymour Martin Lipset and William Schneider, *The Confidence Gap: Business, Labor, and Government in the Public Mind*, rev. ed., (Baltimore: Johns Hopkins University Press, 1987); Herbert McClosky and John Zaller, *The American Ethos: Public Attitudes toward Capitalism and Democracy* (Cambridge: Harvard University Press, 1984); Sidney Verba and Gary R. Orren, *Equality in America* (Cambridge: Harvard University Press, 1985). The loss of

confidence is put into perspective in T. Mitchell and W. G. Scott, "Leadership Failures, the Distrusting Public, and Prospects of the Administrative State," *Public Administration Review* 47 (Nov./Dec. 1987): 445-452.

3. Robert L. Heilbroner, *The Future as History* (New York: Harper & Row, 1960).

4. Nicholas Wade, "Raw Materials: U.S. Grows More Vulnerable to Third World Cartels," *Science*, 183 (18 January 1974).

5. John M. Blair, *The Control of Oil* (New York: Pantheon Books, 1976), 22.

6. Note these excellent books: Robert Stobaugh and Daniel Yergin, eds., *Energy Future: Report of the Energy Project at the Harvard Business School* (New York: Random House, 1979); Daniel Yergin and Martin Hillenbrand, eds., *Global Insecurity: A Strategy for Energy and Economic Renewal* (Boston: Houghton Mifflin, 1982).

7. David Easton, "The New Revolution in Political Science," *American Political Science Review* 63 (Dec. 1969): 1053.

8. Edward Mead Earle, "Adam Smith, Alexander Hamilton, Friedrich List: The Economic Foundations of Military Power," in Edward Mead Earle, ed., *Makers of Modern Strategy* (Princeton: Princeton University Press, 1944), 117-120.

9. Lipset and Schneider, *The Confidence Gap*, rev. ed.

10. S. V. Roberts, "Poll Finds Less Optimism in the U.S. on Future, a First under Reagan," *New York Times*, 21 Feb. 1988, 1 and 8.

11. Philip Selznick, *The Organizational Weapon: A Study of Bolshevik Strategy and Tactics* (Glencoe, Ill., The Free Press, 1952, 1960), 242.

12. Robert Michels, *Political Parties: A Sociological Study of the Oligarchical Tendencies of Modern Democracies*, trans. E. Paul and C. Paul (New York: Dover, 1915, 1959); James Burnham, *The Managerial Revolution* (Bloomington: Indiana University Press, 1941, 1960); Jacques Ellul, *The Technological Society*, trans. J. Wilkinson (New York: Knopf, 1954, 1964).

13. Michels, *Political Parties*, 408. According to Michels, the iron law of oligarchy is innate to organization: "It is organization which gives birth to the dominion of the elected over the electors, of the mandataries over the mandators, of the delegates over the delegators. Who says organization, says oligarchy," 401. The tyranny of expertise comes from the leaders' indispensability: "The leader's principle source of power is found in his indispensability. One who is indispensable has in his power all the lords and masters of the earth," 86.

14. Michels, *Political Parties*, 407

15. Barnard, *Functions of the Executive* (see chap. 1, n. 14).

16. Michels, *Political Parties*, 401. Emphasis in the original.

17. Ellul, *The Technological Society*, 233.

18. Ellul, *The Technological Society*, Chapter 5.

19. George C. Lodge, *The New American Ideology* (New York: Knopf, 1976); Harlan Cleveland, *The Future Executive* (New York: Harper & Row, 1972).

20. This is based upon Charles Perrow, *Complex Organizations*, 3d ed. (New York: Random House, 1986), 62-67.

21. Karl R. Popper, *The Open Society and Its Enemies* (Princeton: Princeton University Press, 1950), 120.

22. Loren Baritz, *Servants of Power* (Middletown, Conn.: Wesleyan Univerity Press, 1960), 198.

3

The Organizational Imperative

In the eyes of large and growing numbers of men, the social and political landscape of America, the most advanced of the advanced states, is no green and gentle place, where men may long abide. The landscape is, rather, a scene of wracked shapes and desert spaces. What we mainly see are the eroded forms of once authoritative institutions and ideas. What we mainly hear are the hollow winds of once compelling ideologies, and the unnerving gusts of new moods and slogans. What we mainly feel in our hearts is the granite consolidation of the technological and bureaucratic order, which may bring physical comfort and great collective power, or sterility, but not political liberty and moral autonomy. All the modern states, with the United States in the vanguard, are well advanced along a path toward a crisis of legitimacy.

—John H. Schaar,
"Legitimacy in the Modern State"

The Transformation of American Values

The American value system has undergone a major transformation since the years of our national founding. The pluralistic forces that early shaped our national character have largely disappeared,[1] as individualism has been diverted into service to modern organization. In contemporary America, the demands of modern organization overwhelm all other considerations, whether of family, religion, art, science, law, or the individual. Because we have thoughtlessly allowed this to happen, we have become a different people than we imagined we would be, than we think we are. In spite of our claims to individualism and cultural diversity, we have become a homogeneous people in our devotion to the values of the organizational imperative.

27

That was not the way it was to be, for the lodestar of the American dream was the complete individual. Central to American individualism was the belief that each person could know and achieve his or her interests better than any collectivity. We were confident that such personal knowledge gave individuals the possibilities of control over their destiny.

But as time passed, the autonomy of individuals became ever more meaningless, as the new organizational collectivities emerged. These vast, complex, technologically based modern organizations synthesized clusters of resources, including individuals, into rationally functioning wholes. Our lives became organizational lives and the organizational environment became as familiar to us as farms were to our ancestors. By now, the organizational way of life is commonplace and we accept its benefits neither gratefully nor ungratefully, but simply as a deserved inevitability.

But in the midst of all this organizationally generated affluence we sense that it has not brought a commensurate spiritual peace. Indeed, as Robert Heilbroner has written, that affluence has unmasked an agonizing "existential hunger."[2] It appears that the organizational way of life, in its present form, is neither natural nor happy for individuals. There is something about technology and organization that is baneful to the human spirit.

The Paradoxes of Technological Progress

Like many often used words, "technology" presumes a common meaning that pertains to the results that come from the application of scientific rationality to machines and to the organization of human labor. But this meaning is unduly narrow. In its larger sense, "technology" refers to an amalgam of empirical research methods, machines, techniques of organization, and a logic of rational analysis.[3] Furthermore, it was assumed that technology, so construed, was value neutral, and could be controlled by human intention. The managerial elite believes it can control technology because it created technology.

This nondeterministic belief was disassembled by Jacques Ellul, in an essay sarcastically entitled "The Machine Is Neutral Object and Man Is Its Master."[4] His point was that although individuals can control single machines, the network of machines and organizations is beyond them: "If man can claim to be the master of a machine, and even of every machine considered successively, can he claim to be the master of the technological whole of which each machine is a part?"[5] It is the whole interlocking network of machines that is the problem.

But who, specifically, has the responsibility to control the whole? Indeed, who has the capacity to even understand the whole, let alone control it? Some make the naive assertion that since scientists and engineers made technology, they are both willing and able to control it. This position is impossible to support. Scientists cannot control technology because the instruments for control are not in their hands. Instead, the managers control its development and use. Thus, more realistically, *the responsibility for the control of technology—and modern organization—lies entirely with management.*

If the responsibility to control technology lies with the managers, then how do they go about solving its problems? We believe they must begin by recognizing that modern organizations pose *ethical* problems. Ellul correctly notes that such organizations are "leading man to [a] new vision of good and evil,"[6] which is the paradox. Can managers solve the ethical problems created by organizations when their personal values have been shaped by those same organizations? This paradox was described by John Platt, who ranked "administrative management" third among the top American crises, surpassed only by total nuclear annihilation and great destruction short of annihilation. Unless we, as a nation, become better at management, our nation faces unbearable tensions. The key, however, is what is meant by "better." Unfortunately, Platt makes the mistake of believing that the answer lies in more "enlightened" management techniques: "the cure for bad management designs is better management designs."[7] Platt's stand will gain nods of assent from orthodox managers. But, like too many others within this circle, Platt has fallen for the deception that good methods guarantee good results: the notion that when practices are useful for the organization, they are thereby good for the individual.

Good management does not automatically result in "the good." Regardless of how well managers perform their jobs, it is unwarranted to suppose that social good will follow. As C. P. Snow has written: "We are immensely competent; we know our own pattern of operations like the palm of our hands. It is not enough . . . It would be bitter if, when this storm of history is over, the best epitaph that anyone could write of us was only that: 'The wisest men who had not the gift of foresight'."[8] In other words, no matter how well we manage, we must still foster leadership, which is quite different from management. Management may serve organizational America in many ways, but the one thing it does not necessarily provide is leadership.

Leadership involves, on the one hand, the capacity to understand the individual's requirements particular to different endeavors and the moral courage to defend such uniqueness. This dictum applies equally to corporations, universities, labor unions, government agencies, and the military. Orthodox managers, on the other hand, will pursue those conventional alternatives that are derived from the organizational status quo.[9] The military historians Richard Gabriel and Paul Savage, emphasized this point in their study of the management (or mis-management) of the U.S. Army in Vietnam. The deterioration of the field army, they claimed, was a direct result of the false premise that good management was good leadership. Discussing Robert S. McNamara's role in promulgating this idea, they wrote

> He was the ideal corporate man, and during his tenure as Secretary of Defense the Army moved ever closer to the modern business corporation in concept, tone, language, and style. Further, the individual military officer became identified with the corporate executive to the point where the functions of command were perceived as identical to the functions of departmental management. More and more of its officers were sent to graduate schools to take advanced degrees, almost all receiving degrees in business management or administration.[10]

The result was too often the loss of the unique leadership necessary for combat: elan, valor, and the ability to instill unit loyalty in the troops. Ideally, leadership has the foresight to extract itself from organizational imperatives.

Thus, the question is not whether modern organizations are governable. They are. Rather, the pertinent question is whether the managers, who have the power, also have the moral wit and moral courage necessary to alter the management value system upon which their power and perquisites depend. The matter is not just one of managerial competence; the more important matter is the need for moral leadership. But that raises the question as to the values managers should adopt. At present, they are locked into the values of the organizational imperative.

The New Legitimacy of the Organizational Imperative

The promise of the modern organization is that it can actually deliver both security and material abundance, and that these conditions are sufficient for a worthy life. From this claim came the new legitimacy of the organizational imperative. It was not the conscious product of a group of organizational Founding Fathers who wrote the propositions. Rather, it evolved as a cultural mutation and has become the major force that has transformed the American Founding Values. "Hence," as Schaar has written, "the test of legitimacy for them is not power's origins but its ends. And from this point of view, the 'public interest' means just about what it has always meant: security and material abundance."[11]

The organizational imperative consists of two a priori value propositions and four rules for behavior. The imperative is based upon a primary proposition which is absolute: *whatever is good for the individual can only come from the modern organization.* The question of the nature of that good is left purposely vague, to be filled in according to the current needs of the organization. What must be beyond doubt is the belief that the only way to achieve anything of significance is through the modern organization. The secondary proposition derives from the first: *therefore, all behavior must enhance the health of such organizations.* These two propositions constitute the primary values of the new legitimacy, especially as they pertain to the place of modern organizations in contemporary society.

From these propositions come four rules for organizationally healthy behavior that define, guide, and measure all managerial performance. They apply to every manager in every organization in modern society, and they constitute the legitimacy of the internal use of power. These behavioral rules require employees: (1) to be obedient to the decisions of superior managers, (2) to be technically rational, (3) to be good stewards of other people's property, and (4) to be pragmatic. Since the concepts of hierarchical obedience, rationality, stewardship, and pragmatism carry heavy burdens of numerous interpretations, we must specify their meaning with respect to the organizational imperative.

Hierarchical Obedience

In the traditional American conception of legitimacy, the flow of approval was upward: from the rank and file to the governors. The assumption underlying the effective functioning of all democratic societies is that those who hold power must be held directly accountable to the governed individuals who *relinquish* that power.[12] But the organizational imperative reversed the flow of accountability, devaluing the abilities of the rank and file to assess the performance of those in authority, while requiring from them obedience to directives from above. As Schaar pointed out:

> The flow is [now] from leaders to followers. Leaders lay down rules, promulgate policies, and disseminate symbols which tell followers how and what they should feel and do.[13]

This reversal of the traditional pattern of legitimacy means that the managerial elite is beyond criticism by those below it. The reason has nothing to do with the realities of executive decision making. It has everything to do with the maintenance of the status, power, and perquisites of the organizational elite.

Rationality

The rule of technical rationality is the common denominator for all scientifically conditioned, technologically oriented organizations in advanced industrial nations. We do not refer to the philosophic tradition of rationalism, but to that form of rationality central to scientific method: the logic of rational analysis. Drawing upon its heritage of science, engineering, and economics, management has made this logic indistinguishable from efficiency—the equation of $E = O/I$. The task of administration, guided by this formula, is to increase the value of E (efficiency) by adjusting the relative values of O (outputs) and I (inputs). While managers often argue over definitional refinements and are sometimes confused by their own rhetoric, this statement must be accepted, along with its behavioral implications, because there are few other satisfactory ways to hold managers accountable for what they do in modern organizations.

Stewardship

The organizational imperative requires competent stewards, but their primary stewardship must be upward: to the organizational imperative and the elite who serve it. They must be defenders of the faith and, beyond that, must proselytize on its behalf.[14] Their secondary loyalty must be downward: to the "others" in whose interests the organization is managed. It does not make a particle of difference who the "others" are: the public at large, the stockholders of a corporation, the members of a consumer cooperative, or the members of labor unions.

The rule of stewardship legitimizes the hierarchical structure of organizations. Stewardship requires the husbanding of organizational resources. If the stewardship rule is successfully executed, the health and wealth of the organization are protected and increased, the welfare of those dependent on the organization is improved, and the fortunes of its managers are advanced. As with rationality, divergent ideas about stewardship are unthinkable within the framework of management theory and practice as it has developed during the twentieth century.

Pragmatism

"Pragmatism" does not refer to the philosophy of Peirce, James, and Dewey, but rather to a contingent practicality. Pragmatic behavior enables the organization to survive in good health in changing environments, as circumstances continually impose different necessities upon managers. The rule of pragmatism requires no more than a devotion to expediency, guided by the primary and secondary propositions. Beyond this, the rule for pragmatic behavior has no other content.

The organizational world of management is one where complex problems of short-term duration must be dealt with expediently in order to advance the a priori propositions. Pragmatism demands that managers direct their energies and talents to finding solutions for practical, existing problems within an immediate time frame. The language, reward systems, and activities of management demonstrate this concern for the present. Its attention to putting out fires, meeting competition, adjusting to "inputs" from the public, ensuring the smooth day-to-day running of departments, and short-range planning horizons indicate its devotion to securing an orderly, purposeful world composed of interesting, narrow puzzles to be solved. This pragmatic puzzle world discourages managers from reflecting on larger, less immediate issues of long-range effects or needs.

Each of the behavioral rules involves the others. To be pragmatic is to be rational, in the sense that efficiency and expediency often amount to the same thing in practice. To be a competent steward means finding expedient solutions to pressing problems within boundaries defined by the logic of rational analysis; and, finally, practicality, rationality, and stewardship are the yardsticks that measure managerial success in organizations dominated by hierarchy. Therefore, the four behavioral rules exist in an interrelated web, the primary purpose of which is to strengthen the a priori propositions of the organizational imperative. What does this mean to American society?

Organizational Morality, Managerial Amorality

The domination of the organizational imperative has created a peculiar moral dilemma for managers. The separation of fact and value was the single most important legacy given to management by Chester I. Barnard's and Herbert Simon's respective works.[15] Barnard's a priori belief in the functional morality of organization opened the door for Simon to suggest that management attends to the discovery and application of administrative facts without the burden of value considerations. Managers were thus relieved of moral concerns beyond organizational functionality. Managers were to be driven by the facts to do whatever was necessary to ensure organizational health, which was their primary moral function.

The Criterion of Organizational Health

At one time, organizational health meant adjusting organizational inputs so that they were minimized relative to outputs. Success in this endeavor was called efficiency, and the object of management was to increase it. Efficiency meant lower costs, lower prices, higher profits, and better competitive status in the marketplace. The continuous growth of efficiency meant that everyone — managers, employees, customers, and, ultimately, all of society — would be better off.

At the time when efficiency measures were about the only formal standards for judging managerial performance, the word "health" was seldom used in connection with organizations. It has appeared more frequently as the metaphor likening organizations to organic systems has gained acceptance.[16] The metaphor assumes that an organization, similar to all living things, must manifest two characteristics to be judged healthy. First, it must be either growing or mature and stable. Of these characteristics, growth was preferable, since the economic system depended on it.[17] Maturity and stability were also acceptable, of course, but not for long; managers get fired for failing to return to growth patterns. (How quickly the organic analogy can be forgotten!) Above all, the organization must never be allowed to decline, contract, or shrink, as these conditions are unhealthy in the organic organization. Second, the organization must be adaptable, since healthy, complex organisms adjust to environmental contingencies in order to survive.

Thus growth and adaptability have been added to the older notion of efficiency as criteria for organizational health. The sum of these factors is now expressed by the term "organizational effectiveness," an ideal for managerial success. Unfortunately, few people are sure what the term means, let alone how to measure it.[18]

The criterion of organizational health has two interesting managerial consequences. The first is that managers must be amoral in order to obtain the most benefits for their organizations. Note, we argue that managers are "amoral," not "immoral." They must keep their value commitments open to the needs of the organizational imperative. Thus, they are also prohibited, by that imperative, from immoral action, on the basis that it is not good for the organization. Second, managers need not worry about the outcomes of their actions if they are expedient, for organizations shield managers from public accountability. We term these conditions the "methods of expediency" and the "shield of elitist invisibility."

The Methods of Expediency

When management theory emerged as a discipline, in the early twentieth century, the theories and methods of natural science were well advanced. One of the basic features of the natural sciences is the separation of fact and value. This separation allowed scientists to avoid troublesome value questions and to concentrate on the comparatively simple world of nature. Scientists confined their inquiries to the puzzles presented by the natural order and developed— concomitant with these puzzles—techniques that enable them to predict, and often to control, the events of the empirical universe. By limiting itself to a world capable of being known, science thus identified research goals that could be objectively verified and replicated. And there are an endless number of puzzles for scientists to solve.[19]

The enormous success of natural science was not lost on management. Scholars and practitioners optimistically presumed that their field could enjoy similar explosive progress by using the methods of science in managing organizational affairs. Accordingly, management began to transpose those methods into guidelines of its own, and scientific management, the earliest movement in that direction, was created by Frederick W. Taylor around 1900.[20]

To an extent, management's borrowing of the scientific method has been justified. Over the years major problems have been solved and management has learned a great deal. Unfortunately, the methodological single-mindedness with which management embraced scientific methods has resulted in a dangerous unwillingness to question values or discuss anything that cannot be treated empirically.

This failure to consider values is risky for any applied behavioral science, and it is lethal in the case of management. Clearly, management's value poverty is not the fault of science. It is the result of a combination of circumstances that elevated a false model of scientific method into a model suitable for management theory and practice. The need for empirical methods, joined with the need for solving the immediate problems of modern organizations, provided the foundation for managerial amorality. The methods of expediency are rooted here.

These methods are largely a practical exercise in puzzle solving. The rational requirements of technology, the coordination requirements of job specialization, and the productivity expectations of society require that managers direct their energies and talents to finding solutions for the immediate, practical, and material problems that confront them. So the pressures for solving these concrete problems have overridden any propensities for thinking about values.

Management has not, however, reluctantly turned away from such thinking. The motivation for it was never there to begin with; organizational puzzle solving is so engaging that serious concern about values is condemned within the management profession as a wasteful excursion into mysticism. Consequently, managers are rewarded only for the expedient solution of organizational problems; those who think about anything else are derided.[21]

So the policies, practices, and thoughts of management are heavily weighted toward the expedient by people who have been trained to consider value questions as closed. Managers, trained in the scientific management of organizations, enter into an orderly, purposeful, and balanced empirical world of puzzles "that only their own lack of ingenuity would keep them from solving."[22] That world offers managers security and status so long as the methods of expediency remain intact. Since questioning values is a threat to this security, there should be little wonder that it is neglected.

But there is a hitch. In the name of organizational health, managers must make decisions affecting the lives of many others, and while these decisions may be organizationally justified, they may also be morally indefensible. Are individual managers accountable to higher public tribunals of opinion for the morality— distinct from the legality—of their decisions? The answer is no, for personal responsibility is inconsistent with expediency. Therefore, managers must be shielded by the organization from accountability.

The Shield of Elitist Invisibility

We have argued for many years that there is a shield of elitist invisibility within organizational America.[23] By this we mean that cardinal decisions about our lives are made by organizational leaders who are both invisible and unaccountable. Some might claim that the exposure, prosecution, and jailing of managerial miscreants disprove this contention, and that there is some ultimate accountability for managers whether they serve in public or private enterprises. Theoretically, this is true, and from time to time dramatic examples of mismanagement or executive misdeeds are exposed. Certainly an epic disaster like the events in Bhopal was well covered by the media. Other indiscretions have also been reported, like the WedTech, E. F. Hutton, and General Dynamics scandals of the 1980s. But these exceptions prove the point that, if for no other reason, the cost and the effort required precludes the exposure of many or even most gross misdeeds.

However, it is not only misdeeds that are hidden; almost all managerial actions are shielded by the impenetrability of modern organizations, whether they be offensive, innocuous, or even gratifying to public opinion. We can recall seeing a picture of a corporate president saying goodbye to one of his subordinates at the gate of a federal prison. He was about to start serving time for a price-fixing conviction. Of course, it was the subordinate who was going in, not the president. The situation was the electrical industry price-fixing case in the late 1950s and early 1960s. The question was then, as it still is, why was the president of the company shielded from conviction and not the subordinate?

Other incidents come to mind. The Senate, investigating oil company practices during the OPEC embargo, simply could not get enough information from testifying executives to determine whether anything shady had been done to restrict oil supplies. But Senate investigators are not the only ones deprived of information for investigatory purposes. The shield of elitist invisibility even protects managers from inopportune inquiries from their own boards of directors. For example, the board of Gulf Oil, looking into the machinations of the company's chief lobbyist, was led astray by the top management through the 1970s. The clash between the board and management came to a head in 1975. It was asked why the board had not done more:

> Why did the directors behave as they did? In part, because they were led astray by the management. Gulf's general counsel and lawyers retained by the company withheld from the board some devastating details that they had turned up while looking into the company's transgressions. And Dorsey (the CEO) kept

secret from the board, for more than a year and a half after the scandal broke, the fact that he had personally authorized the largest political payments—$4 million to the party backing President Park Chung Hee of Korea.[24]

It is often said by public administration observers that government agencies are open with respect to their policies but very secretive about their procedures. The politicization of the U.S. General Accounting Office (GAO) supports this claim.[25] In organizational America it is extraordinarily difficult to get at high-level managers, public or private, to make them accountable for the legality, much less the morality, of their administrative decisions.[26]

One of the most effective shields protecting managerial performance is the reification of the organization in familiar phrases: "the company feels," organizations "do" this or "decide" that, organizations "behave responsibly" or "irresponsibly." This is consummate nonsense and we all know it. Yet we continue to write and speak about organizations as if they were persons. This obscures the fact that it is individuals who make decisions within organizations. To suggest that organizations "do" anything masks these individuals from view and depersonalizes both the value and moral issues implicit in their conduct, thus relieving them of individual responsibility and public accountability.

A second way in which the invisibility of the managerial elite is preserved is that their performance is measured by purely operational criteria. Because Americans are so dependent upon the efficient performance of organizational systems, they tend to hold managers operationally accountable for their actions and excuse all else. In other words, a manager's morality is equated with the utility of his or her actions, as they contribute to the health of the organization. As we have seen earlier, the measures of that utility are efficiency, growth, and adaptability. A manager may behave like Attila the Hun, but, if he or she contributes substantially to organizational effectiveness, all is forgiven. This is not because the public is morally insensitive, but because it lacks the technical expertise needed to understand the modern organization.

There is a third method of shielding, and it is extremely important. The value system of modern organizations has developed behind closed doors, so to speak. Managers continue to do what they must do, and the organizational values that guide their decisions are clear to them. But ordinary people are not privy to the intricacies of that value system. This has led to a widening gap between the popular beliefs about organizations and the actual practices of managers in modern organizations.

The Organizational Imperative: We All Win . . .

The organizational imperative is the sine qua non of management theory and practice. It cuts across organizational boundaries. It changes slowly, if at all. If it is affected tangibly by political and social turmoil, or even war, the imperative is strengthened by them. The organizational imperative is the metaphysic of management: absolute and immutable. It is persuasive (it alters values in order to alter behavior), it is universal (it governs, through the a priori propositions, all collective efforts for achieving major social and individual objectives), it is durable (it is the one source of stability and continuity in a turbulent world), and it is moral (it is derived from the assumptions about functional morality). In short, it constitutes the new legitimacy.

Before explaining these contentions, we must remember that the management of organizations is a practical and mundane effort. Implicit within the pragmatic rule is a warning against philosophizing. Management does the vital job of linking organizations, which are the most elaborate of abstractions, with the people. Organizations are run by managers who must make decisions about goals, policies, and strategies of action that influence human values and behavior, both within and outside the organization. They respond with varying sensitivity and accuracy to the needs and interests of the different groups affected by their decisions. But their loyalties seldom belong to those they affect most profoundly, and certainly they are neither trained nor encouraged to speculate about the value implications of their decisions. The vice-president for personnel of a large company that must lay off five hundred employees is certainly not encouraged to consider the impact of this action upon their lives. Instead, consideration is given to the health of the company.

Conventional wisdom has it that the primary loyalty of managers should be to those who own their organizations: the stockholders, if it is a private company, or the citizens, if it is a public organization. While that wisdom may be have been correct once, it is certainly not so now. *The overriding concern of managers is to keep their organizations healthy*: if their clients are served as a consequence, it is a happy secondary result of the primary managerial concern.

Organizational health is best achieved through management's total allegiance to the organizational imperative. To advance this cause, the values of all persons who influence the organization must be modified so that they complement the organizational imperative. This "imperialism" is a distinctive characteristic of the organizational imperative. Managers, therefore, must discipline themselves, their subordinates, and even their clients to arrange their values, expectations, and practical affairs so that the organizational imperative is served.

This generally requires the modification of traditional beliefs. For instance, the individualism of our pioneer past is more likely to get one fired than promoted in any large organization today, particularly one with a dress code. The required modifications of the older values convert almost all beliefs into organizationally supportive attitudes, which are always alterable to suit the needs of organizations in changing times and circumstances. Changes in employee behavior, however, do not produce changes in the organizational imperative, which holds absolute sway. Such behavioral and value alterations may be spiritually agonizing, but they are not materially painful, for those who are loyal to the organization are usually well rewarded.

As early as 1910, Frederick W. Taylor argued that scientific management had to be used to expand the productivity pie. He taught that individual advantage was best served when human energy was directed rationally toward increasing productivity rather than spent squabbling over the relative size of the shares of the pie. According to Taylor, workers, managers, owners, and consumers had a mutual interest in the continuous growth of productivity. Growth created surpluses in the form of economic abundance, which could be applied to finance still another cycle of growth.[27]

Out of this dream came the belief that material growth was absolutely essential to the vitality of national life and that the material abundance obtained from such growth was limitless. These were the necessary preconditions for the good that modern organizations created for the individual. Whatever Americans sought as individuals, they could find their satisfactions in the consumption of products and services. Material well-being was, to an appreciable extent, the basis for the *consensus* that cemented the social order, especially after the American Industrial Revolution of the late nineteenth century.

There has not been much difference between how Americans define their individual aims and what managers try to accomplish within organizations. Management practices are usually consistent with the expectations of Americans at large, since successful practices are thought to contribute to individual welfare. However, as technology has been carried by modern organizations into nearly every corner of society, a new and extremely important factor has been added to the equation for a good life. This factor has not eradicated customary materialistic conceptions of individual good. Rather, it has converted them to organizational terms. The organizational imperative was this factor, and the single most important change in public attitude it wrought was the creation of the idea that individual welfare can only be realized through the modern organization and its managerial systems.

Thus growth is a good, but the most important growth is organizational. Abundance is a good, but it is an organizationally produced abundance. Consensus is a good, but the crucial consensus is among potentially conflicting interest groups within organizations. For the most part these organizationally derived goods have materially benefited individuals. By managing organizational resources efficiently, growth results in financial and productive surpluses that—when distributed in a reasonably equitable way—promote positive attitudes among the recipients about the validity of the organization and the importance of expanding productivity. The goods of growth, abundance, and consensus have become guidelines for management practice that reconciled the organizational imperative with the people's expectations. Everyone can be satisfied when the productivity pie grows. But there is doubt that everyone can win, that growth can continue.

Notes

1. Henry S. Kariel, *The Decline of American Pluralism* (Stanford: Stanford University Press, 1961). See also David K. Hart and William G. Scott, "The Organizational Imperative," *Administration and Society*, 7 (Nov. 1975): 259–285.
2. Robert L. Heilbroner, *An Inquiry into the Human Prospect* (New York: Norton, 1974), 70.
3. "A machine is, logically speaking, an embodied decision procedure. By going through a finite and unvarying number of steps it arrives invariably, so long as it is not defective, at a definite result. . . . Since technology is merely the embodiment of a logical procedure, and this procedure divides the problem into a number of partial and successive steps, therefore the social accomplishment of the task will be divided into the accomplishment of those component parts. Consequently, we are each assigned our particular slot in society." William Barrett, *The Illusion of Technique* (Garden City, N.Y.: Anchor Press, 1978), 20, 22–23.
4. Jacques Ellul, *A Critique of the New Commonplaces*, trans. H. Weaver (New York: Knopf, 1968), 226–235.
5. Ellul, *Commonplaces*, 228.
6. Ellul, *Commonplaces*, 230.
7. John Platt, "What We Must Do," *Science* 28 (Nov. 1969): 1117.
8. C. P. Snow, *Science and Government* (Cambridge: Harvard University Press, 1961), 84.
9. The military historian Major Andrew Krepinevich discusses how the U.S. Army's dedication to its doctrine (or concept) on the conduct of conventional warfare in the European theater of operations prevented the Joint Chiefs of Staff from structuring an effective counterinsurgency response to the combat conditions in Vietnam. Andrew Krepinevich, *The Army and Vietnam* (Baltimore: Johns Hopkins University Press, 1986).
10. Richard A. Gabriel and Paul L. Savage, *Crisis in Command* (New York: Hill and Wang, 1978), 19.
11. John H. Schaar, "Legitimacy in the Modern State," in Philip Green and Sanford Levinson, eds., *Power and Community* (New York: Pantheon Books, 1970), 289.
12. Louis Fry, William G. Scott, Terence R. Mitchell, and Patricia Nemetz, "Who Evaluates the Evaluator: A Study of Governance Practices in Professional Bureaucracies," (unpublished manuscript, 1988 Annual Meeting of the Academy of Management, Anaheim, Calif.).
13. Schaar, "Legitimacy," 285.
14. Barnard, *Function of the Executive* (see chap.1, n. 14), chapter 17.
15. Terence R. Mitchell and William G. Scott, "The Barnard-Simon Contribution: A Vanished Legacy," *Public Administration Quarterly*, 12 (Fall, 1988): 348–368.
16. Examples are legion, but note particularly Warren Bennis, *Changing Organizations* (New York: McGraw-Hill, 1966).

17. Rolf H. Wild, *Management by Compulsion: The Corporate Urge to Grow* (Boston: Houghton Mifflin, 1978).
18. For an excellent review article on this subject see Richard M. Steers, "Problems in the Measurement of Organizational Effectiveness," *Administrative Science Quarterly* (Dec. 1975): 546–551.
19. See Thomas S. Kuhn, *The Structure of Scientific Revolutions*, 2nd ed. (Chicago: University of Chicago Press, 1970).
20. Daniel Nelson, *Frederick W. Taylor and the Rise of Scientific Management* (Madison: University of Wisconsin Press, 1980). It is suggestive on this point to mention that the first major movement in administrative theory was "scientific management"; later, two key fields of study and practice emerged, called "management science" and "operations research," and at present two of the most respected professional journals are *Administrative Science Quarterly* and *Management Science*.
21. Daniel Katz and Robert L. Kahn, *The Social Psychology of Organizations* (New York: John Wiley, 1966), 55.
22. Kuhn, *Scientific Revolutions*, 37.
23. William G. Scott and David K. Hart, "Administrative Crisis: The Neglect of Metaphysical Speculation," *Public Administration Review*, 33 (Sept.–Oct. 1973): 415–422.
24. Wyndham Robertson, "The Directors Woke Up Too Late at Gulf," *Fortune* (June, 1976): 121.
25. D. Brock, "Politicizing the Government's Watchdog," *Wall Street Journal* (July 16, 1986).
26. Mendes Hershman, "Liabilities and Responsibilities of Corporate Officers and Directors," *The Business Lawyer* 33 (Nov. 1977): 263–308. By and large the courts have been unwilling to cause any major changes in the "prudent man" and "due diligence" doctrine relative to corporate management. Therefore, it is extremely difficult to prove negligence. These rules add to the shield of elitist invisibility because it is nearly impossible by legal action to hold management liable for bad decisions or incompetency.
27. Frederick W. Taylor, *The Principles of Scientific Management* (New York: Harper & Bros., 1919), 6.

4

The Organizational Imperative Realized

> *People grow restive with a mythology that is
> too distant from the way things actually are,
> and as more and more lives have been encom-
> passed by the organization way of life, the
> pressures for an accompanying ideological shift
> have been mounting. The pressures of the group,
> the frustrations of individual creativity, the an-
> onymity of achievement: are these defects to
> struggle against or are they virtues in dis-
> guise? The organization man seeks a redefini-
> tion of his place on earth—a faith that will
> satisfy him that what he must endure has a
> deeper meaning than appears on the surface.
> He needs, in short, something that will do for
> him what the Protestant Ethic did once. And
> slowly, almost imperceptibly, a body of thought
> has been coalescing that does that.*
>
> —William H. Whyte, Jr.,
> *The Organization Man*

We All Win . . . or Do We?

The benefits of organizational America do not come for free; everyone
must pay. And paying that debt has required us to surrender our allegiance to
the traditional values of the American founding and substitute for them the
values of the organizational imperative. As technology, organization, and
management have penetrated more deeply into the social order, collisions of
increasing severity have been unavoidable between those early values that
supported the small-town, agricultural orientations of our past and the new
organizational values.

The result has been a revolution in our value system, which was largely
unanticipated as recently as World War II. But warnings were widely sounded
after the war by many perceptive observers. Among the most important was

William H. Whyte, Jr., whose book *The Organization Man* enjoyed great success in the 1950s. He presented a particularly insightful, accurate, and timely appraisal of what was happening. Whyte argued that America was shifting from an ethic of individualism to an organizational ethic, which was not yet articulated. His contention was that organizations—through their management systems—were imposing their values upon all Americans, in virtually every area of their interaction. He noted that the situation was producing the value-lag described in the epigraph.

Unfortunately, most people misread his message as simply another condemnation of conformity, a nonfiction version of the popular novel *The Man in the Grey Flannel Suit*[1] that had appeared a year earlier in 1955. Thus, the theme of conformity was disproportionately emphasized, while the essential meaning of Whyte's book—his identification of organizational trends that were changing our values—was almost completely overlooked. Whyte was concerned with the same moral dilemma that had plagued philosophers since the beginnings of the Industrial Revolution: that a "society as an engine for the production and multiplication of goods was inherently hostile to society as the moral foundation of personality."[2]

In the turmoil of the 1960s, Whyte's warnings were forgotten. The explosive protests against the status quo deluded us into a belief that the bases of modern organization were being changed and humanized. That was a mistake, for in spite of urban and campus riots, civil rights and peace movements, and all the other distractions of that decade, the organizational imperative grew even stronger. The irony was that as organizations came under fire, they found ever more effective ways to maintain their specific value system, and America drifted even further into the embrace of modern organization.

This becomes clear when one studies the history of the times.[3] Paralleling the rise of the hip generation was a new generation of managers. The contemptible "organization men" of the 1950s became laudable models of managerial dedication: the "best and the brightest," the most visible of whom served in the Kennedy administration. These new managers, products of the more scientific schools of management, rose to leadership in many institutions: business, public agencies, foundations, universities, hospitals, and even churches. And, in order to maintain coherence and security in their lives, to overcome Whyte's value-lag, they constantly exerted pressure to bring social values into a harmonious and reinforcing relationship with the organizational imperative to which they had pledged total allegiance. Their philosophers and spokesmen were intellectuals of the first rank: from the elder statesman, Chester I. Barnard, to the contemporary spokesmen, Peter Drucker, Herbert Simon and Philip Selznick.

So, contrary to the conclusions of the easily distracted media, the ideal individuals of the 1960s were not the "with-it" hippies, the peace activists, the committed and articulate university students, or the humanist psychologists. Rather, they were the superbly trained, functionally devoted, essentially amoral managers. They were us, and most of us became them, if not in actuality, then at least in spirit. The irony was that we presumed we were following another model: John F. Kennedy set a fine intellectual style, as he called for a modern Renaissance, led by a new generation of Americans. But, we did not become like him; we became like those he hired.[4] Whyte's prophesies were fulfilled with only the slightest public recognition of what was happening.

Securing the dominance of the modern organization amid the cultural upheaval of the 1960s has been the major triumph of management in contemporary America. And, because of their vital posts in all organizations, the members of the new managerial elite are now able to influence the substance of popular values: they design the educational curricula; they allocate the funding; they choose which books to publish, which movies to film, which television programs to sponsor.

Through the mediating role of management, the values of modern America now reinforce the organizational imperative. Outrageous as it seemed to activists after the travails of the 1960s, organizational values were clearly predominant by the mid-1970s. The organizational imperative had become the dominant force in the collectivization of America, displacing the more individualistic values of the past.

But this should have come as no surprise. Modern organizations require specific beliefs from all individuals if the organizations are to survive. Therefore, the most fundamental task of members of the managerial elite in maintaining their organizations must be to ensure the inculcation of the values of the organizational imperative in all citizens. The leading role in this process has been openly assumed by the elite management theorists and practitioners, who were, from the outset, the voice, the facilitators, and the arbitrators of the change in American values. Now that that change is complete, they have become the defenders of the entrenched organizational values.

To illustrate our argument, we shall discuss six values, central to the American tradition, that have changed under the irresistible pressures of the organizational imperative. The values have been paired in figure 4.1: the first column sets out a few of the prominent values of our tradition; the second column indicates the values now dominant.

These pairs are not exhaustive, but they do demonstrate the contrasting profiles of what we were and what we have become. Perhaps the most fundamental of the value pairs is the conception of the innate moral nature of the individual.

Figure 4.1

The Changing American Value System: From Individual
America to Organizational America

A	B
The Values of the Individual Imperative	The Values of the Organizational Imperative
Innate Human Nature ————————	Malleability
Individuality ———————	Obedience
Indispensability ———————	Dispensability
Community ———————	Specialization
Spontaneity ———————	Planning
Voluntarism ———————	Paternalism

From Innate Moral Nature to Malleability

To understand any organization, one must begin with an answer to the basic question: what a priori conception of the innate moral nature of the individual instructs and legitimizes the system of authority? Political philosophers have understood the primacy of this issue for centuries:

> Underlying every system of government there is some predominant conception of the nature of man and the meaning of human existence. More often than not, this idea of man is implicit rather than explicit. But if not always explicit, it is always fundamental. For what we think government can and ought to do will depend in large part upon what we think about the capacities of men and the purpose of human existence. If our conception of man's essential nature and ultimate destiny is false, i.e., unreal, we may be led to seek and apply political solutions to human and social problems that at best are useless and at worst harmful.[5]

The same thing is true for any organization, public or private, economic or social. Furthermore, as modern organizations have gotten larger, more overlapping, and more intrusive, the matter of their conception of the moral nature of individuals is of enormous importance, for it determines how they will govern the people within them. Their conception of moral nature will largely determine the substance of our lives.

On the one hand, if the dominant assumption is that people are innately evil, then the manner of governance will be authoritarian, rule-dominated, and perhaps even cruel. It was just such a conception that supported Machiavelli's belief that rulers must be feared more than loved, if they wished to succeed in their reigns.[6] The state that derived from such an assumption was severe and life within it was scarcely pleasant for anyone other than the rulers. That belief, along with Machiavelli's ambitions, explains the most unpleasant prescriptions of *The Prince*. Western civilization has seen many such states. On the other hand, if one assumes that people are innately compassionate, quite a different use of power will be recommended. This is clear when one looks at the prescriptions of Jean Jacques Rousseau or those of most of the philosophers of the Scottish Enlightenment, from Francis Hutcheson to Adam Smith.[7]

Thus the subject of innate moral nature was of enormous interest to the moral and political philosophers of the eighteenth century, and they vigorously debated it. The Founders were very much a part of that tradition and so this matter is of more than passing historical interest: it defines the legitimate uses of power in American institutions. The Founders did not believe humans were completely malleable, capable of being molded into virtually any form, without spiritual damage. From Hamilton's dark distrust of human nature to Jefferson's bright optimism, the Founders believed that the institutions of society had to be designed to conform to that innate nature. What they would not accept was that individuals were nothing until institutions molded them into something—that it was up to the institutions of a society to give shape, meaning, and substance to individual lives.

But that is precisely the conception of innate moral nature required by the organizational imperative, and it has become the dominant image in organizational America. From the outset, management has been concerned with getting people to be obedient to management instructions. Usually these concerns have been subsumed under studies of structures or systems or economic processes. But management also had to create rational ways to bring people, resources, and specialized tasks together into efficiently functioning arrangements.

So, consistent with the methods of expediency, management has created powerful organizational methods of control. But it is rare to find equally forceful attempts in managerial thought to understand the innate nature of the individual who is to be controlled. We do *not* imply that managerial thought does not have a vision of innate moral nature. To the contrary, management has been dominated by a succession of such images. Although these implicit value assumptions are seldom recognized as the foundations of managerial thought, they are deeply embedded in both theory and practice.

In an early essay entitled "The Moral Nature of Man in Organizations," we examined the evolution of these images, comparing the ideas of three management theorists (Frederick W. Taylor, Elton Mayo, and Douglas McGregor) with three political philosophers (Hobbes, Locke, and Rousseau). Noting some basic similarities and differences, we wrote that

> Taylor and Hobbes believed in the need for maximum control to beat back *predatory* man. McGregor and Rousseau, in opposition, agreed to a minimiza-

tion of the institutions of control to allow man's *innate compassion* to be released. . . . Mayo and Locke occupied somewhat the center ground where man, being *basically indeterminate*, had to be formed through education to develop his own rational controls.[8]

The conclusion we drew there was that the view of human nature held by management theorists necessarily influences all their prescriptions for the management and design of organizations. A Frederick W. Taylor would prescribe differently from a Douglas McGregor. This particular point is so obvious in management thought that the models of the individual proposed by Taylor and McGregor are often used as examples of the extremes in organizational government: autocracy and democracy, respectively.

But theoretical fashions change, and the good-evil, democracy-autocracy polarities in the old management thought faded away. A new vision of innate moral nature has become predominant. It can be seen lurking in the shadows of the currently fashionable ideas that hold that there are no morally right or wrong ways for management to organize and control. The new idea of what managers should do depends upon the practical demands of organizational size, environment, and technology. Thus, management thought not based upon moral and ethical relativism, upon a conception of the individual as malleable, is condemned.

This pragmatic approach grants managers a marvelous plasticity in adapting themselves and the people in their organizations to technological change and environmental tempests—whatever happens and however often. This conviction about human malleability is, in fact, the necessary condition required by the organizational imperative; thus it is embedded solidly within every modern organization. This image is based on the belief that the individual is, by nature, nothing and has the potential to be made into virtually anything. Therefore, organizations must be designed to mold individuals, since there is nothing in their nature to prevent their adapting to whatever value premises and organizational contingencies are required. There can be little doubt that in the eyes of management the contemporary image of the individual's nature is one of malleability.

The psychologist Elton Mayo postulated, in the 1930s, the notion of human malleability in a way that management found extraordinarily useful. In his influential book *The Human Problems of an Industrial Civilization*,[9] he argued that the individual has an indeterminate nature. This vision of innate malleability has solved some serious personnel problems.

The technology upon which our society is built is so complex and expensive that it is more cost-effective to change people rather than systems. The means used to accomplish this goal is the education curriculum and standard management practices. They all bring pressure onto the individual to change to what the organization needs. Since it is assumed that the ultimate ends of the modern organization are functionally moral, little thought has been given to whether the presumption of malleability is harmful to the individual. We have simply accepted our pliant role.

This is a dangerous situation, because it does not allow for the serious consideration of whether it is morally right to act upon the presumption that individuals are malleable. Management gravitates toward the tangible realities of immediate organizational solutions that work and do not disturb the organizational cosmos.

The presumption of malleability means the individual need not get in the way of technological and organizational requirements, since nothing innate in individuals will cause them to resist adaptation if the rewards are sufficient. In other words, management theory assumes individuals can be shaped, by psychological interventions, into anything the organization wants them to be. The problems of the individual are reduced to empirical puzzles. This presumption has become a third a priori of the organizational imperative: *the individual can be shaped or, given a shift in events, reshaped for maximum organizational utility.*

There is no moral obligation to the individual as an individual in the management theory of human malleability. This allows management to focus its attention upon human behavior that is reducible to statements of fact that are subject to empirical verification. This absolves managers from any need to consider individual rights to liberty or justice, or from any personal responsibility for the lives of the people they manage, because human behavior is a scientific problem and not a moral one.

A sophisticated variant of Mayo's image of the individual is dominant in contemporary management thought. This position may be far beyond anything Mayo wanted or anticipated,[10] but it is now the orthodox belief. The only element still needed for the fulfillment of this vision is for individuals to accept their own malleability. Not only must all people believe they are, by nature, malleable, they must also accept this condition as positive.[11] When that happens, the managerial domination of society will be complete.

This is a major cultural renovation of America. The change began in the 1920s, when influential writers like Elton Mayo, A. A. Berle, G. C. Means, and Chester I. Barnard were struggling to understand the then-emerging national managerial system. It was clear to them that management was in just the strategic position for planning and bringing into being changes in values. Barnard, in particular, foresaw that management had to be the final arbiter of social values. He wrote: "The distinguishing mark of the executive responsibility is that it requires not merely conformance to a complex code of morals but also the creation of moral codes for others."[12] Mayo and Barnard never dreamed how prophetic they were about the evolving managerial society.[13]

Managers have set the tone of society by their influence on values. Since managers control modern organizations, they can write programs of social control for people who cannot hope to accede to managerial power but whose support is absolutely necessary for maintaining the managerial regime. These are the "insignificant people," discussed in chapters 6 and 7, who must be convinced of their malleability and insignificance. But such persuading is not a part of managerial responsibility, in any sense justified by the Founding values. Regardless, management scholars and practitioners have not only accepted the premise of innate human malleability (without a trace of philosophical reflection), they have become its primary spokesmen. This demonstrates a moral bankruptcy, for individuals are not completely malleable.

From Individuality to Obedience

De Tocqueville, among others, correctly observed that Americans have ranged, with marvelous inconsistency, from individuality to conformity. Nevertheless, individualism has held a unique and dominant place in our tradition because it is associated with the principle of liberty that Americans esteem. Individualism has been interpreted in many ways, but central to them all was the confidence that people knew, or could know, what was best for themselves. As John Stuart Mill wrote: "With respect to his own feelings and circumstances, the ordinary man or woman has means of knowledge immeasurably surpassing those that can be possessed by anyone else."[14]

Legitimacy was conferred upon American social, economic, and political institutions when they conformed to the individual's perception of right and wrong. Granted, this was an ideal, but it was nonetheless an ideal we tried to put into practice. David Riesman provides a definition of that individuality in his description of the "inner-directed man."[15] The most significant justifications for action came from the individual, and the satisfactions derived from such personal actions were infinitely superior to those that came from obedience to collectivities. The ideal of individual freedom was the essential foundation for our notions about representative government and the free market.

In our time, the organizational imperative requires individual obedience to it. What is more, organizational obedience is now considered of greater worth than individuality. Unreflectively, the leaders of most American organizations still proclaim on public occasions the importance of individuality, while demanding utter obedience from their employees. When are they to exercise such individuality? Certainly not on the job. Given that reality, our allegiance has shifted quietly from individuality to obedience to the organizational demands. The claim is now made that obedience to organizational rules results in far superior personal satisfaction. In short, it is good for individuals to be obedient. Obedience is, therefore, the foundation of hierarchy, and modern organization is unthinkable without the chain of command. There are two particularly important aspects of obedience: homogenization and organizational morality.[16]

Psychologist Stanley Milgram distinguished between conformity and obedience as follows: "Conformity [is] the action of a subject when he goes along with his peers, people of his own status, who have no special right to direct his behavior. Obedience [is] the action of the subject who complies with authority."[17] Americans are conformists, but that is of less concern than the fact that we have become an obedient people. We have accepted the supposed realities of organizational life and now look to the managerial elite for direction. Employee obedience and loyalty have been approvingly elevated by the management scholar Dennis W. Organ to define organizational citizenship behavior (OCB) as the "good soldier syndrome."[18] The conventional wisdom that holds that America is a land of diversity is false. We have become an extremely homogeneous people, conforming to the standards of a mass culture. But, more significantly, we have also become homogeneous because we have, perversely, made individual decisions to be obedient to organizational authority.

In a sense, we have become like the members of a religious sect. They become the same from observing the same standards, *not* from observing each other. In a similar manner, individuality has been lost because we accept the same organizational values.

Furthermore, the higher one rises in an organization, the more his or her values must be synonymous with organizational values. Individual idiosyncrasies cannot be allowed to impede the effective operation of the organization. Hence, the desired attitude for those who would advance within the organization is the willingness to substitute organizational values for personal preferences. In order to be of the greatest usefulness to the modern organization, individuals must be personally amoral and organizationally moral. That is, they must willingly internalize the values of the organization as their own values, without a qualm. This requires that they accept the premise that the organizational imperative is morally superior to any conflicting individual moral commitments.

Such commitments are not new. Human history is full of accounts of "true believers," individuals who gained meaning for their lives by committing themselves totally to a cause or a movement.[19] What is new is that the organizational imperative does not require the fanaticism so common to mass movements. Indeed, the organizational way of life is very nearly the antithesis of fanaticism. But one central feature of mass movements is present: the substitution of the collective absolute for personal values.

The values of the organizational imperative are clear and easily understood. Further, their application has produced observable and beneficial results; this is the stuff of conversion. However, individual values are not easily determined and held in the best of times. When confronted with the clarity and force of the organizational imperative, conflicting individual values are easily swept aside or, more likely, converted into organizationally useful values. By adopting the organizational imperative as the foundation of personal values, the agonies of introspection and the articulation of personal value commitments are removed and purpose is given to individual lives.

The situation is reinforced by the fact that such a conversion is usually painless, materially rewarding, and brings with it the approbation of one's employers. The rule that emerges, which is nearly universal throughout our institutions, is that efficient performance in the service of organizational values is considered good behavior. Thus, our standards of personal morality are defined by their usefulness to organizational goals: in other words, functional morality.

So something like the following sequence has occurred. First, because of the successes of the modern organization, conventional wisdom has elevated its imperative over individual values. Second, since organizational values are given precedence over individual values, individuals are invariably rewarded for believing in their personal malleability. Third, once individual malleability is accepted, individual morality becomes synonymous with organizationally useful attitudes and behaviors. Individuals are rewarded for "adjusting" their personal attitudes and behaviors to bring them into congruence with the organizational imperative. The result is the substitution of obedience for individualism, so the organization will be better served.

From Indispensability to Dispensability

An important value in the American tradition has been the belief that individuals were justified in feeling indispensable to the groups, organizations, and communities of which they were a part. Honorable people had the right to expect that their absence would have a profound effect upon those who worked and lived with them. For example, when the great historian Frederick Jackson Turner was a young assistant professor at the University of Wisconsin, in 1889, a senior professor of history died: "His passing plunged the university into mourning; classes were canceled, the massive pillars at the entrance to the campus were draped in black, and all social events were put off until after the funeral, three days later."[20]

The community was sorrowfully diminished by the passage of one individual. One might ask what would be the response of a major university today upon the death of a single professor? At best, the deceased would earn a mention in the mimeographed notes of the next faculty senate meeting, and perhaps a minute of silence at the beginning of that meeting. During that observance those attending would surreptitiously look at their watches so that they could be first to be recognized by the chair after the inconvenience was over.

Throughout history, including parts of our own, people have dispensed with one another in callous and brutal ways, and most people have probably never really felt indispensable. Nevertheless, the ideal of personal indispensability has been central to our tradition, and its attainment has been held out as one of the most important rewards of an honorable life. Simply, indispensability meant that individuals could have a sense of being necessary to their kin and their communities.

But the organizational imperative requires that no one be indispensable and that, indeed, dispensability be a prized attribute. Modern American society is built upon the dispensability of things, and our economy is founded upon the necessity of the dispensability of products through the consumption cycle. The major purpose of obsolescence is to enrich organizations. Our lives are spent in surroundings of constant material replacement because our technology and our economy have made it more efficient to dispose of things rather than to reuse them.

All of this is well known. What is less well understood is how individuals in a society that exalts dispensability might eventually come to view themselves. Further, how does a society that demands that nothing (save modern organizations) be indispensable come to regard individuals? The answer is that people are required to believe they are dispensable and, further, that this is a good thing.

Modern organizations cannot tolerate necessary individuals. If they did, organizations would become dependent upon them, and such a situation is anathema to managerial thought and practice. For example, consider a familiar metaphor of the organization as a machine. In a machine, each part is linked as efficiently as possible with all the other parts. Each performs its specific tasks in a productive rhythm with all the others. If there is an ample supply of spares, any part of the machine is dispensable, even though some parts are more expensive to replace than others. The engineer must not only keep the machine running, but also ensure an adequate supply of spare parts.

In the modern organization, the manager, analogous to the engineer, must keep the organization running as efficiently as possible. Like the engineers, managers must ensure that an adequate supply of spare parts, including their own, is immediately available through the personnel department. The motto of the modern manager demonstrates the principle: "I've trained my own replacement." At all levels and in all capacities, personnel must be replaceable by others of similar abilities with a minimal loss of efficiency during the transition. If there are enough human spares, there need never be any major upheavals because of turnover. The difficulty here is that while no machine part needs to be convinced of its dispensability, a human being does.

The organizational imperative demands that people accept the principle of dispensability, and one of the main tasks of the American educational system is to reinforce that idea. From the earliest grades on, books, articles, teachers, and professors hammer away at the theme that individuals have no right to expect that they might become necessary, nor should they attempt to do so. It is stressed, as a fact of life in the real world, that the dream of personal indispensability is selfish and, even worse, organizationally intolerable.

One of our graduate students, when asked to comment on what an MBA program should do for him, observed that he wanted us to consider him as a sausage being prepared for consumption by a large organization. He argued that nothing should be stuffed into him that would give his employer (who would consume him!) indigestion. Some variant of this sentiment is drilled into students as an essential part of the managerial attitude they should take with them to the job. Certainly it is quickly learned the moment students are employed.

But this process of organizational socialization does not stop at the boundaries of the employing organizations. As the organizational imperative has affected more and more social values, the attitude of dispensability has extended into all areas of our lives, and there is now a widespread belief that indispensability is an illusion, nowhere to be found.

If individuals do indeed have an innate need to be necessary in their world (and they do), this particular value transition is destructive. A society of people convinced of their personal dispensability has many baleful characteristics, from alienation to nihilism. And the condition worsens with age, for the aging and the elderly are the most dispensable.[21] And so the terrible paradox: as people flee more deeply into the organization, searching for security, they find only that there they are the most dispensable commodity of all.

From Community to Specialization

Part of America's magnificent inconsistency has been a stubborn commitment to the seemingly contradictory values of individuality and conformity to community norms, be they of family, farm, small town, ethnic group, church, occupation, or whatever. But the values of community and indispensability went hand in hand, for individuals prized for their personal qualities contributed something unique to the continuity, warmth, and support found in community.[22] When they were gone, the quality of those multiple community virtues was lessened, community life was diminished, and those people who were left behind realized that the bell tolled not only for those departed but for them as well. The life of the community could never be experienced again in quite the same manner.

The organizational imperative has transformed the value of community, as it has the other values discussed here. In this instance, the organizational imperative requires that the individual's dedication be primarily to a specialty that is harmonious with, and contributes to, the systemic needs of an organization. Clearly, specialization does not exist for its own sake. For specialization to have any meaning, it must have utility for the organization. So, regardless of the functions managers perform, the stewardship of their responsibilities is measured by their utility to the organization. Loyalty must not, therefore, be given to the work group, to the place, or to some abstract ideal of honor, hospitality, or obligation; rather, loyalty must be to the specialized function, the successful performance of which adds to the whole organizational effort. The present emphasis on "professional bureaucracies" simply increases the importance of specialization;[23] while personnel, projects, departments, and jobs may come and go, specialization goes on forever.

The criteria by which an individual's worth is evaluated in a community are quite different from those by which an individual's utility is assessed in an organization. The organizational imperative requires a denial of community. An individual's worth, in organizational terms, is not measured by the quality of his or her relationship with others. When has friendship ever been considered a standard in wage and salary administration? Instead, worth is measured quantitatively, wherever possible, by the level of one's specialized performance relative to the achievement of organizational goals.

Finally, specialization and dispensability are comfortable, even necessary, partners. Specialization has always been considered impersonally in management. The efficient way to manage people in modern organizations is to objectify their jobs and to assign quantitative standards in order to judge their performances. These standards allow little room for affective considerations other than those with organizational utility, such as interpersonal competence, which helps people work together temporarily in more effective teams.[24]

There is no room for community, in the traditional sense of the word, within modern organizations, since it requires individuals to become indispensable to one another. No modern organization could tolerate such real interpersonal relationships. The loss of meaning in one's life because of the absence of community cannot be replaced by the dispassionate rewards that come from specialization. Yet specialization predominates because it is required by the organizational imperative.

From Spontaneity to Planning

Another value central to the American tradition has been spontaneity. As usual, it has been interpreted in a number of ways. Its most dramatic example was the entrepreneur who was willing to stake everything on high-risk ventures for the sake of personal gain. There was a spontaneity, also, among the pioneers who opened the West. But the most significant form of spontaneity was found in problem solving. Americans believed that the really serious problems would most often be solved by individuals through spontaneous, creative action. While such individual spontaneity, by definition, could not be anticipated in detail, it was assumed that it would somehow occur, in mysterious ways and at appropriate times, to the benefit of society in general or specific organizations in particular. The spontaneous, creative, enterprising individual would work wonders in all areas, from farming and industry to politics and governance. The result would be a better way of doing things, creating on the way more jobs, goods, and services, and ending with improvement in the welfare of society.

Thus, spontaneity became an integral part of the American business character. The moral lesson in the Horatio Alger and Frank Merriwell stories was simply that anyone with "pluck and luck" would succeed. "Pluck" meant the motivation to act creatively in unforeseen circumstances to solve problems. "Luck" referred to the risk that a plucky person had to assume if he was to make his way. The implication in these stories was that if individuals took action from an intuitive knowledge of what was right, Lady Luck would bend in their favor. Individual, spontaneous action was prized because it brought favorable outcomes for all concerned, especially when guided by a sense of moral rectitude. In this way, the uncertainties of life were seen not as fearsome but as sources of opportunity.

Management needs in modern organizations have changed this. The world of management is composed of short-term, complex, immediate problems. But the future must also be taken into account in setting goals, mapping strategies, making budgets, establishing policies, allocating resources, and so on. In short, managers must plan. However, they cannot plan spontaneity. Therefore, there is not only a low premium placed upon spontaneity in management theory and practice, it is also seen as harmful. The future cannot be left either to chance or to spontaneous individual reactions. Organizations need systematic and informed projections about the future.

As more investment capital is committed to plant and equipment, as the time span between the beginning and the end of tasks or projects lengthens, as more specialized personnel are hired, and as the flexibility of an organization diminishes in relation to its increased fixed resources, planning activities expands dramatically. First, managers must eliminate as much guesswork as possible. This requires the development and application of better forecasting techniques. Second, managers must control as many external variables as possible, because they influence the direction of the organization in uncertain ways. By controlling these variables, today's forecasts become tomorrow's self-fulfilling prophecies. Third, managers must reduce the possibilities that aberrant, including *spontaneous*, individual behavior will unpredictably alter the course of planned future events. Finally, managers must control behavior in the planning process itself. This means that planning ideally should be a collective activity, because group performance is more measurable and predictable than individual performance.

That control and planning are conceptual counterparts is a frequently cited management adage. However, it is certain that as managerial planning grows, controlling also grows, if for no other reason than to prevent random or deviant occurrences from confounding plans. This explains why spontaneity is by now a doubtful and even dangerous behavioral commodity. It is unpredictable, hence, uncontrollable. And while the organization may lose some advantage from spontaneously creative acts, this loss is offset by the more easily controlled behavior that arises from collective planning activities.

From Voluntarism to Paternalism

In the past, when individuals required concerted action to achieve common aims, it was assumed that they would combine voluntarily into interest groups and that their communal efforts would be effective. Associations of freely participating individuals were so much a part of the American way of doing things that the traditional political theory of pluralism and the economic theory of countervailing power rested,[25] to a substantial degree, upon the principle of voluntarism. This principle underlay the familiar American ideals of industrial democracy, collective self-determination, federalism, decentralization, and government by consent.

The labor movement is a dramatic example of how voluntarism worked. Samuel Gompers was aware that American public opinion, around the turn of the century, was not receptive to radical, politically oriented labor movements, so he rooted the organizational philosophy of the American Federation of Labor in two tenets—voluntarism and economic unionism. In its early days, the success of the A. F. of L. vindicated his judgment. No small reason for its survival, when other attempts at labor federation were failing, was due to the fact that the ideas of free association and economic self-interest corresponded to widely held American values. So, while the unionization of workers was a bitter prospect for many in business and government, they began to realize after a long struggle that it was better to have a labor movement congruent with prevailing values than one that subscribed to alien, revolutionary philosophies.

Voluntarism, of course, had many adherents outside the labor movement. Farmers, accountants, consumers, doctors, professors, engineers, business-people, lawyers, and many others have formed voluntary associations at different times, with varying degrees of success. Our point is that voluntarism reflected a compromise between individualism and collectivism, presenting us with an ingenious amalgamation of these extremes.

Americans have traditionally believed that social structures were the result of deliberate decisions traceable to individual acts. This belief implied autonomy, free will, individual responsibility and accountability, and generally accepted cultural values that guided the conduct of individuals in making choices. It is also true that we believed in the usefulness of collective action, especially when additional leverage was required to advance one's own interest in the face of opposing collective interests. So voluntarism allowed the people to retain the rights and privileges of individualism, but also permitted them to take advantage of the power of concerted action within a self-governing organizational framework.

Voluntarism was an effective but fragile compromise. It was always under assault from both individualist and collectivist fronts. Even the most conservative craft unions still are condemned in some quarters because they allegedly curtail individual autonomy. The argument used against the unionization of university professors is that individual freedom, for many the essence of scholarly excellence, will be destroyed. But the most devastating attack upon voluntarism now is not coming from those who advocate individualism but from those who advocate and practice organizational paternalism.

Paternalism, the antithesis of voluntarism, is nothing new to organizations. The benevolent concern of management for the welfare of their employee "children" has been prevalent, especially in Great Britain and the United States, for a long time. Paternalistic feeling initially grew out of the social doctrines of Calvinism, which imposed upon the elect the responsibility for the collective spiritual welfare of their charges. Following the Industrial Revolution in England, many owners tacked up on shop walls and worker residences the "Code of Conduct" they believed appropriate for the moral and spiritual welfare of their employees. Regardless of how primitive, convoluted, and cynical this early paternalistic thinking may seem to us now, it was defended by its practitioners as a manifestation of deep religious commitment.

Paternalism changed as social innovations swept through the industrial Western nations. The religious justification for paternalism correspondingly diminished with the secularization of America and Great Britain, and organizational and economic benefits became the dominant reason for management's interest in employee welfare. As Andrew Carnegie put it: "The employer who helps his workmen through education, recreation, and social uplift, helps himself."[26] Responding to the challenge of unionism in the 1920s, management adopted the paternalistic "American plan" as a counterstrategy. In the American plan employees would be given benefits directly by the employer that they would otherwise have to bargain for indirectly through their union.

Thus, by the first part of this century, paternalism was used by management for practical purposes: fighting unions or raising worker productivity. But while the focus of paternalism shifted from the spiritual to the temporal, it remained basically a collective undertaking, ideologically justified as the means of promoting general employee welfare. However, there was nothing in business paternalism that encouraged the voluntaristic principles of self-determination.

Another shift in the doctrine of paternalism occurred in the 1930s, against the backdrop, interestingly, of changes in criminal justice philosophy. These changes were partially attributable to the growing dominance of organizations in America and to the increasing influence of the behavioral sciences, particularly psychology, on social policy making. The legal scholar Nicholas N. Kittrie, discussing the changes from a legal perspective, stressed that criminal justice systems progressively de-emphasized the punishment of deviant behavior and substituted psychiatric treatment for it. The impetus behind this change stemmed from a rising humanist sentiment, a broadened conception of the welfare function of the state, and the spreading importance of the behavioral sciences in the welfare sphere. The net effect was that the state applied therapeutic means even more in the treatment of antisocial behavior.[27]

Concomitantly, paternalism changed even more with the rise of professional managers during the 1930s. It did not take long for those managers to extend their control from the material and financial resources of the organization to the human resources. The more modern version of paternalism took a therapeutic turn: deviant behavior in organizations is a sign of illness, which should be treated medically (psychiatrically). It is not a very long step from this point of view to the next: the prescription of measures to prevent such organizational mental illness. As E. Fuller Torrey wrote: "Prevention is powerful, efficient, and American."[28] To illustrate, an acquaintance interviewed for a job with a large national management consulting firm. The interviewer carefully described all the employee benefits, including the offer to pay for his attendance at twice-yearly sensitivity-training programs. Our friend said that he really didn't want to attend that training, to which the interviewer replied: "But don't you want to be happy?"

What does this anecdote reveal about therapeutic paternalism? At one level it says that management knows best what contributes to good employee mental health. But at another level it demonstrates the proposition that, given appropriate standards of mental health, there should be no incompatibility between the goals of organizational performance and individual satisfaction. In other words, there is an optimal cluster of behaviors and attitudes that contribute to both these goals. This cluster defines "normal" behavior. It does not take much to move from here to the next stage, wherein the norms for employee mental hygiene are specified. A deviation from these norms defines mental illness, organizationally speaking. Therefore management, following the model of therapeutic paternalism, ought to use all the means at its disposal to prevent employees from getting "sick."

The preventative methods of mental hygiene were quickly learned and put into practice with the assistance of psychologist-consultants. These methods are based on the following premises. First, people are organizationally maladjusted if they do not accept organizational rules because the rules define normality. Second, management has sovereign power and responsibility to inculcate organizational rules for the employees' own attitudinal welfare. Third, organizationally deviant employees should be cured by using applied behavioral-science techniques rather than punished by disciplinary action.

Organizational paternalism has come a long way, beginning with a concern for spiritual welfare, moving through the economic considerations, and ending with the mental welfare of employees. Of them all, the last is the most insidious, because in our age the best way to ensure obedience is to create a state of psychological dependency. This is exactly what the new form of paternalism does. It defines anything but the most innocuous expressions of self-determination, autonomy, and other conditions of individualism as illness. Consequently, the authority of management is complete, for there is no more despotic authority than that of "father," the manager, who righteously legislates the terms of mental health for his "children," the employees.

New Values—New Puzzles

The organizational imperative that has displaced the Founding Values is now the central part of a new, well-entrenched system of American values. Obedience is essential to organizational discipline, dispensability is necessary for organizational change, specialization is required for organizational efficiency, planning is needed to reduce organizational uncertainty, and paternalism is the psychological justification for management's dominion over the work force. But, most of all, the denial of an innate moral nature has thrown open the door to the complete domination of most Americans by the organizational imperative.

Not all Americans are committed to these values. There are many people who live in ignored corners of our society who have little to do with them, including large numbers of the "invisible people" who we discuss in the next chapter. But regardless of them, most of us in the production and consumption mainstream of American life are inextricably involved in, and perhaps committed to, these values. They are contemporary articles of faith that we must embrace if we expect to gain any rewards from the system we have made for ourselves. They are the definition of organizational America.

It is important to reemphasize this point: the organizational imperative is dominant because we made it so. *It was a moral choice*, made because we believed that the modern organization would provide us with material affluence, physical safety, and peace of mind. We were not aware, in the beginning, that we would need a whole set of new values to accompany the organizational imperative. Once the organizational imperative was set in motion, it became so powerful that we lost our sense of how to control it, let alone how to turn it off.

Yet, in spite of negative feelings, we seemingly cannot escape. The basic values of modern organization are at the root of our national malaise, and there is no way we can ever return to a simpler life. Would we, or could we, voluntarily go the "small is beautiful" route if we had a choice? Probably not. We are too enchanted with material abundance to turn our backs on it. We have no Cato the Censor calling for a reassertion of the old values. Instead we have legions of politicians calling for an increased Gross National Product (GNP), and we will probably continue to cling to the status quo unless it is unhinged by some global disaster.

But, if we are willing to adapt ourselves to the value system of organizational America, why should anyone fret? There are at least two reasons. The first is because ordinary people are trying to run a nation of almost hopeless complexity. In plain language, management cannot cope with this complexity by any technical or governmental means yet devised. But management is urgently seeking new technologies and management systems in a desperate attempt to impose a new order of control on our society. This desperation does not bode well for us, for if history teaches us anything, it is that control achieved in the face of panic is almost always authoritarian.

This leads to the second reason. This new set of organizationally fostered values offends our deepest sense of humanity. The combination of management, organization, and technology holds both promise and danger. In the authors' view, the danger of this combination is out of proportion to its promise because of the unwillingness of those who should know better (e.g., management scholars) to reflect upon the implications of the values that underlie modern organizations. The fact that the discussion of values in management has not progressed along with the development of our core technologies and our organizational designs creates pressing human problems that cannot be ignored, unless one believes that our present condition is acceptable.

It may seem unfair to blame managers for not being concerned with value questions. After all, their responsibility is to their organizations. Why, then, should we insist that managers be moral philosophers, any more than are scientists, teachers, physicians, or engineers? The answer is simple: because managers have power.[29] Those who manage, and those who theorize about management, are the human agents of organizational power. That power is based upon their control of certain essential organizational assets. They control the material resources and the technical knowledge necessary for continued development. They control the communications and decision networks in private industry and government. They have this power because of their unique managerial skills, which are quite different from the skills of science and engineering, and that allows them access to the significant jobs in organizations. Without management, large-scale organizations would be impossible. The managerial function is indispensable, which gives managers more influence over public attitudes than any other group in society.

In a democratic society, however, power carries moral obligations and the greater the power, the greater the obligations. Top managers exercise the greatest power in our nation; they should be sensitive to their moral obligations. But nothing in their training prepares them to follow moral philosophy, nor does it give them a concern for their moral obligations. The question is, why have we failed to recognize the ethical dimensions of management?

Notes

1. Sloan Wilson, *The Man in the Grey Flannel Suit* (New York: Simon and Schuster, 1955).
2. J. G. A. Pocock, *The Machiavellian Moment: Florentine Political Thought and the Atlantic Republican Tradition* (Princeton: Princeton University Press, 1975), 501.
3. Note, for instance, the rather disillusioned popular history by one of the major players: Todd Gitlin, *The Sixties: Years of Hope, Days of Rage* (New York: Bantam, 1987).
4. The story was well told by David Halberstam, *The Best and the Brightest* (New York: Random House, 1972).
5. John H. Hallowell, *The Moral Foundation of Democracy* (Chicago: University of Chicago Press, 1954), 89.
6. Niccolo Machiavelli, "Discourses" in *The Prince and the Discourses*, ed. M. Lerner (New York: Modern Library, 1950), Book 1, Chapter 3, 117.
7. For a survey, see Gladys Bryson, *Man and Society: The Scottish Inquiry of the Eighteenth Century* (New York: Augustus M. Kelley [1945], 1968).
8. William G. Scott and David K. Hart, "The Moral Nature of Man in Organizations: A Comparative Analysis," *Academy of Management Journal* 14 (June

1971): 255. Note the criticism of this position by Don Hellreigel, "The Moral Nature of Man in Organizations: A Comparative Analysis: Comment," *Academy of Management Journal* 14 (Dec. 1971): 533–537.

9. Elton Mayo, *The Human Problems of an Industrial Civilization* (Boston: Harvard University, Graduate School of Business Administration, 1933), especially 150–151.

10. Richard C. S. Trahair, *The Humanist Temper* (New Brunswick: Transaction Publishers, 1984).

11. This point is of the utmost importance. When all individuals believe their nature to be malleable, they make themselves completely susceptible to the values and behaviors demanded by administrators. For examples: John Taylor, *The Shape of Minds to Come* (New York: Weybright and Talley, 1970); Gordon Rattray Taylor, *The Biological Time Bomb* (New York: New American Library, 1968).

12. Barnard, *Functions of the Executive* (see chap. 1, n. 14), 279.

13. Barnard and Mayo had contemporaries who were not so optimistic about the new managerial society. However, their voices were not heard, at least to the extent of influencing the corpus of management thought. Perhaps the most influential critics were Adolf A. Berle, Jr. and Gardiner C. Means, *The Modern Corporation and Private Property* (New York: Macmillan, 1933). We have also referred to James Burnham in chapter 1. See also Oswald Knauth, *The Managerial Enterprise* (New York: Norton, 1948).

14. John Stuart Mill, "On Liberty" in *John Stuart Mill, Utilitarianism, Liberty, and Representative Government*, Everyman's Library (New York: Dutton, 1950), 178.

15. David Riesman et al., *The Lonely Crowd* (Garden City, N.Y.: Anchor, 1953), 29–32.

16. An excellent discussion of the topic is contained in Stanley Milgram, *Obedience to Authority* (New York: Harper & Row, 1974), especially 123–168. In addition, ideas central to our discussion are presented in Irving L. Janis, *Victims of Groupthink* (Boston: Houghton Mifflin, 1972).

17. Milgram, *Obedience to Authority*, 113.

18. Dennis W. Organ, *Organizational Citizenship Behavior: The Good Soldier Syndrome* (Lexington, M.A.: Lexington Books, 1988).

19. Eric Hoffer, *The True Believer* (New York: Harper & Row, 1951).

20. Ray Allen Billington, *Frederick Jackson Turner* (New York: Oxford, 1973), 86.

21. This most serious problem cuts across cultures, but seems to be heightened in advanced industrial societies. See, for instance, Simone de Beauvoir, *The Coming of Age*, trans. P. O'Brian (New York: Putman, 1970, 1972). For the American situation, see the Pulitzer Prize–winning book by Robert N. Butler, M.D., *Why Survive? Being Old in America* (New York: Harper & Row, 1975).

22. There is extensive literature dealing with the concept of community. The following books are most useful: Robert A. Nisbet, *The Quest for Community* (New York: Oxford, 1953, 1969); Maurice R. Stein, *The Eclipse of Community*, expanded ed. (Princeton: Princeton University Press, 1972); Wilson Carey McWilliams, *The Idea of Fraternity in America* (Berkeley: University of California Press, 1973).

23. Henry Mintzberg, *Structure in Fives: Designing Effective Organization* (Englewood Cliffs, N.J.: Prentice-Hall, 1983).

24. Patrick E. Connor and William G. Scott, "Reward Protocols in Technical Organizations: Interpersonal versus Technical Competence," *Human Organization* 33 (Winter, 1975): 367–374.
25. For example, see Kariel, *Decline of American Pluralism* (see chap. 3, n. 1), and John Kenneth Galbraith, *American Capitalism: The Concept of Countervailing Power* (Boston: Houghton Mifflin, 1952, 1956).
26. Andrew Carnegie, *The Empire of Business* (New York: Doubleday, Page, 1902), v.
27. Nicholas N. Kittrie, *The Right to Be Different* (Baltimore: Pelican Books, 1973), 5.
28. See E. Fuller Torrey, *The Death of Psychiatry* (Radnor, P.A.: Chilton, 1974), 97.
29. Berle and Means, *Modern Corporation and Private Property*.

5

Organizational Roles

> *Both [capitalism and communism] are devel-*
> *oping into managerial societies, their inhab-*
> *itants well fed, well clad, having their wishes*
> *satisfied, and not having wishes which cannot*
> *be satisfied; automatons, who follow without*
> *force, who are guided without leaders, who*
> *make machines which act like men and pro-*
> *duce men who act like machines. . . .*

> —Erich Fromm,
> *The Sane Society*

Values and Roles in Organizational America

Very few people consciously and actively go searching for the origins of their values, in order to confirm their validity and to learn how to act. For every René Descartes or William James, there are a million George Babbitts. Rather, people accept unthinkingly the operational values of their society, as they are made evident in the tangible realities of their daily lives. In simpler societies, those values structured kinship, community, and religious actions, as well as attitudes toward economic endeavors and governance. Individuals have always been socialized from birth to be alert to behavioral cues, which are everywhere present in a society.

But as societies became more complex, such commonplace behaviors began to attract the attention of behavioral scientists. These behaviors became "roles": "a set of expectations applied to an incumbent of a particular position."[1] Social, economic, and political roles thus mediate between cultural values and individual behavior. They convert the abstractions of values into concrete role expectations, from which people learn the orthodox attitudes and how they should behave in everyday life. The primary mission of education became training in appropriate role behaviors.

However, we are required to play not one role, but many of them. They exist in a multitude of configurations and, as George Simmel noted, the nature

65

of the configuration, this web of primary group affiliations, makes each individual—and thereby each society of individuals in the aggregate—different from each other.[2] These webs of roles are very complex, and sometimes specific roles within them are conflicting.

For instance, the realities of our consumer society were artfully dissected by Sinclair Lewis. In the 1920s, as in all the decades since, people chanted a litany of "rugged individualism," where individuals "stood on their own two feet" and "spoke their own minds." Lewis's protagonist, George Babbitt, was the noisy booster of those clichés; all the while he was the personification of another role: the malleable, consuming citizen that an emerging organizational America required:

> Just as he was an Elk, a Booster, and a member of the Chamber of Commerce, just as the priests of the Presbyterian Church determined his every religious belief and the senators who controlled the Republican Party decided in little smoky rooms in Washington what he should think about disarmament, tariff, and Germany, so did the large national advertisers fix the surface of his life, fix what he believed to be his individuality. These standard advertised wares—toothpastes, socks, tires, cameras, instantaneous hot-water heaters—were his symbols and proofs of excellence; at first the signs, then the substitutes, for joy and passion and wisdom.[3]

Babbitt was the composite of roles assigned to him as a consumer, a Republican, and a Presbyterian. And yet, pathetically, there lurked within him the knowledge that somehow he was more than his roles.

In response, the generation of the 1960s called upon everyone to "do their own thing." In the cry and the result, Americans came to see how completely their lives were dominated by the roles of organizational America. We did not know how to do our own thing for the simple reason that we did not know ourselves. As David Norton has so aptly written: "Indeed, I offer it as our ranking malaise that that about which we instinctively believe we can be most certain—ourselves—is in fact our sorest bewilderment."[4] We had become the reflection of the authorized roles of organizational America.

Today, one may be a hyperconsumer, an MBA graduate, and a politically liberal Unitarian. It does not really matter. The multiple roles people must play in America are defined for them externally by schools, television, corporations, government agencies, and many other socializing organizations. Whatever conflicts might occur in these roles can be resolved by reference to the overarching framework of values from which they are derived. For example, the time demands of one's role as corporation manager might conflict with the role of parent. However, the conflict is settled by the parent's belief that the organizational commitment will provide economic benefits for the family, and they will make up for the absences. Such beliefs are reinforced by organizational rewards: but only if the corporate roles are satisfactorily performed.

The multiplicity of roles was, for a while, described as the "wearing of different hats." Thus, during a day an individual might start off with her mother-hat and send the kids off to school. At work, she switches to a peer-hat to greet her colleagues. She whips that off and dons a subordinate-hat for a meeting with her boss—and then puts on her own boss-hat to run her division. After work, she can sport a friendship-hat at the office watering hole, then hurry home for her mother-hat again. Her husband has on his yuppie-hat and is washing their BMW. When the kids are down, they can pull on their husband-wife-hats before heading off to bed. The list could be expanded, but the message is clear. The symbolism of the different hats is a recognition that roles, while they differ, are always present, whether one is on or off the job.

The point here is not whether role theory is good or bad, but rather the question of what values determine the roles of organizational America? If they are the internalized Founding Values, then we might laugh at the visions of hats dancing in our heads. But if the values are those of the organizational imperative, then the roles become just that: artificial roles to be enacted, but not lives to live.

The Two Organizational Mega-Roles

Modern organization has given a new emphasis to the concept of "role." The reason is clear: all human attitudes and behaviors must enhance the health of modern organizations. The multiple roles of our pluralist past have been swept away, and modern organization has canonized two *mega-roles*: the job-role and the leisure-role, subsumed under the overarching role of a believer in the organizational imperative. The mega-roles are both moral roles, in that the performance of the role expectations is now a moral obligation. The primary obligation of the job-role is to contribute to organizational health. The primary obligation of the leisure-role is consumption. The performance of the two mega-roles is self-reinforcing. Finally, all of the lesser roles defined by the modern organization are derived from the two mega-roles.

The job-roles and leisure-roles are organizationally specified, and conformity to them is required if an individual desires the rewards that come from being a citizen in organizational America. Granted, some slack is allowed in the performance of these roles; nevertheless, it is obvious that our lives are channeled through them.

The reason for this emphasis upon roles is clear. Organizations need workers but, more than that, they need workers who are reliable. But "reliable" has taken on a new meaning. It not only means that workers—and especially white-collar workers—must show up on time and do their work in a conscientious manner, it also means that they must be predictable, that they must act in ways approved by the organization. It might be thought that while this applies to people of lesser rank, it does not hold true for those higher up. Such is not the case, for two reasons. First, the heads of modern organizations are increasingly being drawn from the ranks of university-trained managers: graduates of management programs, possessors of MBAs, MPAs, and MHAs. The essence of their education has been their indoctrination into the demands of the organizational imperative, as made manifest in the two mega-roles. They come to their jobs as true believers. Second, these people are never free from organizational interdependencies. They must interact with peers and command subordinates, all of whom are similarly indoctrinated. Thus, there is no escape from the mega-roles of the organizational imperative.

The higher one rises in the organization, the more one is dominated by the entailments of the managerial roles. Promotions seldom bring more freedom, even though they bring more money and perquisites, with their leisure-role requirements for conspicuous consumption. Instead of increasing freedom, promotion actually ensnares the individual more, by requiring greater personal commitment to the values of the organization. But what about those at the very top? Surely when they arrive at the pinnacle of their organization they can do whatever they wish. Not so. One of two things usually happens. First, in order to get to the top, managers have had to internalize their organizational roles more intensely than others. Thus, it is difficult for them to separate their organizational persona from whatever remnants are left of their individuality. Second, however, some do arrive at the top with their personal values still intact. But they find that even in the rarified atmosphere of the executive suite, they do not have the power to make fundamental alterations in the primal *value orientation* of the organization. The situation is not hopeless, but for leaders to make changes in value orientations, it is necessary for them to have an extraordinarily strong moral character. They must be moral heroes.

And so the mega-roles of modern organization have become the defining reality for almost all Americans. But even with the obvious problems, management theorists and practitioners accept the clarification of roles as a good thing. Its worth is beyond discussion. Employees, from the top to the bottom, can thus talk objectively about the substance of their jobs and, more importantly, exactly who has authority over whom (and what) within the organization. Such role specification reduces uncertainty—more, however, for the managers than the managees. Further, it allows for both planning and prediction. To a certain extent, this is beneficial. The problem is that when the benefits of role specification cease, control, for its own sake, takes over. But because of the individual and organizational benefits, the role specification abuses are masked. Three abuses must be mentioned.

First, there is the illusion that one can compartmentalize one's internal life: that the moral commitment to the role requirements of one's job will not bleed over into one's personal life. But that is an egregious error and we know it. Powerful role expectations, such as are found in the modern organization, determine how individuals will perceive themselves and others, and even arrange their priorities of what they consider important in life. The human personality is an integrated whole and, unless there is psychic disorder, no aspect of our lives can be walled off. The notion that one can behave like Mac the Knife at work and then return home as a parental Mr. Chips is a dangerous myth. Consequently, those who manage, especially at the middle and upper levels, inevitably allow their organizational roles to seep into their most private relationships. Profound commitment to the values of the organizational imperative is the touchstone of success in their working lives. That commitment does not stay behind at the office.

Second, the required intensity of commitment to authorized roles leads people to define their total selves in terms of those dominant roles and in terms of the organizational processes that these roles require. It is commonplace to observe how often Americans, when asked *who* they are, respond with the title of their job. The response is almost instinctive. But contrast the response of a three-year-old, who tells you proudly that he is "Steven Matthew Turek" (with full childish knowledge of just who he is), with the middle-aged academic, who unthinkingly responds that he is "a professor of management at the university." There is a real and qualitative difference. When people define their identities solely in terms of their organizational roles, it suspends their possibilities for attaining a wholeness of the integrated self essential for self-actualization. As A. G. Ramos wrote: "Only a defective self can find in contrived systems the adequate milieu for his actualization."[5]

Third, the excessive reliance upon organizationally defined roles creates a much greater potential for human control. The most graphic illustration comes from totalitarianism, which the political scientist Carl J. Friedrich referred to as "historically unique and *sui generis*."[6] We maintain that totalitarianism is the only modern form of government because it is the only one entirely dependent upon modern organization for the control of the people. That control is complete, as Harold D. Lasswell and Abraham Kaplan wrote: "A system of maximal regimentation is called totalitarian; the scope of the power is all inclusive. . . . All practices are coercively controlled; in the familiar phrase, everything that isn't forbidden is obligatory."[7]

The key lies in that final sentence. Total control is obtained by placing rules upon everything, positive and negative, and enforcing obedience to those rules: totalitarianism is rule by rules. Thus, all roles are defined authoritatively, and behavior outside the official role structure is illegitimate. We would expand upon sociologist Lewis H. Coser's assessment and argue that modern organizations are "greedy institutions," demanding total obedience at all times,[8] in off-the-job as well as on-the-job roles.

With these preliminaries in mind, we can now turn our attention to the characteristics of the two mega-roles.

On-the-Job Roles

Like Gaul, the organizational world is divided into three parts, as figure 5.1 illustrates (although there are four parts of the figure):

Figure 5.1

On-the-Job Role Hierarchy

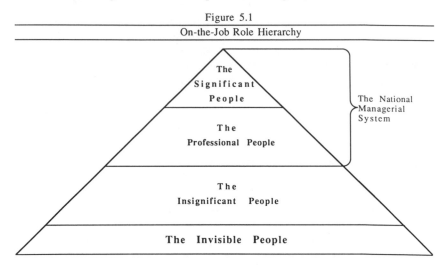

The "significant people" are at the top of the hierarchy because they occupy the most important positions, the "significant jobs." Those positions are significant because their incumbents must make cardinal choices among organizational strategies that ultimately affect the lives of everyone in organizational America. Those choices range from the obviously significant (i.e., the manufacturing abroad of all television components) to the subtle (i.e., the programs seen on television). The quality of all our lives is influenced by those choices.

Below this set of roles is the technical core of the organization,[9] composed of scientists, engineers, and technicians, as well as a vast cadre of middle managers ranked according to function and position. We have termed them the "professional people." They make the technologies run, make the policies work, do research, perform routine housekeeping tasks, and, in general, maintain the health of the organization by keeping its internal affairs tidy. In short, the professional people staff the bureaucratic apparatus of the modern organization and operate its technological systems. It is important to understand, however, that if those who belong to the core want to move up the ladder into significant positions, they must abandon their specialized fields and adopt managerial values and frames of reference. The rule is unavoidable: access to power in the modern organization comes almost exclusively through higher *managerial* positions.

Taken together, the significant people and the professional people make up the national managerial system. One's status in this system is identified by one's role in the managerial hierarchy. The degree of personal influence in the national managerial system is based upon the strategic importance of the job within an organization. It must be noted that the national managerial system exists without an intentional solidarity among the incumbents of these organizational roles. They do not meet in secret to determine the fate of organizational America. Finally, it must be noted that one's personal qualities, good or bad, have almost nothing to do with one's place within the national managerial system. A significant person may be a saint or a swine; what counts is the position he or she occupies.

The lowest on-the-job roles are occupied by the majority of the people, those who perform the ordinary tasks of the organization, whether assembling automobiles, taking dictation, frying hamburgers, operating computers, or selling clothing. We have termed them the "insignificant people." The insignificant people are treated as production units although they are euphemistically called "human resources" in the personnel management trade.

A production unit is a functional, completely interchangeable, low-priority component of the organizational machine. Units no longer have a sense of unitness—a sense of solidarity with other units. As with the higher members of the modern organization, the work lives of the insignificant people only take on meaning through the roles they perform. They may feel isolated or alienated, but such feelings only become important to modern organizations when they interfere with productivity. Thus, units must understand that their primary role is to serve as elements in the total organizational environment. They must believe that they are powerless to affect it, and that their best course is to adapt as often and as well as possible.

The on-the-job relationships of all individuals in the modern organization, which we have briefly summarized, is ordered hierarchically according to the utility of an individual's contribution to the production of goods or services. This aspect of our argument is so important that we devote a separate chapter to a discussion of each group. We must emphasize, however, that while the organizational role content differs dramatically as the hierarchy is ascended, the significant, professional, and insignificant people have one overwhelmingly important thing in common. They all *work* in socially approved occupations. (A socially approved occupation is one which figures into national accounting data, the GNP.)

This puts them in sharp contrast with the "invisible people," who have no organizational role at all. They do not work in socially approved occupations. They are casualties of organizational America, to be locked in a metaphoric back room so as not to trouble our collective conscience.

Off-the-Job Roles

One of the most pervasive myths in contemporary society is that, regardless of what people must do on the job, when they leave work, their time is their own. Further, it is assumed that in leisure time, satisfactions not found on the job can be fulfilled. The sacrifices and responsibilities that organizational obedience entails are amply rewarded by salaries that enable people to exploit their leisure time to the fullest. This is a cruel deception.

There is really no such thing as leisure time in organizational America, in the sense that people can be free of the binding rule of service to the organization. The reality is that what one does away from the job is also determined by the needs of the organization, even through the range of options is great. Because of vast possibilities for choice, the illusion exists of the free use of leisure time. This illusion masks the fact that most options, and therefore most choices, are organizationally predetermined.

Some years ago, Alvin Toffler wrote about the problem of variety in the American future. To make his case, he pointed to a "new family sportscar": with all of the various options available in that model year, from engine size to paint color, the consumer had 25,000,000 varieties of the same car to choose from.[10] But he missed the point entirely, for they were not different cars. Had the choice been among even five hundred cars as dramatically different as a Mustang, a Shelby Cobra, a Lotus Elan, and a Morgan, then the consumer would have a time of it. The illusion of variety is confirmed in television programming, franchise foods, clothing, and virtually anything else the public consumes in mass quantity.

But, then, the predetermination of leisure activities is a logical extension of the second proposition of the organizational imperative: that all behavior must enhance the health of modern organizations. Service to the organization must be constant. The rule is: *The primary obligation of the individual off the job is to consume.* The economist John Kenneth Galbraith made this clear in his discussion of the importance of the production-consumption cycle in a technological society:

The small volume of saving by the average man, and its absence among the lower-income masses, reflect faithfully the role of the individual in the industrial system, and the accepted view of his function. The individual serves the industrial system not by supplying it with savings and the resulting capital; he serves it by consuming its products. On no other matter, religious, political, or moral, is he so elaborately and skillfully and expensively instructed.[11]

One of the most fascinating aspects of leisure time is that it is when people in organizational America are most equal. The "blithe and jocund peasantry mingle with their superiors"[12] with scarcely any recognition on either's part that there are any on-the-job role differences between them. When hunting, one is just as likely to encounter a bank manager as a teller, a corporation lawyer as a court clerk, an aerospace engineer as an aircraft mechanic, a hospital administrator as a food-service worker. It is virtually impossible to tell them apart since they have similar vehicles, similar clothes, and similar access to the hunting terrain, which is frequently federal land. The same can be said for other leisure pursuits, such as skiing, fishing, mountain climbing, and jogging. Those are all participant activities, of course, and most people prefer to attend spectator sports, concerts, movies, and other entertainments where they can relax. But in those halls and arenas, too, almost all differences disappear.

Organizational America has democratized leisure time, but this has *not* relieved its citizens of the obligation to support modern organizations continuously through consumption. Some will argue that where consumption is concerned, people are unequal because of the differences in their disposable incomes. But this misses the point. We are equal in our responsibility to consume up to the limits of our disposable incomes and, through credit, beyond that. Is this overstating the case? No. Actually, we are understating it. Since the early 1950s, personal debt has risen astronomically and is now at an all-time high. If all people do not consume as much as possible, then most modern organizations will fail, and that is an unthinkable proposition.

The personal pleasure derived from consumption in off-the-job pursuits takes a distant second place from the standpoint of the modern organization. The primary purpose of consumption is to enhance organizational stability. But the personal pleasure does have a lesser use for the modern organization. For the vast majority of people, their off-the-job activities are organizationally so determined that they will create no debilitating incongruities with what they must do on the job. R and R (rest and recreation) is necessary for continuous organizational efficiency. Individuals should come back to their jobs refreshed and better able to perform their organizational roles.

Everyone needs a break with routine; but beyond that, there is a training purpose to leisure-time consumption. Our supposed recreation teaches us, subtly, to appreciate technology in countless ways. We cannot play tennis or golf, ski, jog, or bicycle without using and appreciating the irresistible new technological products that abound. For instance, the jogging craze that swept through America in the late 1970s produced an innovative explosion in the technology of running shoes; in the late 1980s a computerized bait-casting fishing reel automatically adjusts spool tension to eliminate backlash. The same thing happened (and is happening) in nearly every participant sport. In the spectator sports—such as football, basketball, or hockey—a singularly important lesson is taught: the futility of individual effort, as compared with teamwork.[13] The on-the-job usefulness of teamwork and organizational dependence is constantly reinforced. Even television viewing is but an endless round of obedience-training in consumption, and there is growing evidence that television may be the most powerful training tool in the arsenal of modern organizations.[14]

Out-of-Organization Roles

Now we must turn to those who cannot fulfill either of the mega-roles, the invisible people. Historian Paul Fussell observed that the people at the extremes of the class system are out of sight.[15] Those who are at the very top and the very bottom of America's status hierarchy are invisible. We have noted how the shield of elitist invisibility works for those on top to protect them from accountability. It is necessary here to consider the plight of a far larger number of invisible people at the bottom of the hierarchy.

There are many Americans who cannot or will not participate in authorized leisure or work activities. Those millions are the casualties of organizational America. They do not match the rest of Americans in their responsibilities to work or consume because it is impossible for them to do so. They compose a distinct class. Some have lost their organizational identities through unemployment or retirement. Others never had an organizational role and thus were nonpersons. For instance, we attended an MBA party and were a part of a group of students, all of whom were dressed in John Malloy–authorized, MBA garb. Dark, subtly pin-striped suits prevailed. We noticed an attractive woman in a red dress in another group. Someone asked who she was. One of the female MBA students replied: "She's nobody. She's just a wife." That is the summation of invisibility.

Journalist Tom Wicker, drawing from census data for 1985, observed that "33.1 million Americans—14 percent of the total were poor in 1985. . . . Sixty-nine percent of those poor were white, up from 66 percent in 1979. Whites accounted for 81 percent of the net increase in the poverty population between 1979 and 1985."[16] Political scientist Frederick Thayer commented that "we are living in the third worst jobless period in 100 years,"[17] because "callous statistics" conceal widespread unemployment. Besides the growth of poverty rates among whites, the tragedy of chronic black unemployment still has not been solved, nor are things much better for Hispanic or Native Americans.

Those in the culture of poverty have been alienated from the mainstream work-life of the dominant culture, and the leaders of our society have decided that it is not worth the effort to provide them with work. The problem can be handled by welfare. In fact, the movements toward increased automation in the work place, the increasing technical service industry, and other changes in the nature of work in organizational America is exacerbating the problem. Thus, the net loss of jobs for all people at the lower end of the skill level is great, with estimates in New York City ranging from the disappearance of 492,000 low-skill jobs and the creation of 239,000 higher-skilled ones. [18]

However, the issue is more than unemployment. The invisible people form a class of those irrelevant to modern organizations. For instance, enough has been written about the plight of the elderly that we need not discuss it here. Suffice it to say, their problem is not just a matter of having enough to live on. Rather, it is the larger problem: What do you do with people who have been trained to make the heads of pins and have spent their lives in such work? What can retirement mean to them? They have lost their definition of self with the disappearance of their organizational role.

So an invisible underclass is growing in America. While it can be defined in terms of unemployment, race, ethnicity, gender, or age, its distinctive features are poverty or invisibility or both. They exacerbate the feelings of hopelessness and alienation that those who are in that class must feel toward organizational America. At the same time, the underclass assaults the equanimity, if not the conscience, of better-situated Americans. The distinctions between the haves and the have-nots are real, and they are apparent.

Therefore, we are compelled to do something for the homeless, for the old folks, for the teens on the street, for the women who are single parents, for the drug addicts and alcoholics, for the technologically displaced, for the functionally illiterate, and so on. We try to be kind to our casualties. But, just as the primary mission of an army is not the care of its wounded, so the primary mission of the organizational culture is not the care of its casualties. There is real tragedy in the blighted lives of America's wounded, but the modern organization is not to be deterred from its main goals by sentimentality.

But sentimentality notwithstanding, the underclass of invisible people could be the undoing of organizational America. Ironically, despite our deep concern for the organizationally useful, the useful themselves are condemned ultimately to the anomie of the invisible class that awaits the ends of their careers.

Notes

1. Neal Gross et al., *Explorations in Role Analysis* (New York: Wiley, 1958), 67.
2. George Simmel, *The Web of Group Affiliations* (London: Collier-Macmillan, 1955).
3. Sinclair Lewis, *Babbitt* (New York: New American Library, 1922), 80–81.
4. Norton, *Personal Destinies* (see chap. 1, n. 11) 3–4.
5. Alberto G. Ramos, *The New Science of Organizations: A Reconceptualization of the Wealth of Nations* (Toronto: The University of Toronto Press, 1981), 87.
6. Carl J. Friedrich, "The Unique Character of Totalitarian Society" in Carl J. Friedrich, ed., *Totalitarianism* (New York: Grosset & Dunlap, 1954), 47.
7. Harold D. Lasswell and Abraham Kaplan, *Power and Society: A Framework for Political Inquiry* (New Haven: Yale University Press, 1950), 222.
8. Lewis A. Coser, *Greedy Institutions: Patterns of Undivided Commitment* (New York: Free Press, 1974). While we do not agree entirely with his argument, his idea about "greedy institutions" is most applicable.
9. James D. Thompson, *Organizations In Action* (New York: McGraw-Hill, 1967), develops the notion of the "technical core" in some detail.
10. Alvin Toffler, *Future Shock* (New York: Random House, 1970), 230.
11. John Kenneth Galbraith, *The New Industrial State*, 2nd ed. (Boston: Houghton Mifflin, 1971), 36–37.
12. Thomas Oakleigh, Esq., *The Oakleigh Shooting Code* (London: James Ridgway, 1837), 118. Reflections of the author on the day before the opening of the grouse-hunting season in Scotland.
13. This was the major purpose of the game of *Rollerball*, in Norman Jewison's vastly underrated film of the same name. The point was stressed by the Director of Energy when discussing the purpose of the game. The directors of the great corporations were trying to convince the highly popular professional player, Jonathan E., to resign from the sport. Unfortunately, most film critics did not have the wit to understand the theme or the importance of the film.
14. For an excellent survey of the literature, see George Comstock et al., *Television and Human Behavior* (New York: Columbia University Press, 1978).
15. Paul Fussell, *Class* (New York: Ballantine Books, 1983).
16. Tom Wicker, "Always with Us," *New York Times*, 19 Nov. 1987, 27.
17. Frederick C. Thayer, "Callous Statistics," *New York Times*, 20 Dec. 1987, 19 (E).
18. Don Sycliff, "Why the Underclass Is Still Under," *New York Times*, 16 Nov. 1987, 18.

6

The Insignificant People: The Strategy of Mass Domination

Among the constant facts and tendencies that are to be found in all political organisms, one is so obvious that it is apparent from societies that are very meagerly developed and have barely attained the dawnings of civilization, down to the most advanced and powerful societies—two classes of people appear—a class that rules and a class that is ruled. The first class, always the less numerous, performs all political functions, monopolizes power and enjoys the advantages that power brings, whereas the second, the more numerous class, is directed and controlled by the first, in a manner that is now more or less legal, now more or less arbitrary and violent, and supplies the first, in appearance at least, with material means of subsistence and with the instrumentalities that are essential to the vitality of the political organism.

—Gaetano Mosca,
The Ruling Class.

The "Weenie Syndrome"

Many years ago, Harold D. Lasswell made an important observation about the nature of power. Power, he wrote, "is an interpersonal situation; those who hold power are empowered. They depend upon and continue only so long as there is a continuing stream of empowering responses."[1] Thus, any form of governance, including organizational governance, boils down to the ability of the leaders to obtain and maintain the support of the people necessary to the organization—that flow of empowering responses. This is true at two levels: there must be both internal support and external support.

77

Management cannot take mass support for granted; it must be actively cultivated. As rule by the managerial elite has become evident, and as the quality of life in organizational America is deteriorating, more and more people are asking questions about the sagacity of that elite. Increasingly, managers are confronted with the age-old political problem of how to gain and keep public support. They are trying to solve that problem by using both the assumptions and techniques most familiar to them—techniques derived from managing their subordinates.

The two assumptions they draw upon are: (1) that the individual, relative to the organization, is insignificant and; (2) that innate human nature is malleable. The first assumption justifies the modification of the individual, while the second means that managers need not worry about harming something innate within the individual. These assumptions have been central to management theory and practice for decades. Thus, management can actively pursue policies in which molding, shaping, changing, modifying, and controlling human behavior are legitimate parts of their responsibility. The major project is convincing people of their insignificance and malleability.

Many people are willing to accept the premise that there is a managerial elite, which means that there must be a nonelite—a mass who are less significant to the total society than the leaders. This also means that there must be a theory of the elite that is, again, an acceptable premise. But what is less understood is that there then must be a corollary *theory of the insignificance of the nonelite*. Gaetano Mosca, who is quoted in the epigraph, did not mince words, because he realized the necessity for an insignificance theory, which is the seamy side of elite theory. Although insignificance theory is a part of contemporary management, it is seldom ever discussed, because it entails mass domination, a subject of dangerous consequences in a democratic society.

But the silence—in management theory and practice—about insignificance and mass domination does not negate the fact that they exist. But now an almost poetic paradox is forcing managers to face the realities of the theory of insignificance. As modern organizations have grown increasingly more complex, it has become necessary to educate more employees to handle the increasingly technical demands of their jobs. And therein lies the peril for the elite. Education prompts people to think, and in thinking lie notions disruptive for the organizational imperative. Thus, training and education are necessities, and, in spite of their pedestrian nature, they nevertheless require people to think; thinking may lead people to contemplate the nature of their jobs. Most of them will not be altogether happy with what they find.

They probably will not find the horrors of industrial jobs so common in the last century. But they will find routines and monotonies that are corrosive of life. This is not inevitable, of course, for many technical jobs can be fascinating. For example, a young person may enlist in naval aviation and, because of scores on various selection tests, be trained in advanced radar gunnery systems. The training will be very intense and the pay low, but the probability is very high that the sailor will find the work personally rewarding: the intellect is engaged and the person is important to a team and part of a tradition.

Alternatively, another young person may be employed by a large supermarket chain, to handle the computer-based checkout stands, which also maintain an inventory-control system. The new employee will be trained in its operation. Yet it is safe to argue that within a week the graduate of that program will find the job dull, routine, and personally unrewarding: the intellect is irrelevant, there is no sense of teamwork, and there certainly is no tradition. In short, that person is trained for insignificance. In organizational America, more people tend boring machines than sophisticated electronic gunnery systems.

Thus, if the employees of organizational America were ever to comprehend the life-destroying implications of their jobs, there would be a frightful turmoil. Escapism through leisure-time consumption is the prescribed method of offsetting the problem of doing dumb things eight hours a day. But there is a big problem, for continuously growing consumption patterns may be impossible to sustain in the future. Therefore, much more conscious managerial attention will be given to adjusting the attitudes of the mass of people. They must be indoctrinated, from their earliest days through their retirement, to understand and accept the insignificance of their individual lives in relation to the more exalted collective goals of the modern organization. Put differently, they must be scared enough at the start so that they will understand their extreme personal vulnerability and will gladly accept the security of managerial paternalism.

This adjusting of attitudes is what has happened, and we have termed this phenomenon of vulnerability and dependence the "weenie syndrome." In the previous chapter, we gave an account of one of our students who demanded that we treat him as a weenie—a sausage to be stuffed with appropriate attitudes to make him digestible to his employer-consumer. The members of the managerial elite generally believe they are the stuffers, and all other employees, from the professional to the insignificant people, are the stuffees. This is not, in fact, the case, since managers get stuffed themselves.

With respect to the insignificant people, the weenie syndrome involves the assumption by the elite that the mass of people are empty of understanding and that they must be stuffed with relevant instructions. The world of the modern organization is far too complicated for them, and they therefore must quietly await instructions from an elite. Stuffing implies quite a bit more than just on-the-job instructions. It provides correct attitudes and values about one's entire life. Furthermore, since the managerial elite provides jobs and entertainment—bread and circuses—the insignificant people will care little about the moral conduct of their leaders.

A classic example of the weenie syndrome was President Nixon's casual dismissal of the furor over the early Watergate revelations in 1973. He passed it off with the argument that since the pro-football season was then just getting under way, the public would forget Watergate in about three weeks. The assumption was: give the weenies a six-pack of beer and plenty of television, and they will be quiet. This proved to be one of the more impressive miscalculations in American history. The weenie syndrome implies that people want to be led and that the managerial elite performs an altruistic and selfless task when it takes upon itself the burden of leadership. Watergate demonstrated, to the contrary, that the rank and file could be both interested and informed, and act upon those feelings.

And so the elite divides the world in two: those who manage (the minority) and those who are managed (the vast majority). In America, most managers would publicly deny that they conceive of the world this way, but their actions betray this conception. They firmly believe that only managers have the arcane knowledge and intuitive understanding to integrate all of the diverse efforts within an organization into a harmonious whole. They believe that only managers can guide people through the mazes of technology and intricate organizational interdependencies. Thus, the managerial claim upon elite status has a definite messianic ring. Managers are the secular priesthood of modern society, and their authority is symbolized by conservative suits and the appropriate graduate degrees. They alone are privy to secrets of how to run technologically sophisticated organizations. Without them, the mass of people would not have the comforts and securities that organizational America has been constructed to provide.[2]

It is tempting to write exclusively about these interesting and powerful people.[3] But, in spite of their importance, they are nothing without the masses. Leaders require followers, for to have power, they must have empowering responses. Mass support is a necessity for a managerial elite. While this assertion has been muted in the past, it is getting louder and louder, and management is listening. Management must obtain popular support that justifies its positions and practices, or it will lose its claim to legitimacy.[4] The attempt of the managerial elite to establish its right to rule is the essence of mass domination.

Mass Domination: Some Strategic Considerations

Insignificance

The conviction by the individual of personal insignificance is the base from which the new mass domination must begin. However, the proposition that individuals are insignificant contradicts our most basic heritage. That heritage includes Locke's educational ideal that almost completely unformed children must be taught to be industrious and virtuous citizens, in ways consistent with their potentials.[5] But care has to be exercised to preserve the essential moral autonomy of the individual.[6] The education of a child is similar to delivering an uncut diamond of rare size and quality to a stonecutter in Amsterdam. The stone must be shaped from its primitive state into a form that will maximize its beauty and value, based upon the potential inherent in the pristine stone. A wrong blow will shatter the gem into worthless chips.

People are not diamonds, for they are conscious of themselves, and this self-consciousness can cause problems. It can lead individuals to prize some characteristics over others. A diamond awaits the cutter's vision: it cannot demand to be cut into one shape, in preference to another. But humans prefer some shapes and choices to others, especially in the American tradition. This tradition emphasized the development of a moral character that gave unique meaning to the individual, making him or her significant to family, community, and society.

The insignificance that is required by the modern organization demands that the individual has no meaning until the elite impresses upon him or her an organizationally significant purpose. Hobbes put it bluntly: "the common people's minds . . . are like clean paper, fit to receive whatsoever by public authority shall be imprinted in them."[7] This view is an essential proposition for the modern organization. But to convince individuals of their insignificance is no easy task!

To demonstrate this point for your own satisfaction, go up to an acquaintance and say, "Scott (or Zelda), you are insignificant." Most of the time a clouded look will cross your friend's eyes while he or she tries to decide if you deserve to be punched. This little experiment should show, even the most skeptical, that considerable effort is required to change the term "insignificant" from an insult to a compliment. Most American people understand that they have little or no significance for their organizations, but they certainly do not want to be reminded of it. We all want to hold on to our treasured notion of our importance and uniqueness. These American attitudes are still deeply ingrained, and they will not go away easily. But go they must; the traditional American vision of the individual is not consistent with the needs of the modern organization.

As a result there is a tension in modern life between how we would prefer to conceive of ourselves and how we are forced to conceive of ourselves by organizational realities.[8] The tension comes from the incongruity between our traditional Founding Values (such as freedom, indispensability, etc.) for which we still express personal preferences, and the beliefs required by the modern organization (such as obedience, replaceability, etc.) This tension is exacerbated for most younger Americans, who are just entering the job force, because they think they still have a choice. They believe they are free to select, among different organizational realities, the one that best fits their concepts of themselves. The illusion of choice helped preserve each individual's conviction that his or her life had a truly special meaning.

But the illusion of choice has become just that, an illusion, for those who have been on the job for any length of time. In the past, choice was possible, because jobs were often qualitatively different in different kinds of organizations. But today, one organizational reality is very much like another. Changing one's job, for example, changes an individual's circumstances in only marginal ways, for the roles required by the organizational imperative uniformly pervade virtually every modern organization.

The tension generated between notions of the conception of self and the needs of the organization are highly disruptive to the managerial equation.[9] Therefore, individuals must be convinced that their ideas of what they want to be are meaningless if they differ fundamentally from what the managerial elite wants. One of the most important missions for the managerial elite is to convince people that such tensions are not real, that the highest good is the harmony that is produced when the values of the individual and the organization are the same. Furthermore, the values of the organization are superior, so whatever changing must be done must be done by the individual. The essence of this harmony is simply that individual preferences are insignificant when compared with the overwhelming collective well-being that comes from integration into the modern organization.

The strategy of insignificance for the managerial elite is to gain mass acceptance of this organizational ideal by assaulting the foundations of our faith in individual worth. These foundations are innate moral nature, intellect, and work.

Innate Moral Nature

Since we discussed the subject of innate moral nature in some detail in chapter 4, we will just make a few additional observations here. As noted, all organizations are built upon assumptions about the innate moral nature of individuals. In the past, that innate nature was considered unalterable and was, therefore, accepted as a constant to be worked with, but not changed.[10] That being the case, human action arose from forces within the individual. Whatever these forces were termed—soul, mind, ego, self, personality—they were rooted within each person, and human history was ultimately the result of the interaction between the individual's internal qualities and the external forces of the world. Obviously, if that nature was constant, it could then be predicted and planned for.

One aspect of that older approach was that innate moral nature was, in the final analysis, beyond human powers of explanation. As Jeremy Bentham, the utilitarian, observed about his own basic conception of human nature:

> Is it susceptible of any direct proof? It should seem not; for that which is used to prove everything else cannot itself be proved: a chain of proofs must have their commencement somewhere.[11]

The dual ideas of innateness and inexplicability are anathema to the modern organization, which must ascribe causality to all things in its domain, if it is to control them.

Management theorists and practitioners turned to the behavioral sciences to overcome the problem. In the nineteenth century, as science mastered more and more of the physical world, some behavioral scientists became confident that individuals could be completely understood and that their behavior could be both predicted and controlled. Then the inaccessible ghoulies and ghosties of innate nature would be banished forever. This approach, which we call "externalism," has gained adherents and influence. The old convictions of innateness have given way to new externalistic explanations, in which individual behavior is seen as a reaction to the pushing and pulling of external forces.[12]

The acceptance of externalism is understandable, even without invoking the consuming desire of management for behavioral control. The enormous complexity of the physical, biological, human, and organizational events surrounding us has made the search for innate explanations of anything seem quixotic. It is best, so the argument runs, to assign complex matters like the brain, or the organization, or the relationship between the individual and the organization, to the status of a black box. Since only the inputs and outputs of the black box are scientifically knowable and controllable, these are the interesting empirical variables that should dominate our attention.

Many complex phenomena can be regulated by controlling their inputs. The only necessary assumption is that the black box has a structure that causes it to respond with predictable outputs to controlled inputs. Black-box thinking, which is an intimate part of externalism, rejects any philosophy that inquires after the essence of things. Instead, it exalts technology that allows for the manipulation of things. Externalism requires an engineering perspective on human behavior—outside causal forces determine behavior. Once these forces are identified and regulated, the individual will be as controllable as any other physical process, especially through the assignment of specialized roles.

But, in spite of the preeminence of science, technology, and modern organizations, the triumph of externalism is not complete. It demands for all to *believe* that the individual can be psychologically disassembled and then reassembled with the best behavioral technology, to suit organizational needs. Until the last holdouts for individualism get over the idea that these are unseemly and scientifically unachievable goals, externalism cannot completely sweep the field.

Unfortunately, the sad truth is that these objections are being overridden. So many things point this way: the triumph of the organizational imperative; the compulsion of managers to reduce all problems, including ethical problems, to technical puzzles; the steady diminution of the status of the individual; the manipulative control of organizational culture; the triumph of external explanations of human behavior; and the public's unwillingness to counter the totalitarian tendencies in the organizations of America. All that remains is to convince the individual that the innate self is a chimera that must be replaced by an organizational reality.

This new reality, consistent with the requirements of externalism, defines the individual as innately nothing. Each person is but a series of chemical and electrical processes that have the capacity to be shaped into just about anything necessary to suit organizational needs. Since the Industrial Revolution, that image of the individual has been useful in organizational design. Nevertheless, the lingering notion persisted that there was some small corner of personality where innateness could flourish—some internal space and time within which the human spirit could flourish.

But even that minuscule amount of innateness was too restrictive to the modern organization, for it contained too much opportunity for variability in behavior. In order for behavioral science to make real progress in its service to organization, innateness had to be expunged. Further, these sciences needed an ideology justifying the conception of the individual as totally malleable. The cause has found its most effective spokesman to date in B. F. Skinner. He attacks the most fundamental principle of innateness, the possibility of individual autonomy, by taking aim at the institutions in which it is embedded: "autonomous man is still an important figure in political science, law, religion, economics, anthropology, sociology, psychotherapy, philosophy, ethics, history, education, child care, linguistics, architecture, city planning, and family life."[13] Skinner rejects any possibility of free will and condemns any institution based upon it. For him, real scientific progress can only take place when all people accept that all of their behavior is determined by external forces. Understand external forces and you understand individuals.

Skinner's most important contribution in this respect is not scientific or psychological: it is moral and political. As Skinner admits, there is no final empirical justification for a malleable, externalistic image of human nature. Acceptance of the premise of malleability requires an act of faith, and while he marshals much scientific evidence to justify his theory, what he is really after is the conversion of all people to his vision of the individual. In this quest, he reinforces the managerial elite, for his image of human nature is the optimal image for the organizational imperative.

Therefore, the first and indispensable step in the strategy of insignificance is to gain mass acceptance of the idea of individual malleability, since no other single idea is more important to the modern organization. Skinner is wide-ranging in his attack on free will, blasting some of the bastions of innate human nature, such as autonomy, choice, independence, uniqueness, person-ality, and soul. In our time, the main source of strength, for those conducting the "rearguard action" referred to by Skinner, is a belief in intellect. In order to demolish the idea of innateness, this belief must also be altered, for in it is a major defense against individual insignificance.

Intellect

Intellect is a major barrier to mass domination[14] because it is the basis of human difference. "But," a modern manager will say, "the very complexity of modern organizations requires that we employ greater numbers of intelli-gent people. How can modern organizations, therefore, be opposed to intel-lect?" The problem lies in differentiating "intellect" from "intelligence." They are two different things, and the difference is critical.

We follow the distinction made by the eminent scholar Jacques Barzun in *The House of Intellect*. Early in the book, he set the lines of debate:

> There is an important reason for not calling this domain more simply the House of Mind. Mind is properly equated with intelligence, and by Intellect I most emphatically do not mean intelligence. Intellect is at once more and less than Mind. The House of Mind may turn out to be as large as the universe; to treat it would require dealing with the mental prowess of apes and bees and, for all I know, of fishes and flowers. Mind or intelligence is widely distributed and serves an infinity of purposes.[15]

A little further on, he wrote: "Intelligence is the native ability of the creature to achieve its ends by varying the use of its powers—living, as we say, by its wits."[16] Therefore, it may be said that a person is very intelligent but is not intellectual. The obverse does not hold true—intellectuals are al-ways intelligent. They may be frivolous or lack common sense or something else, but they are intelligent.

Intelligence, while it does not preclude intellect, can be applied to solving puzzles within the conventional framework of modern organizations. Indeed, an intelligent, literate mass is essential to the organizational imperative. The job force must be intelligent enough to contribute to modern organizations. As the complexities of production and consumption in technological societies increase, people must be prepared to cope with them in the course of their day-to-day lives. Mass education is the method for meeting this need, because it requires educated people to appreciate, purchase, and use such gadgetry as miniature electronic calculators, microwave ovens, compact disc sound systems, megavitamins, and running shoes. One must have intelligence to be a good consumer nowadays.

Consequently, we must amend our statement about malleability and insignificance: the cultivation of intelligent, malleable citizens is of critical importance to the modern organization. Organizational values in America must encourage advanced education as a matter of high priority in order to ensure the continuous flow of persons who are able to produce and consume intelligently. At the same time, educational policy must be controlled to ensure that the forms of intelligence that are fostered serve organizationally useful purposes. Therefore, intelligence alone does not foster individual autonomy, especially since the prized intelligence is that which advances the cause of modern science and modern organizations. One can be intelligent and still be convinced of one's insignificance and malleability.

Conversely, there is no easy way to grasp the meaning of intellect. Let us return to Barzun's definition:

> Intellect is the capitalized and communal form of live intelligence; it is intelligence stored up and made into habits of discipline, signs and symbols of meaning, chains of reasoning and spurs to emotion—a shorthand and a wireless by which the mind can skip connectives, recognize ability, and communicate truth. Intellect is at once a body of common knowledge and the channels through which the right particle of it can be brought to bear quickly, without the effort of redemonstration, on the matter in hand.[17]

Upon a quick reading, Barzun's statement may seem to complicate matters. But from a careful rereading, the missing element emerges. Intellect is the individual ability to perceive quality.

Intellect enables people to transcend the commonplace, to judge quality, and to appreciate variety. Intellect does not necessarily work within conventional frameworks, for it has the capacity both to rise above them and to comprehend inconsistencies within them. It is intellect that is able to distinguish between moral, as opposed to legal, issues of right and wrong. Intellect has the capacity to determine excellence as opposed to mediocrity. In other words, intellect cuts through appearances and exposes essential differences. In fact, this ability to identify, judge, and appreciate the quality of differences is perhaps the main factor that sets intellect apart from intelligence.[18] Intellect applies to qualitative differences in people, in material goods, in entertainment, in art; indeed, it applies in every case where it is necessary to say that something is better or worse than something else. Intellect is not democratic, nor is it necessarily action-oriented. It despises uniformity, and it is utterly opposed to fecklessness. Reason, employed in the service of intellect, is the primary means of identifying the unique and inviolable "self."[19] So intellect is more than making discerning judgments. As noted above, Barzun described intellect as a "capitalized and communal form of live intelligence." As such, intellect exists in its own right, larger than any single intelligence, in fact, greater than the combined intelligence of all living people. It is evident in language, law, architecture, science, and all other human endeavors that represent the accumulated experience, thought, and wisdom of centuries.

It is very instructive to note how the sorties against intellect proceed. Most are based on a single premise, which is repeated over and over in the media and the schools. This premise is simply that those characteristics that people share are more important than those that make people different. Barzun uses the photographic art book *The Family of Man* to demonstrate the premise of commonality.[20] *The Family of Man* is a glorification of sameness, and it presents photographic evidence to support the idea that sameness is better than difference. Even the word "family" in the title suggests the point of view. But what is it that people have in common, according to *The Family of Man*? Mainly, it is biology, expressed in human survival behaviors and the consequences thereof: sexual love, infancy and childhood innocence, toil or "earning bread by the sweat of the brow," misery, joy, and death.

While there is much that is grim and desperate in *The Family of Man*, its overall message is overwhelmingly optimistic. This optimism is summed up by the last picture, which shows two innocent children walking hand in hand, down a dirt road lined with trees, toward a glowing horizon. The message is: Be like children, believe in the essential goodness of people, understand that true wisdom is "earth wisdom," and above all put your trust in your animal functions. If all this is done, the human condition will improve.

Why is the glorification of sameness a critical strategy for the promulgation of insignificance? First, it reduces the number of variables that managers must manipulate in order to control mass behavior effectively. Second, behavioral technology requires it because, in assuming away differences, the amount of variation in behavior to account for is diminished. Third, an essential criterion of the organizational imperative is served, since organizations must treat people uniformly as producers and consumers. Therefore, the emphasis on common elements of humanity is of the highest usefulness to organizations and the managers who serve them, whereas the needs of intellect are downright dangerous. Nevertheless, intellect will not be altogether abolished, if for no other reason than that it has some assets that are valuable to the organizational imperative. Just think of the mess if every new generation of managers had to rediscover everything known about organization. Barzun's House of Intellect preserves such knowledge.

The connection between intellect and the organizational imperative is not obvious because they are very nearly polar forces. Intellect allows the individual to say: "I am different, and this difference is important." The private decision to participate in the life of intellect is an ultimate expression of autonomy. But the organizational imperative requires an entirely opposite commitment to homogeneity, or commonality. This conflict between intellect and the organizational imperative has led to the only possible practical form of resolution: the control of intellect by making it appear undesirable to the majority. In operational terms, the value of intellect must be demeaned so that the motivation of most individuals to participate in intellect is destroyed. One does not get ahead in a modern organization by being an intellectual. The few who are left clinging tenaciously to the option of exercising intellect can be easily identified and, if necessary, discredited. In totalitarian societies, if intellectuals will not join the party, they become a serious threat to the state. They are declared psychopaths and sent away to lunatic asylums to unlearn dangerously deviant values. This has been illustrated by the work and experiences of Russian dissidents like Alexander Solzhenitsyn and Vasily Grossman.

In America, freedom of intellect has generally been respected. Granted, the way of intellect has not been easy. America was founded by those of intellect, but it has also had a dark undercurrent of anti-intellectualism running through it, surfacing occasionally with disgraceful results—from the Know-Nothing party and the fundamentalist wars against a mythic Darwin, to the vicious purges run by Senator Joseph McCarthy and his followers and the never-ending attempt to censor schoolbooks.[21] Nevertheless, in the more open environment of the American past, the intellectual could usually find space to do his or her thing: Mary Parker Follett could lecture on management; Henry Thoreau could retreat; Walt Whitman and Samuel Clemens could wander; Emily Dickinson could compose; Charles Sanders Peirce, William James, and John Dewey could even stay within organizations and exercise intellect.

But in swarming, teeming organizational America, the intellectuals are no longer a threat to modern organizations, because they are either co-opted or ignored. Freedom of intellect is now under a much more subtle, much more dangerous attack: in education, in television, and in psychotherapy.[22] The denigration of things intellectual by the organizational imperative has very personal consequences. As intellect is phased out in organizational America as the chief means for persons to discover and to differentiate themselves, organizational values will be substituted. Since they include malleability, dispensability, and paternalism, they reinforce the legitimacy of the managerial elite and reduce individual responsibility for choices and actions.

Work

The distinction between work and labor is as fundamental as that between intellect and intelligence. The problem, again, is how to make it clear. Work means an activity, both mental and physical, whereby individuals can impress their personal identity upon a tangible object: a painting, book, machine, accounting problem, or food preparation. Work, therefore, is an aspect of intellect closely allied to creativity. When persons create a work of art, the implication is that the artists have achieved something distinctive: an object that differentiates them from all other artists working in the same medium. The idea of work does not apply solely to art, but to just about any activity that permits the expression of individuality and responsibility.

Labor implies toil, but much more as well. The activity of labor does not permit one person to be differentiated from another. It does not allow individuals to impress their distinctive character upon an object. What room is there for individuals laboring in a mass-production automobile factory to stamp their personality upon an engine piston? A cook in a fast-food franchise labors; a chef in a fine restaurant works.

Work does not preclude labor and, in fact, requires it. Much labor goes into writing a book: for example, typing rough drafts of manuscripts. Nevertheless, work is present in the writing process in the form of making a distinct, personal, and unique creation. Through work, individuals try to express excellence in their lives. Hannah Arendt wrote: "The standard by which a thing's excellence is judged is never mere usefulness . . . but its adequacy or inadequacy to what it should look like."[23] Some individuals are better able than others to perceive "what things should look like" and then to translate these perceptions of form and style into tangible artifacts.

However, labor often conspires against work, and, interestingly enough, this conspiracy exists in its most pernicious form at two extremes of a technological continuum. At one end is a sort of tribal toil for the necessities of life, where people are pitted against a hostile nature with primitive technologies, trying to extract a livelihood from the earth. *The Family of Man* depicts toil of this kind in the mistaken belief that there is something noble in the struggle of backward peoples to survive. While laboring people must never be scorned, labor is not ennobling; it is poignant perhaps, but certainly not noble. Nevertheless, the myth persists that the undifferentiated struggle of individuals against nature for the collective welfare of family or tribe is lofty and purifying. This myth remains in our culture partly because that kind of fidelity is expected of the employees of modern organizations.

At the opposite end of the technological continuum is labor of another sort, equally undifferentiated and depersonalized, but light-years more advanced in terms of tools and processes. Toil in the modern office or factory is a form of labor noticeably de-emphasized in *The Family of Man* photographs. Nevertheless, it is obvious that the personality of an employee has no place in putting compressors in refrigerators or programming computers. One reason why the machine is interposed between the employee and the task is to prevent the taint of the individual's personality from being impressed upon the product. The product made or the service rendered must not be contaminated by individual differences.

The analogue of the machine in the factory is the rule in the office. It evokes a standard of predictable performance so that no individual will disrupt the uniform flow of paper through the organization. Further, the rules of bureaucracy have invaded the factory just as the office has become mechanized. Rules and machines in nearly every activity of large organizations have united to prevent people from exercising discretion in performing their tasks. While interposing rules and machines between people and tasks has alleviated some of this concern, it has also taken a sense of personal responsibility for the product from the workers. Ironically, of all the world's leaders, Secretary General Mikhail Gorbachev spoke most directly to the national consequences of such systematized irresponsibility. They are economic stagnation, managerial paralysis, and moral decay.[24]

That the lot of most people is to labor is an ancient and dreary fact of history. But what is fascinating in our society are the efforts made by apologists to elevate this situation. With few exceptions, the argument is that individual sacrifice for the good of the collectivity is ennobling. Collective welfare supersedes individual welfare, and this formula applies across the board, to a tribe in New Guinea, to a large insurance company, and to an automobile assembly line.

The estrangement from the collective enterprise of people who only labor has been a long-standing issue for management. Too much depersonalization of jobs brings about alienation — a consequence that no one wants, least of all managers. Considerable effort and money, therefore, have gone into creating harmonious and satisfying organizational environments wherein people will find collective comfort for their sacrifice of individuality.

Few people who seriously follow trends in management practice have not heard of human relations, organizational development, job-enrichment programs, or quality circles. These programs emphasize individual involvement in a group engaged in collaborative decision making, known as participatory management. This phenomenon is widespread in Europe and America. Participation in job design and goal setting is seen by many as the way present and future organizational societies will achieve maximum effectiveness, with minimum alienation of the masses. While these programs still have little room for intellect and work, it is assumed that the individual employee can be convinced that collective participation in job decision making is an adequate, indeed a superior, substitute.

But the key question is: Why should people participate? One answer given with increasing frequency is that it is good for them. Carole Pateman argues that some form of true industrial democracy at the grass-roots level of work-ers' councils is an essential preliminary to the re-inculcation of democratic values into society at large.[25] The participation movement in organizations is, according to Pateman, a modern version of the classical ideal of human ennoblement through political activity.

If organizations are, as some contend, a contemporary substitute for the polis in ancient Greece, it follows that some process that satisfies a basic human need for political activity must also be substituted, if alienation is to be averted. This argument is persuasive and it has numerous adherents, par-ticularly in the field of public administration. However, it fails in one critical respect: modern organizations are not analogues of the polis as described by Plato and Aristotle.

Another answer to the participation question is more accurate: people should participate because it is good for the organization. Management does not use participation for human ennoblement; it uses it for organizational efficiency. Participation in this respect is a rational management practice for making better use of human resources. There is much support for this contention in behavioral science research.[26]

It would be easy, but wrong, to say that the sole aim of participation is to make people happy and productive in their labors. The participatory process is far more significant than this. When people are convinced that they can achieve higher satisfaction from participation, they often will become more obedient, since they feel they are making a direct contribution to the decisions affecting them. This is correct psychological theory. However, the psychol-ogist A. S. Tannenbaum observes that participation actually increases the power of managers over employees.[27] Research in several industrial coun-tries, including the United States, supports this contention.[28]

One of the facts of modern organizational life is that labor has changed. It is no longer the grinding toil shown in *The Family of Man*, but a process in a collective enterprise, and a rather comfortable one at that.[29] At no other time have so many people with so many roles and skills been involved in so fundamental a social transformation. It is by the mutation of labor to a phys-ically comfortable activity that justification is made for ignoring the absence of work in the daily lives of the insignificant people. This change requires that people become effective contributors to the organizational process so that what ensues is seen by them as neither work nor toil but as something else, *the modern job*, whose comforts they are conditioned to prize above work and intellect.

Of the three concepts we are discussing—work, labor, and the modern job—it is the modern job that concerns most Americans. They make a living from it; they get agitated over it; they derive multiple levels of satisfaction and dissatisfaction from it; and they are alternately depressed and gratified by it.

Table 6.1

Strategic Beliefs in the Role of Insignificance

Positive Beliefs	Negative Beliefs
1. The malleability of human nature allows it to be shaped to suit the needs of the organizational imperative.	1. There is no such thing as innate human nature, and therefore there is no such thing as innately necessary human needs.
2. Intelligence is necessary for rational production and consumption, and therefore, its cultivation is important to the modern organization.	2. Intellect is a dysfunctional form of personal fulfillment for most people, since it tends to separate people from the collective enterprise of the modern organization.
3. The modern job is the chief source of personal satisfaction for people committed to the collective enterprise of the modern organization.	3. Work is an undesirable means of individual expression in the modern organization because it results in variabiltiy rather than uniformity.

The physical and mental activities people perform on the job are the focus of their attention and consume a great deal of their energies. The modern job embodies the tangible, concrete factors of human existence in organizational America. Therefore, to be able to manipulate how people regard their jobs is as essential to management as how people perform them.

Modern jobs are sensitive to the influence of the organizational imperative because most of them are performed within large organizations. For example, the total employment of the *Fortune* 500 corporations in 1987 was 13.1 million. This was 69 percent of the total manufacturing employment in the private sector and 15 percent of the total nonagricultural, nongovernmental employment nationally. The 1987 *Forbes* magazine survey of 796 companies in the private sector, which included both manufacturing and non-manufacturing firms, showed a total of 20.5 million wage-and-salary employees, or 24 percent of the total employment, in the private sector. (In order to qualify for the *Forbes* list, a company had to apperar in at least one of its set of four criteria for company size.) Many of the gainfully employed are with the government, at all levels. In December 1987, the number of people employed by federal, state, and local governments was 17.3 million. Roughly, then, in 1987, about 36 percent of the total work force, or 37.8 million people, were employed in large organizations in either the public or private sector.[30]

These organizations are at the forefront in applying the principles of modern management, and they spend considerable effort and money to change attitudes toward jobs. But the importance of these large organizations does not end there, for they are the managerial exemplars for all the smaller organizations that follow their lead. This vast employment network includes nearly every working adult in the United States. In the end, the loss of the opportunity to work must be made as palatable to people as the loss of opportunity to use their intellect. Technology and the modern organization have not made work available to the masses, as promised. Rather, the insignificant people have been trapped by a mutated form of labor called the modern job.

But our argument is not complete, since we have not demonstrated how the strategy of insignificance, summarized in table 6.1, will move people from obsolete beliefs about human nature, intellect, and work to the organizationally necessary beliefs about malleability, intelligence, and the modern job. The strategy of mass domination is implemented through its tactics.

Notes

1. Harold D. Lasswell, *Power and Personality* (New York: Viking, 1948), 10.
2. Milovan Djilas, *The New Class* (New York: Praeger, 1958), 59–69. Milovan Djilas wrote mainly about the rise to power of bureaucrats in communist parties, and some of the points he makes about managerial class structure are instructive. He observes that this class did not arise by deliberate design, that it is not conscious of itself, but that "the phenomena of careerism and unscrupulous ambition are a sign that it is profitable to be a bureaucrat." Also, he points out that the ranks of the new class are filled by people from the broadest possible strata of society. The "democratization" of access to the ruling class of managers with technical and organizational expertise is an obvious characteristic of the managerial class in noncommunist as well as communist societies.
3. For an interesting and useful summary, see T. B. Bottomore, *Elites and Society* (Baltimore: Penguin Books, 1964).
4. Consensus is central to the legitimization of a dominant managerial value system. This point is clearly made in Rolf Dahrendorf's analysis of managerial attitudes about the "pathology of conflict," in *Class and Class Conflict in Industrial Society* (Stanford: Stanford University Press, 1959). The functional value of consensus is interlaced through the value structure of contemporary management theory and practice. This aspect of management is so fundamental that it is easily overlooked; yet it is the basic historical continuity that links modern theory and practice with the past. For a further elaboration see William G. Scott, "Organization Theory: A Reassessment," *Academy of Management Journal*, 17 (June 1974): 244–246.
5. "At the same time, one should not fail to observe how far Locke is from the other allegedly Lockean extreme of asserting a total human malleability and equality, which emerged in Helvetious and Condillac and continues into our own time. The tabula rasa applies absolutely only to knowledge, not to abilities, temperaments, or desires. As always, Locke is sensible." Nathan Tarcov, *Locke's Education for Liberty* (Chicago: University of Chicago Press, 1984), 109.
6. The issue is discussed in Raymond Polin, "John Locke's Conception of Freedom" in John W. Yolton, ed., *John Locke: Problems and Perspectives* (Cambridge: Cambridge University Press, 1969), 1–18.

7. Thomas Hobbes, *Leviathan*, ed. M. Oakeshott (Oxford: Basil Blackwell [1651], 1957), 2:221.

8. James M. Glass makes this point in an imaginative way by contrasting the behavior of the main characters in two novels, *The Man in the Grey Flannel Suit* and *Something Happened*, in his essay "Organization and Action: The Executive's Personality Type as a Pathological Formation," *Journal of Contemporary Business*, 5 (Autumn 1976), 91–111.

9. This is the major theme of the organizational humanists, made quite clear by Chris Argyris, *Organization and Personality* (New York: Harper & Bros., 1957). Much has been written on the subject of changing either personality or organization so that a closer harmony between the two might be achieved. The idea is simply that disequilibrium among the component parts of a system reduces organizational effectiveness. Humanists like Argyris, Warren Bennis, and Rensis Likert want to modify behavior and organizations so that they are more compatible. The approach is within the consensus tradition of management theory and practice.

10. William G. Scott and Terence R. Mitchell, "The Problem or Mystery of Evil and Virtue in Organizations," in Konstantin Kolenda, ed., *Papers on Ethical Individualism* (New York: Praeger, 1988).

11. Jeremy Bentham, as quoted by Lee Cameron McDonald, *Western Political Philosophy* (New York: Harcourt, Brace and World, 1968), 462.

12. Internalistic versus externalistic causes of behavior are discussed by Pitrim A. Sorokin, *The Crisis of Our Age* (New York: Dutton, 1941).

13. B. F. Skinner, *Beyond Freedom and Dignity* (New York: Knopf, 1971), 19. Skinner answered his critics in *About Behaviorism* (New York: Knopf, 1974), but his position remains the same.

14. Jacques Ellul argues that the only defense against modern propaganda, and thereby mass domination, is the individual intellect. Jacques Ellul, *Propaganda*, trans. K. Kellen and J. Lerner (New York: Knopf, 1965).

15. Jacques Barzun, *The House of Intellect* (New York: Harper & Row, 1959), 3–4.

16. Ibid, 5.

17. Ibid, 4.

18. Robert M. Pirsig, *Zen and the Art of Motorcycle Maintenance* (New York: Morrow, 1974), especially 189–212.

19. We will not develop the idea here, but we are impressed with the fact that reason is a two-edged sword. Outwardly, as intelligence, it is essential to successful paradigmatic puzzle solving. Inwardly, as intellect, it is the means of discovering the inviolable self. This assumption is central to an understanding of John Rawls, *A Theory of Justice* (Cambridge: Harvard University Press, 1973).

20. Museum of Modern Art, *The Family of Man* (New York: Macro Magazine Corporation, 1955).

21. See, for instance, Richard Hofstadter, *Anti-Intellectualism in American Life* (New York: Vintage, 1963); John H. Bunzel, *Anti-Politics in America* (New York: Knopf, 1967); and Russell Jacoby, *The Last Intellectual* (New York: Basic Books, 1987).

22. That psychiatry is the ally of those seeking collective support of the communal values is a point made by E. Fuller Torrey, particularly in his discussion of the "mental hygiene" movement. *Death of Psychiatry* (see chap. 4, n. 27), especially chapter 7. The use of psychology as a management tool is developed in Baritz, *The Servants of Power* (see chap. 2, n. 22).

23. Hannah Arendt, *The Human Condition* (New York: Doubleday Anchor Books, 1959), 152–153.
24. Mikhail Gorbachev, *Perestroika* (New York: Harper & Row, 1987).
25. Carole Pateman, *Participation and Democratic Theory* (Cambridge, England: Cambridge University Press, 1970). The arguments about participation are discussed in David K. Hart, "Theories of Government Related to Decentralization and Citizen Participation," *Public Administration Review* 32 (Special Issue, Oct. 1972), 603–621.
26. William G. Scott, "The Management Governance Theories of Justice and Liberty," *Journal of Management*, 14 (June, 1988), 277–298.
27. A. S. Tannenbaum, *Control in Organizations* (New York: McGraw-Hill, 1968).
28. M. Rosner, B. Kavcic, A. S. Tannenbaum, M. Vianello, and G. Weiser, "Worker Participation and Influence in Industrial Plants in Five Countries," *Proceedings of the First International Sociological Conference on Participation and Self-management* (Zagreb, Yugoslavia: Council of Yugoslavia Trade Unions Federation, 1973).
29. See the delightful book by Allan Harrington, *Life in the Crystal Palace* (New York: Knopf, 1959).
30. The figures were compiled from the following sources: *Fortune* (8 May 1987), 239; *Forbes* (15 May 1987), 286; *Economic Report of the President* (Washington, D.C.: U.S. Printing Office, 1987), 290, 297.

   Some comparisons can be made between the 1977 data reported in the first edition of our book and these 1987 data drawn from the same sources. The *Fortune* 500 manufacturing corporations employed 2.2 million fewer people in 1987, with their percentage of the total private sector employment dropping from 22 percent to 15 percent. These data in part reflect the general contraction in conventional heavy industry manufacturing that the *Fortune* survey reports. The *Forbes* survey showed a decline of just 200,000 employees in the same reporting period. *Forbes*, however, includes companies in service industries as well as manufacturing. These service companies probably maintained the *Forbes* totals at comparable levels with those 10 years earlier. Nevertheless both the *Forbes* and *Fortune* "largest" companies lost similarly in terms of percentages (7 percent) of their employment to total employment. The *Forbes* firms moved from 31 percent in 1977 to 24 percent in 1987. These data from these surveys document the well-known: between 1977 and 1987, private sector employment was expanding mainly because of business startups and growing small firms.

   Government employment increased between 1977 and 1987 by 1.8 million. However, this increase came mainly at state and local levels. Federal government employment increased in these years by just 200,000 people, whereas state and local governments added 1.6 million employees. This change may be accounted for in part by two factors: the incorporation and professionalization of many city governments in the U.S. and the transfer of responsibility for federal welfare and educational programs to state and city governments.

7

The Insignificant People:
The Tactics of Mass Domination

> *Only if you get people acting, even in small ways, the way you want them to, will they come to believe in what they are doing.*
>
> —T. J. Peters and R. H. Waterman,
> *In Search of Excellence*

The tactics of mass domination are the behavioral techniques management uses to convert the insignificant people into obedient and productive employees. These tactics are the applied and instrumental corollaries of the strategies of mass domination discussed in the last chapter. Our concern with these tactics is that they are similar to those used by totalitarian regimes. In the mid-1950s, Carl J. Friedrich and Zbigniew Brzezinski described various tactics used by totalitarian regimes to control their populations.[1] While most attention is given to the violent aspects of control, the sinister aspect of totalitarianism lies in the nonviolent tactics, such as official ideology, propaganda, and the use of the behavioral sciences to structure a totalitarian personality.

A thorough examination has not been made of the tactics of mass domination used within the organizations of modern democratic societies. When they are viewed independently of the totalitarian context, these tactics do not seem so terrible. They address, in a scientific, problem-solving fashion, management responsibilities for coordination, cooperation, orderliness, productivity, morale, and the achievement of mutual interests between the leaders and the led. However, when laid alongside the totalitarian perspective, the similarities between the two are evident and, therefore, worrisome. Three tactics seem most important in organizational America: manipulation, preemptive control, and integrative propaganda.

The Tactics of Manipulation

Manipulation is the deliberate attempt by people with power to alter the perceptions of objective situations by others without their awareness of alternative interpretations, choices, or values. Manipulation is wholly instrumental, since its purpose is to change attitudes and behaviors by deceit, in order to achieve the manipulators' goals. Thus, manipulation is closer to propaganda than to education. Its use is justified by its efficiency—managers do not have to waste time explaining why employees must obey. Manipulation provides a direct route to obedience, that bypasses intellect. As with propaganda, many manipulative techniques have come from the applied behavioral sciences. These techniques aim at two targets: individual employee attitudes and the overall organizational culture.

The Manipulation of Individual Attitudes

Individual motivation has been one of management's chief concerns, because its control assures management's influence over the human resources at its disposal. Consequently, applied behavioral scientists have devoted a large portion of their efforts to the development of techniques that address this management interest. At present, many such techniques derived from these scientific labors are used by management in organizations great and small. They include participatory management, democratic leadership, management by objectives (MBO), quality circles, organizational development (OD), the managerial grid, sensitivity training, management initiated grievance systems (MIGS), and a plethora of combinations and repackagings of all the foregoing. These techniques are thought to induce higher productivity and job satisfaction, more effective goal setting and performance appraisal, smoother organizational change, and better decisions about day-to-day work practices.

These modern motivational practices are the result of a long development of applied behavioral techniques. By the time Chester I. Barnard and Herbert Simon published their seminal books, in 1938 and 1947, respectively, a substantial amount of behavioral research and application had been done.[2] No one saw the implications of this work more clearly than Barnard and Simon. They focused management's attention on employee attitudes, and they argued persuasively that the successful manipulation of these attitudes lay at the heart of effective management practice.

Exchange theory was the framework upon which Barnard and Simon wove their argument. This theory is a psychological interpretation of individual decision making. Barnard and Simon believed that employee attitudes about their jobs were determined by their perception of job inducements (I) versus job contributions (C). Employees, they claimed, did a mental cost/benefit analysis, where they weighed their I's (benefits) against their C's (costs). Depending on how this analysis turned out—that is, whether employees perceived net I's or net C's from their exchange with the organization—they would decide to work diligently (I > C), or decide to do the minimum necessary to keep their jobs (I = C), or quit (I < C). Barnard and Simon held that this theory was the bedrock upon which rested human motivation on the job.

Utility theory in economics predated Barnard's and Simon's views by at least a century. Early economists who followed this theory held that human motivation could be interpreted as the pursuit of pleasure (benefits, inducements) and the avoidance of pain (costs, contributions). Although Barnard and Simon accepted the general assumptions of utility theory, they made two critical modifications of it. First, they thought that inducements and contributions were mainly subjective employee perceptions of job-related incentives and disincentives. These perceptions were largely based on employee feelings, emotions, attitudes, and sentiments. Thus, an employee's I's and C's included far more than merely a rational economic calculation of the monetary reward for doing a job, as opposed to the time and effort taken to earn it. Second, as a corollary to the foregoing, they considered that employees did not make objective or logical economic decisions.

These modifications to utility theory led Barnard and Simon to their most important generalization: employees could be motivated to higher performance by changing what they *thought* were inducements and contributions. Therefore management can and should intervene in employee decision-making processes to induce them to act in ways that improved organizational performance. Furthermore, since employees did not make rational decisions, they should be persuaded that some of their decisions were not in their best interests, while management's were. This would lead to higher employee satisfaction. The tactical management problem was to gain access to those mental processes underlying employee decision making. As Barnard and Simon saw it, the behavioral sciences provided this access.

The elaborate theory of human motivation presented to management by Barnard and Simon did not spring fully formed from their heads. It was preceded by research and application of psychological techniques that began in industry at the turn of this century, with psychological testing of employees for job selection and placement. However, after World War I, the field of industrial psychology flourished, and it evolved in two directions.[3] First, testing programs in business expanded to include employee psychological profiles: intelligence, personality, aptitudes, vocational preferences, trade knowledge and skill, manual dexterity, and so on. Second, an embryonic version of ergonomics took shape, joining physiology and psychology. Scientists of the 1920s took interest in the relationship between physical fatigue (measured by blood pressure and pulse rate) and the level of employee productivity. Other studies looked at the relationship between drug and alcohol use and attention spans. Many studies were designed to determine the job environment causes of accidents, absenteeism, and turnover. Experiments were conducted on the effects of color, noise, and even music on worker productivity and satisfaction.

The pioneer industrial psychologist Hugo Munsterberg believed that a true "scientific management" had to include psychology. Summing up, he wrote: "All business is ultimately the affair of minds. It starts with minds, it works through minds, and it aims to serve minds."[4]

It was in this 1920s context of managerial optimism about the promises of industrial psychology that the Hawthorne studies were begun at AT&T's manufacturing subsidiary, the Western Electric Company. These studies were first conceived in 1926 and they were conducted under the general supervision of Lawrence Henderson and Elton Mayo through their Fatigue Lab at the Harvard Business School. The studies were designed originally as straightforward ergonomic research. However, as the initial findings came in, they were dramatically transformed. The researchers at the plant found that their very presence in the study setting produced anomalous results: the famous "Hawthorne effect."[5] Workers did not behave as anticipated when changes were made in their physical environment. It was assumed that productivity would increase as the environment was made more pleasant, and indeed it did. But to their great surprise, productivity also increased even though the researchers made the environment worse. Therefore, it was concluded that far more powerful factors than physical conditions influenced employee job behavior. These factors were emotional and attitudinal.

The Hawthorne studies added a revolutionary dimension to applied psychology. They showed that workers responded positively to someone in authority giving them recognition, allowing them to participate in job-related decisions, and communicating with them about their job performance. The Hawthorne studies also found that small groups, informal organizations, had a significant impact on individual behavior. These groups within the formal organization of the company set norms of behavior for their members. The studies showed that these norms often were different, and frequently more powerful, than the standards of conduct set by a company.

Although many of the Hawthorne findings are now discredited, no other single piece of psychological research has had as great or as lasting an impact on management thought and practice. It opened the floodgates for the behavioral sciences to inundate management with new perspectives and techniques for manipulating employees. *They demonstrated that management could enter the realm of the employees' subconscious to manipulate their job attitudes.* Until these studies, the subconscious had been explored systematically only by Freud, Jung, and their followers, in clinical cases of psychoses and neuroses. The Hawthorne studies suggested that "normal" people had natural, but unmet, subconscious desires and impulses on the job, which shaped their attitudes and influenced their performance. Thus, the studies concluded that management could improve employee motivation by discovering and satisfying these unmet employee needs.

Barnard and Simon developed their approach to employee motivation within this context of burgeoning behavioral theory, research, and application. They joined many research findings, theories, and concepts of behavior into an elegant integrated paradigm that had meaning for the effective management of human resources. Simon, especially, established that the behavioral sciences were the only legitimate source of appropriate facts about individual and organizational behavior. And finally they understood that management could use these facts to design techniques to manipulate employee job attitudes.

The informal organization, however, defied similar management interventions. Barnard and Simon did not address how management could influence the group functions of role prescription and norm development. Little was done in this area until management realized that the culture of the organization was a major force that shaped, not only individual attitudes, but also the norms of small groups.

The Manipulation of Organizational Culture

Management discovered culture in the 1980s, but it was not precisely a discovery. Rather, management learned that some well-established anthropological concepts could be applied to modern organizations to improve their performance. The most important of these concepts was culture, and it was understood by anthropologists as a system of shared symbolic meaning expressed by rituals, myths, legends, heroic sagas, fictions, and fairy tales.

Employees in organizations perform many symbolic acts as a natural part of their job interactions. Found in organizations are rites of passage for promotions and retirements that range from beer-busts to sedate garden parties; legends about the amorous or drinking exploits of maverick employees; role-model stories about super salespeople, creative designers, innovative product managers, and outstanding engineers; sagas of heroic proportion about the founders of firms; myths about social responsibility; and an inexhaustible fund of fables about people, places, and events that sustain and enrich organizational life for all manner and levels of employees.

These and many other symbols are woven into elaborate tapestries of images and metaphors that comprise "patterns of culture," as anthropologist Ruth Bendict called them. These cultural myths give meaning to people's job roles because they fit the individual into the larger mythic context of the organization. By doing so, they enrich the meaning of self for each person.

Although the culture of formal organizations provides valid research opportunities for some scholars, it must have an instrumental use in order to be attractive to management. The management consultants T. J. Peters and R. H. Waterman in their book *In Search of Excellence*[6] pointed out the benefits to the organization that came from manipulating that culture. Their insight was a logical extension of the manipulation of employee attitudes: if management intervenes in the decision-making processes of individual employees to increase organizational effectiveness, they should also intervene in the *meaning-making* processes of the organizational culture for the same reason.

Both Barnard and Simon flirted with this idea, because they recognized that organizations furnished meaning in people's lives. They did not, however, acknowledge culture as the source of meaning. The astounding success of *In Search of Excellence* was because the authors demonstrated emphatically that the manipulation of culture will result in improved organizational performance. Managements that manipulate their cultures most effectively are in charge of America's best-run companies, according to Peters and Waterman.

Stimulated by this high-voltage inspiration, management scurried to climb on the culture bandwagon. From 1983 to 1988, the *Academy of Management Review* published no fewer than thirteen major articles on the subject. This was in addition to a number of books that appeared in the same period that dealt with corporate culture. Junk mail abounds with advertisements from full-time management consultants announcing their programs to train managers to do cultural meaning making. Finally, some academics, combining research and consulting roles, shroud cultural manipulation with the scholarly legitimacy of their management-oriented speeches, books, and workshop activities.

Consequently, although the idea of cultural meaning making seems abstract, there is no shortage of examples that detail what it is and how it is practiced. Books by Ian Mitroff and Garath Morgan describe a variety of concepts, techniques, and specific practices that can be used to shape images, metaphors, and symbols to improve organization performance.[7]

Cultural manipulation strikes directly at employee values. It can be used to mold employee's attitudes about their innate moral nature, the importance of intellect, and the nature of work. Thus, cultural manipulation is influential in getting the insignificant people to conform to the organizational values of effort, productivity, teamwork, and striving for excellence. Current research emphasizes that management is symbolic action, and current theory takes the position that management must manipulate employee values through the symbols of the corporate culture.

The Categorical Imperative of Manipulation

The tactics of manipulation stand Kant on his head. They hold that management *must* make instrumental use of people. One does not have to dig deeply to understand why the manipulation of individual attitudes and organizational culture strikes management's instrumental nerve. The successful use of these tactics promises to motivate action, reduce disagreement, increase employee commitment to organizational values, and cement managerial authority. Taken together, these manipulative tactics cause employees to have a pleasing view of their organizational world.

But do these ends justify the means? Kant answered this question categorically: *never* must people be used instrumentally. Since management ignores Kant, it must have its own moral justification for manipulation. It is found in two interrelated metaphysical premises.

The first premise is management's assumption that people do not have an innate moral nature. As long as there is nothing innately inviolable in human nature, management can and should intrude upon employee decision-making processes. The second premise is the philosophical assumption that denies or discounts an objective moral reality. It calls for the suspension or negation of individual judgment in discerning what is right and just, or even what is real in organizations. The culture, then, can be whatever management wants it to be.

The moral justification for manipulation follows from these two premises. Since people are void of meaning, having no innate nature, it is morally praiseworthy for management to create meaning for them through the culture of the organization. Consequently managers are justified in cultural manipulation because positive employee values are created by them in what would be an otherwise empty vessel of individual innate nature. Management receives its moral halo by intervening, since the lesser people of the organization would be without values if it did not provide appropriate attitudes and cultures for them.

The cynical aspect of manipulation is that the myths management creates are not based necessarily on belief. Management not only manipulates people to believe in certain values, but it also constructs these values without itself having any real adherence to, or belief in, them.[8] Management imposes organizationally useful values on employees because it has the power to do so. Management's intentions do not come from the milk of human kindness, but from a desire to use those behavioral techniques to enhance their own authority and to improve the performance of their organization.

Manipulation is the master tactic of mass domination. However, it is not a very reliable means—yet. People see through its cynicism rather quickly. But, though they do, management continues to use and perfect these and similar means of mass domination. Why bother? Because these tactics hold the promise of working well, once the bugs are ironed out. As propaganda has worked in nations, so might cultural and attitudinal manipulation work in organizations. This devotion to manipulation is troubling because, as the political philosopher Hannah Arendt pointed out, it is a hallmark of totalitarianism.[9]

The Tactic of Preemptive Control

All modern organizations have planning systems. Control, the necessary adjunct of planning, prevents random or deviant events from confounding future expectations. Going one step further, preemptive control is even more effective. It is the conscious managerial effort to control *in advance* all organizationally critical variables in accordance with the managerial policies. In other words, through prior intervention, certain problems are taken care of before they arise. Ideally, preemptive control makes managerial plans self-fulfilling prophecies.[10]

The desire to move toward more effective preemptive control is clearly present in management theory and practice. Computer technology and management information systems have given it its biggest boost in the last twenty-five years. However, while technology is necessary for effective preemptive control, it is not sufficient. There is an ancient military adage that says a commander should give battle only when the conditions are favorable to victory. In managerial language this means that preemptive control is possible only when managers have the power to influence and to manipulate the strategic variables in an organization's environment. Thus power is essential, since managers can only use preemptive control when they get at the main variables.

For instance, the managers of a public utility projected that its company's size would double over a ten-year period. This doubling was the long-range plan. Further incremental, short-term increases on a year-by-year basis were also forecast. Reviewing the plan at the end of ten years, the managers found that not only had the long-term objective been met, but that each intermediate yearly goal had also been met according to plan. Everyone congratulated one another on what marvelous planners they were. Actually, the managers had nearly complete control over many important variables—the market area, the financial resources for expanding plant and equipment, the supply of fuel necessary for generating energy—so that their projected outcomes were nearly inevitable from the beginning.

This is instructive of the kind of preemptive control that occurs in managerial situations where the top managers have the power to mold such variables to the shape of the plan. The problem is not planning for an uncertain future, but controlling the strategic variables in an organization's environment to ensure that the desired future emerges as forecast. The extent to which preemptive control can be practiced depends, of course, on the type of market in which a business or government agency operates. Different market structures have different degrees of uncertainty with varying susceptibility to control. But as management reduces these uncertainties, it increases its chances to exercise preemptive control. Uncertainty reduction is, therefore, the name of an important managerial game.

However, critical unplanned changes often occur outside the planning framework. Americans have traditionally welcomed unanticipated change as necessary for progress. The positive benefit of such change was believed to provide opportunities for organizational growth. One might be led to believe, then, that there is a managerial dilemma between the desirability of unplanned change versus preemptive control. However, no such dilemma exists because the organizational imperative has resolved it in favor of preemptive control. Planning has become less a matter of crystal-ball gazing and more a matter of manipulating strategic factors in the environment. Hence the managerial response to crisis and change is not spontaneous, creative adaptation; rather, it is the construction of predictive models based on the assumption that managers can preemptively make events flow in a predetermined course.

This a very large order, but it is not as great as it might first appear. Simulation models have gone far to account for many of the confounding variables, so crises and unplanned changes can be offset by anticipatory managerial actions. These actions are based upon three tactical requirements: (1) organizational variables must be made amenable to control; (2) those variables not immediately susceptible to control must be converted to become so; and (3) if a variable cannot be converted, it must be eliminated.

These conditions have been met in modern organizations to a surprising degree. However, the individual is the one crucial variable in the organizational environment that has eluded preemptive control. If individual behavior can be made predictable in organizational life, many conceivable crises and changes can be planned for within a framework that is optimal for the organizational imperative. Thus, *the primary target for preemptive control must be the individual*.

Preemptive control requires the fusion of managerial and organizational technology into a tactical assault on the human variable. This assault has a single aim: *to homogenize all people as a requisite aspect of organizational culture*. Preemptive control operates on the lowest common traits in human behavior and manages them in ways that result in predictable organizational outcomes. Human behavior is reduced to a scientific problem, an engineering puzzle to solve.

The organizational imperative provides the necessary justification for preemptive controls, especially its second proposition that all behavior must contribute to the health of the organization. This makes managerial efforts to impose preemptive control for mass domination both right and reasonable.

However, right and reason are not in themselves enough to accomplish the tactical objectives of manipulation and preemptive control. These tactics must be reinforced by integrative propaganda.

The Tactic of Integrative Propaganda

Like manipulation and preemptive control, integrative propaganda is a recent phenomenon, made possible by modern communication techniques and the behavioral sciences. The popular and old-fashioned view of propaganda is largely incorrect. This view held that propaganda consisted of "the big lie." Conventional wisdom had it that propaganda is based upon falsehood and is used to inflame emotions against an enemy. That is correct, but it is the least important use of propaganda. Modern propaganda is designed to integrate, rather than agitate, people. Jacques Ellul observed this change and it led him to distinguish between agitational and integrative propaganda.[11] Agitational propaganda is used to incite people to frenzies of loyalty or animosity. But integration is the primary objective of propaganda. Furthermore, it is nearly invisible, and is congruent with, and supportive of, the dominant social values.

Integrative propaganda is directed within, toward resolution of conflict and toward the promotion of consensus among people. It has a single vision, that humanity is a harmonious whole in which people share essential similarities. The purpose of integrative propaganda is to stimulate and to reinforce this vision of harmony, either in one organization or in a whole society. Modern propagandists concentrate upon integrating attitudes; they teach us to appreciate similarities in the in-group, because this promotes intraorganizational harmony.

The ideal of harmony was given added impetus after World War II, partly in revulsion against the horrors of the Nazi era and the war. This attitude was reinforced by the egalitarian sentiment that swept over Europe and America at the same time. It was further strengthened, as the military historian John Keegan pointed out, by the change in public attitudes toward violence.[12] Integrative propaganda, based upon nonviolence, suits the needs of organizational America. Agitational propaganda, which encourages antagonists to hate each other, is not organizationally useful at this moment.

The fact that integrative propaganda suits the needs of the modern organization gives an unprecedented twist to the function of propagandists. There are two sides to their role. One side, already mentioned as the cultivation of consensus, is well understood in management thought.[13] The need for organizational harmony, as opposed to conflict, is a widely documented managerial belief that has persisted as a central theme in management for years.[14]

The other side of the propagandist's role is less well understood, since it reduces individual alienation. Clearly employees who are at peace with themselves will be more apt to reach harmonious accommodation with their organizations.[15]

The subject of organizational alienation has not gone unexamined.[16] The problem is that within management, alienation was perceived as a personal ailment. Moreover, it was seen as an illness that was not responsive to conventional means of treatment, because alienation transcended any single management group's capacity to cope with it directly. More pay or job enrichment or greater participation in decision making were like Band-Aids over a ten-inch laceration. They were palliatives, not cures. Through them and similar techniques, the individual does not necessarily rise to a self-accommodation with the imperatives of organizational living.

Can integrative propaganda reduce alienation and promote consensus? There are reasons to believe that it can, to a rather large extent, and more now than ever before. The modern propagandist has available advanced information about the human mind from the findings of medical and behavioral sciences. More is known about processes that alter individual attitudes. Further, the technologies of communication now available to the propagandist are considerably more formidable than earlier technologies. If nothing else, television provides the most expeditious access to the masses in history.

Of great importance to the integrative propagandist is the fact that the people are already in their seats. In other words, they are inextricably involved with, and reliant upon, modern organizations. The propagandist will not have to chase around looking for an audience; it is already gathered into receptive and interdependent clusters. But the real power behind integrative propaganda rests upon the foundation of corporate culture, whose symbols and myths can be manipulated. As Ellul wrote, one cannot propagandize a single, thinking individual. Finally, the promulgation of externalism has eliminated any notions of individual moral autonomy. Thus, the propagandist can act as the molder without any silly pangs of conscience. The way is cleared for a systematic attempt to mold and maintain insignificant people in a pre-selected, role-reinforcing, organizationally healthy model.

This raises some questions about method. The most effective means of integrative propaganda is through the manipulation of language. The tactical principle is straightforward: people can only act collectively upon what they can think about. Conversely, they cannot act wrongly if there are no words to identify the wrong collective behavior. This was the most important message in George Orwell's novel, *1984*. It was stated explicitly in the little-heeded appendix, which explained the principles of "Newspeak."[17] While there is obviously no propaganda program to create an American newspeak yet, the corruption of our language is well under way. Its purpose, usually implicit, is to strengthen support for the organizational imperative among the mass of people.

Language emasculation works on other planes. The jargon of academics, the buzz words of managers, and the acronyms of technologists remove from the realm of thought the possibility of passionate expressions, humane sentiments, and, indeed, even the necessity of thought itself. Suffice it to say, the importance of the place of language in integrative propaganda cannot be overemphasized. It is the key to controlling employee attitudes and organizational culture.

The Creation of the Ideal Organizational Person

There is, in the literature of socialism, the phrase "the socialist man." The idea is that there is a perfect personality suited for the success of socialism, and the task is to create such people. Similarly, there is great force in the creation of an ideal, prototypical "ideal organizational person," and full use of it will be made by propaganda in the service of the organizational imperative.

The "ideal organizational person" is defined by the propositions and rules of the organizational imperative. Now the task is to bring the ideal into being. There is no shortage of advocates. For instance, the public administration scholar Harlan Cleveland argues that executives must deal with one another as "functions," not as individuals: with the objective of "growing" the ideal organizational person.[18] These are not the words of people with sinister designs, but rather of people who want to create more effective organizations, staffed by ideal organizational people. For them, this new breed of people will solve so many of the problems that plague humankind. Our argument is that these assumptions and tactics will destroy the last vestiges of individualism.

Notes

1. Carl J. Friedrich and Zbigniew K. Brzezinski, *Totalitarian Dictatorship and Autocracy* (Cambridge: Harvard University Press, 1956), part 4.
2. Barnard, *Functions of the Executive* (see chap. 1, n. 14) and Herbert Simon, *Administrative Behavior* (New York: Macmillan, 1947).
3. For an analysis and criticism of this movement from a historical perspective, see Baritz, *Servants of Power* (see chap. 2, n. 22).
4. Hugo Munsterberg, *Business Psychology* (Chicago: La Salle Extension University, 1922), 5.
5. The report of the Hawthorne studies is contained in F. J. Roethlisberger and William J. Dickson, *Management and the Worker* (Cambridge: Harvard University Press, 1939).
6. Thomas J. Peters and Robert H. Waterman, Jr., *In Search of Excellence: Lessons from America's Best Run Companies* (New York: Harper and Row, 1982).

7. Ian Mitroff, *The Stakeholders of the Organizational Mind* (San Francisco: Jossey-Bass, 1983); and Garath Morgan, *Images of Organization* (Beverly Hills, Calif.: Sage, 1986).

8. William G. Scott and Terence R. Mitchell, "Markets and Morals in Management Education," *Selections* (Autumn 1986), 4.

9. See especially, Chapter 11, "The Totalitarian Movement," in Hannah Arendt, *The Origins of Totalitarianism*, 2nd ed. (Cleveland: World, 1958), 341–388.

10. See William G. Scott, "Executive Development as an Instrument of Higher Control," *Academy of Management Journal* 6 (Sept. 1963), 191–203.

11. Ellul, *Propaganda* (see chap. 6, n. 14).

12. John Keegan, *The Face of Battle* (New York: Viking Press, 1976), chapter 5.

13. Dahrendorf, *Class and Class Conflict* (see chap. 6, n. 4).

14. Scott, "Organization Theory" (see chap. 6, n. 4), 245.

15. Although from reading James Glass's commentary on Heller's book, *Something Happened*, one might be led to the opposite conclusion—that psychic turmoil is the only way a person has to cope with an insane organizational world. Glass, "Organization and Action" (see chap. 6, n. 8), and James M. Glass, "Consciousness and Organizations," *Administration and Society* 7 (Nov. 1975), 366–384.

16. Robert A. Nisbet, *The Quest for Community* (London: Oxford University Press, 1970), viii–xi. See Richard Schacht, *Alienation* (Garden City, N.Y.: Anchor, 1970), and the bibliography therein.

17. George Orwell, *1984* (Baltimore: Penguin, 1949), 241–251.

18. Cleveland, *The Future Executive* (see chap. 2, n. 19), 25–26.

8

The Professional People

The rule of the functionary is . . . identical with the rule of the professionals, *the so-called "specialists"—even though it is only a subordinate kind of rule exercised by those who carry out orders. The specialist is the prisoner of his department; he lives in the ghetto of objectivity. He is "utilized"—the term itself is characteristic; he is assigned his role in the termite state. He is the distinctly "disengaged" man and is therefore liable to become the tool of a degenerate humanity.*

—Helmut Thielicke, *Nihilism*

The Occupants of the Professional Jobs

This chapter treats a new class of people in organizational America. We do not refer to those who lead the great organizations, the significant people, but rather to an essential intermediary layer between them and the insignificant people. These are the people directly responsible for carrying out the policies of those at the top. Without them, the leaders would not be able to lead: their skills are essential to the functioning of the modern organization. Using a military metaphor, Thorstein Veblen termed "these expert men . . . the indispensable General Staff of the industrial system; and without their immediate and unremitting guidance and correction the industrial system will not work."[1]

These subordinates of the managerial elite are identified by sociologist James Thompson as the "technical core" of an organization.[2] But that suggests a narrower role for these people than they actually have; therefore, we term them the professional people, for they are the occupants of the middle-mangement and technical jobs in modern organizations. In the private sector, they are the middle managers and the technical specialists: corporate librarians, regional sales managers, accountants, supermarket managers, chemical engineers, factory superintendents, planning analysts, and public-relations directors. Their jobs require special education and training. Their jobs are varied: some are technical (such as engineering); others are semiscientific (such as financial analysis, cost accounting, computer programming, and product research and development); many are managerial. Without the skills of the professional people, the modern corporation would grind to a halt.

There are legions of professional people in the public sector as well: their jobs—in housing, welfare, tax collection, education, space exploration, agriculture, broadcasting regulation, or forest management—also require specialized knowledge and the supervision of specialized tasks. Demagogues condemn them as bureaucrats who feed at the public trough, without producing anything tangible in return. That is nonsense, for they are both productive and indispensable. Their aspirations are also virtually indistinguishable from their counterparts in the private sector.

Our main concern in this chapter will be with the professional people who perform middle-management functions, rather than technical functions. As Chester I. Barnard wrote: "Executive work is not that *of* the organization, but the specialized work of *maintaining* the organization in operation."[3] The key word is "maintaining," since the critical task of professional managers is to ensure that all internal organizational processes run properly and in accordance with the policies formulated by top management. The performance of these managerial jobs is absolutely essential for organizational survival. Without them, the organization would collapse.

The professional people transmit the instructions of the significant people to the lower echelons and ensure their compliance. They provide the contact between the managerial elite and their constituencies, both internal and external. They mediate disputes, hear complaints, adjust morale, and see to the welfare of organizational personnel and clients. Veblen was correct: they are indispensable.

Because the professional people are charged with maintaining the organization, they understand what it takes to keep organizations alive and healthy. Thus, they are in the direct line of succession to top management. Furthermore, their aspirations conform to the values of the significant people they serve, for many hope to join the ranks of significance. Their demonstration of competence in organizational maintenance is a necessary, but not a sufficient, condition for career advancement leading to the top. It is also required of them that they demonstrate loyalty to the "managerial code."

Given the absolute importance of the managerial function, it stands to reason that there should be a code that defines the moral requirements of those jobs. That is indeed the case, although the code is unwritten. Professionals must make acts of faith and demonstrations of loyalty toward the organization and its leadership, through their acceptance of this code. Professional competence and loyalty to the managerial code are key ingredients for accession to the significant jobs.

Solving the Paradox of Professional Obligation

The paradox of professional role obligation comes from the fact that the professional people must be committed to two codes of organizational conduct, both requiring advanced education and varying amounts of practical experience. The first, the "technical code," regulates the practice of a specialty; the second, the "managerial code," pertains to the managerial activity. The managerial code is far less specific, but by far and away the more important, because it deals with the exercise of power inherent in all managerial transactions.

The technical code is quite clear: one is obligated to perform one's technical function with the utmost skill and dedication, according to the dictates of one's hierarchical superiors. Since this code refers to the specialized components of the professional job—such as engineering, computer programming, accounting, selling, or manufacturing—the rules are rather clear-cut. To greater or lesser degrees, these job components have standards of professional performance. Sometimes these standards are written and monitored by independent professional associations, as with corporation lawyers or certified public accountants. In other instances, however, the standards are unwritten, unmonitored, and contain norms that are generally understood by the practitioners. Examples include personnel managers, advertising executives, sales managers, and the like.

The managerial code, on the other hand, is more difficult to comprehend, since it involves the obligation of exercising power to manage other people. The obligation is very general: the manager must do whatever organizational maintenance is necessary to keep the organization healthy. The managerial code is not a written code, nor is it monitored by a professional association. Nevertheless, the managerial responsibility, in both theory and practice, has priority over the specialized functions, because the performance of the managerial function is essential to the survival of the organization. The bulk of this chapter will explain its entailments.

From this brief description of the responsibilities of the two codes of the professional job, certain conclusions can be drawn. Some professional jobs require only specialization: many electrical engineers do their jobs without any managerial responsibility. They are managees, not managers. However, the reverse is not true. A professional who manages others must also have a specialty, such as quality-control management, sales management, or the management of legal services. These professionals are said to have *line* management authority as well as specialized expert authority. The word "line" refers to a position of authority in a chain of command.

The amount of line authority relative to the amount of specialization in a professional job varies directly with the level of that job in the organizational hierarchy. Thus, the higher the job in the chain of command, the more important is the management function related to the specialized function, as figure 8.1 illustrates. Note that the insignificant jobs are entirely specialized and that the significant jobs are entirely managerial. It is only in the middle ranges of the organization that a combination of these two components exists, with the exception of the technical specialist who has no managerial responsibility.

Figure 8.1

Relative Job Components in a Chain of Command

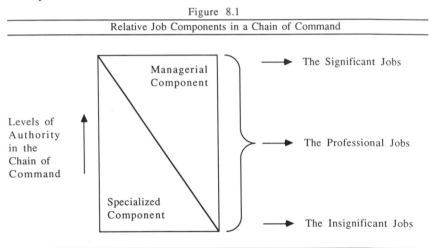

These organizational realities are reflected in job titles. The titles of middle managers always indicate rank and function, such as those in the Internal Revenue Service—branch chief-audit, assistant regional commissioner-audit—or in a business organization—regional sales manager, vice-president of marketing. For insignificant jobs, the title of the specialization alone is sufficient—machinist, typist, cook. For the significant job the title of the rank is enough—president, CEO, chairman of the board.

The relative emphasis given to job components has been a source of serious conflict in middle management. These problems have been observed for years and thoroughly discussed. Veblen thought, incorrectly, that technical specialization was a foundation for class consciousness among professionals. But as John Kenneth Galbraith and Nicole Salinger wrote: "I do not believe the conflict cited by Veblen exists, at least in the form he described. . . . Engineers need managers and organization if they are to be useful."[4]

Early organization theorists thought that the separation of organizations into operating line management functions and supporting specialized staff functions created a conflict of interest between staff specialists and line executives. These theorists believed that while both activities were essential to complex organizations, the conflict potential inherent in them had to be eliminated.[5] Social psychologists after World War II found distinct personality and attitude differences between people whose jobs were heavily weighted toward specialization and those whose jobs were largely managerial.[6] They also saw these differences as harboring potential conflict.

Peter Drucker recognized the disparity between specialization and managerial responsibility and devoted an entire chapter of his influential book, *The Practice of Management*, to it. He made several recommendations for resolving these differences. One suggestion was to establish a separate promotion ladder for specialists,[7] such as apprentice chemist, junior chemist, senior chemist, and finally, manager of the chemical engineering function.

Drucker was wrong about this. If anything, separate promotional ladders would exaggerate the differences between specialists and managers rather than reconcile them. Structural, psychological, and financial palliatives are not able, in themselves, to resolve the conflict inherent in job content. True solutions are based upon two conditions. The first is that modern organizations have sufficient influence, or power, to change the standards of professional associations to suit their requirements; some organizations do have such power. The second condition is that professional people be converted to the management code, and many of them have. Thus, the code is central to resolving conflict in job responsibilities. Through it, professional standards, diverse specializations, and management are homogenized into a whole in which agreement about essential values is possible.

All professionals, regardless of how their jobs are weighted, must be committed to the codes of both specialization and management, and therein lies the paradox. Sometimes the demands of the technical speciality contradict managerial needs. The paradox has been bluntly resolved: the codes cannot be equal and because the managerial function is the more important, the managerial code must always predominate. Thus, while managers must acknowledge and support specialization, they can never allow it to interfere with the smooth operations of the organization within which it takes place.

While professionals must be faithful to the canons of their specialization, they must always recognize the secondary status of that specialization in relation to the needs of the organization. This is nowhere more evident than in the fact that if any of them hope to get away from their "ghettos of objectivity" and move up the organizational hierarchy, they must be converted to the managerial code more than to the technical codes of accounting, chemistry, law, or whatever.

This means that the managerial code must contain an emotional commitment not present in the technical code. Managers, in other words, must believe. Thus, we contend that it is more appropriate to use the word "credo," rather than code, because it entails belief. One may observe a code, one believes in a credo. Thus, the most important aspect of management education has become the inculcation of the managerial credo.

Credo in Unam Ordinationem

The Latin phrase *credo in unam ordinationem* is a statement of belief in "one orderly system of government." In the light of this credo, personal and selfish interests in specialization disappear. They are replaced by an overarching faith that the professionals have mutual interests in serving the organizational imperative. The credo exalts professional obedience and organizational loyalty.

Thorstein Veblen focused his incisive critical eye on a problem similar to the one under discussion here: how does a ruling elite ensure the loyalty of its professional functionaries? Veblen was more specific, since he was concerned with how capitalists guaranteed the loyalty of the engineers they hired. This problem interested Veblen in 1921, because he was writing *The Engineers and the Price System*, and he was mulling over the possibility that the engineers might overthrow the capitalist ruling class and replace it with a technocracy. Veblen thought that the engineers, roughly his equivalent of our professional people, had distinct class interests. Veblen concluded that a revolution from this quarter of society was unlikely, since the engineers had been wholly bought off by the capitalists.

However correct Veblen might have been in 1921 about the distinct class awareness of engineers (and there is reason to doubt its validity even then),[8] his argument is inaccurate with respect to organizational America. While Veblen believed in a disparity of class interest between engineers and capitalists, such a disparity does not exist between the significant people and the professional people.

If professionals want to advance their careers, they must show their unalloyed loyalty to top management and the credo. Such loyalty must be demonstrated beyond question. However, people are not born with innate tendencies in this direction. Correct attitudes and behaviors are learned in the educational process, which begins in youth. They are codified in BA, MBA, and MPA programs, culminating when the professional internalizes the manager's credo, which we summarize as a set of six beliefs. While future managers *learn* the credo in school, the most critical period for *belief* is during the individual's service as a professional within the modern organization. The meaning of the six articles of faith are confirmed, as they are revealed by the concrete experience of managing and being managed.

Credo 1: We Believe in the Decency of Managerial Intention

Contrary to the media and literary depictions, most of those who occupy positions of mangerial power in organizational America wish no ill to other people and, in fact, are receptive to ideas that might make their managerial practices more humane. But too often those decent intentions get lost in the practices of organizational life. It is hard to consider managers as essentially decent when thousands of workers are laid off, when toxic wastes are covertly dumped, or when dangerous products are knowingly sold to the public. Why is there this disparity?

Where the decent intentions of managers are lost is in the glorification of means over ends, and the failure of managers to think about the moral consequences of their actions. Managers, most of whom are neither barbarians nor robots, need to believe that their endeavors are worthy. But modern organizations cannot have managers questioning the morality of policies and actions. It is both inefficient and corrosive of the managerial authority. Contemporary management has solved this means-ends problem in a fascinating manner, by fusing the behavioral-science techniques of managerial control with humanistic psychology.[9]

The idea guiding early human developmentalists in the late 1940s, such as Kurt Lewin, Gordon Allport, and Carl Rogers, was that individuals have considerable latent potential that is not released because of the inhibitions imposed by their organizational environment. Consequently, the humanists wanted to alter this environment so that it would promote individual psychological growth. It did not take long for this appealing doctrine to be applied to management by such psychologists as Abraham Maslow, Chris Argyris, Douglas McGregor, Warren Bennis, and Rensis Likert. Their leading theme was expressed by Maslow as "self-actualization." Maslow held that self-actualized persons integrated their work with their personal identities, making work psychotherapeutic.

This argument is convincing, up to a point, if people in organizations actually did work instead of performed jobs. As it now stands, humanistic techniques—such as OD, organizational transformation, and organizational imagization—are used to manipulate people into identifying with that mutant form of labor we call the modern job. The techniques of these applied versions of human development are packaged and marketed by a staggering number of management consultants. Many companies have become converts to these management technologies: first, because they seemed to produce more effective employees; second, because they were seemingly more humane; and third, because they promised to help people cope with the pressures of organizational life.

By infusing humanistic values into management techniques, managers would not be provoked into questioning the moral worth of the ends chosen by the leaders or the means chosen by themselves. In that way, their efforts to be more knowledgeable about managerial means would have a seemingly moral justification. This fusion was brilliant, for it appeared to provide management with ethics built into both the ends and the means. Then managers would not need to engage in fuzzy and unscientific evaluations about the moral worth of their actions. They need only become more proficient at their jobs. They could be confident that the more pervasive and intensive the application of their managerial skills, the more humane society would become.

This confidence is the essential feature of the first credo: namely, the need for managers to believe that the application of good means will automatically produce good results and better people. If this is believed, the consideration of values becomes unnecessary, even wasteful. Managers need look no further than to the humaneness of their techniques. This credo is nowhere more obvious than in the technique of participatory management.[10]

The reasoning is that since participation is democratic, it is therefore good, producing both harmony and good people. Nothing more need be said since the proposition is self-evident: good procedures produce good people. But it is erroneous to believe that discussions about an organizationally good decision adequately replace serious thought and moral discourse about individual rights and the embodiment of those rights in both structure and action. They are two different endeavors and must not be confused.

Nevertheless, there is a consensus among those in the national managerial system that their intentions are decent and that the honor of their intentions is plainly demonstrated by their professional eagerness to find more humane means to organizational ends. That consensus is reinforced in nearly every book they read, nearly every class they take, and nearly every management training session they attend.

Credo 2: We Believe in the Humaneness of Managerial Escalation

Management escalation refers to the desire of managers to extend their influence into ever more areas. If one accepts Credo 1, it follows that modern managerial practice represents the most humane way to govern large numbers of people. Implicit is the expectation that the more extensive the influence of management becomes, the happier people will be. Furthermore, managers believe in the evolutionary premise of science, which states that continuous behavioral research will automatically advance the state of the management discipline. As a result, life within all organizations so managed will progressively improve.

This assumption justifies the extension of management techniques not only into formal organizations, but also into the most sensitive private areas of life, from religion and marriage to child rearing and education. This has happened, in fact, and the 1980s have witnessed the steady encroachment of management techniques into each individual's personal affairs. By the end of the decade, there were no havens from management influence.

But the real beneficiary of escalation is management itself. If management is extended into education, organizations may be assured an uninterrupted supply of the right sort of employees. If it is extended into matters of taste, then organizations may be assured of an uninterrupted demand for their products. The list could be extended, but the point is that management escalation makes both the internal and external environments of the organization less uncertain, and management is thus able to plan for and control them.

The promise of escalation to management was caught by the political philosopher, Sheldon S. Wolin, who wrote: "for what would be more hopeful than to know that the political and social world is deliberately fashioned to produce regular and predictable behavior?"[11] As more of the uncertainties of life are brought under the control of management, people will be made secure from random events. The further the control extends, the more efficiently the entire society can be planned for. Surely such security will increase the net happiness of these people, for they will be watched over by humane managers.

Credo 3: We Believe in the Job over All Else

Given Credos 1 and 2, the happiness and security of the nation depend upon the extension and maintenance of humanely managed organizations. Since the burden for attaining those organizational goals lies with the professional people, it is necessary that they have their priorities straight. They must understand the seriousness of their jobs in relation to the other nonjob influences in their lives. The job must come first.

A venerable adage in personnel management sums it up: Jobs are built around functions and not around personal desires. A quality-control manager sees that appropriate measures are applied to ensure that the quality of flashlight batteries is maintained. Being a good parent means nothing so far as this job is concerned, whereas the job may mean everything to one's ability to support one's family. The job must be done according to criteria established by the organization, or the manager may as well forget about sending the children to the university. The essential point of Credo 3 is that the job is more important than the person who occupies it.

This is heralded by some influential writers as progress, rather than as a stultifying requirement of the modern job. The perfect example of such doublethink is found in Harlan Cleveland's *The Future Executive*. For him, the reduction of self to a series of organizational functions represents a positive aspect of organizational evolution. He argues that the modern organization must be a psychologically neutral place, because tensions between personal and organizational interests impede management processes: "Tension, drained so far as possible of its *personal* content, is what makes modern large-scale organization possible."[12] In other words, the modern organization requires that the job must never be tainted by an individual's preferences.

This credo states that if the professional people will put their jobs first, the world will be a better place. Surely that justifies subordinating personal and family desires to it.

Credo 4: We Believe in the Homogeneity of Management

Another old saying in management is that it is universal. It can be practiced anywhere without regard to organization or specialty. This universality is reflected in fields as diverse as marketing, finance, and accounting, when they are identified as marketing management, financial management, and managerial accounting. A manager can practice this universal art in business, government, and educational organizations without having to learn a new management process for each institution.

Indicative of the faith in management, universality is the rise of generic schools of administration; their major purpose is to train interchangeable managers, who can move with ease into managerial jobs in virtually any organization.

What universality also means is that the managers are homogeneous. The reason why Credo 4 is vital for modern organizations is that by accepting it, professionals are homogenized through believing in a common core of organizational values. Modern organization prizes such homogeneity because it makes the control of the professionals easier. It guarantees reliable and, thus, predictable performance. The desirability of homogenization is a long-standing, orthodox management dogma. Chester I. Barnard observed that it is cheaper and more effective to have employees psychologically committed to serve a managerial system, than it is to buy their willingness with economic inducements. Barnard would agree that homogenization through belief in organizational values is the best way to ensure the loyalty and obedience of professionals.

Seldom is the rationale for management homogeneity made explicit, and when it is, it is not greeted with much enthusiasm. Years ago, William G. Scott, a social churl, wrote a satirical article entitled "Executive Development as an Instrument of Higher Control."[13] In it he made the modest proposal that executive development programs incorporate brainwashing principles to ensure the reliability of professional people in their performance of strategic organizational functions. Brainwashing would certainly be the most efficient way to obtain homogeneity.

The manuscript was sent initially to the *Harvard Business Review*. The editor returned the manuscript with a very long letter saying that the reviewers debated at length on whether the author was kidding or serious about that proposal. They finally concluded that he was serious and that there was not sufficient data to support the view that brainwashing was an effective means of behavioral control. The unmistakable message was that when satire comes too close to stating dangerous truths, it is better left unprinted.

Since management, then, is universal and managers are homogeneous, it means that they could move with ease among jobs and organizations within the national managerial system. Homogeneity permits mobility. But does this highly vaunted mobility really occur? Not as frequently as one might imagine. Most managers remain in the same type of organization or in the same organization where they began their careers. They tend not to move to different organizations, *although they could*. So mobility is not the reason for stressing management universality; homogenization is.

Credo 5: We Believe in the Vocationalization of Education

The most effective way to guarantee appropriate attitudes is through an educational system that will indoctrinate people in the requisite vocational beliefs. This means that vocational specialization is presented as a superior goal, to which all should aspire, with the expectation of being generously rewarded. A fully developed vocational educational system ensures an adequate supply of professionals with appropriate skills and attitudes before they are needed by the modern organization.

It has been often observed that middle-class Americans have been prepared from childhood to accept roles as professionals, with a minimum of attitude adjustment when they finally enter the job force. The major responsibility for the development of the requisite character belongs to the educational system, and it has accepted this responsibility with enthusiasm, at all levels.

Particularly dramatic are the enlarging segments of the student body in higher education who are choosing majors in administration: whether of businesses, governments, educational institutions, hospitals, or hotels. In most universities and colleges, traditional fields of learning in the arts and sciences are suffering serious declines in student enrollment as more and more students seek admission to professional programs, as the social critic Alan Bloom has lamented.[14]

In all areas of academic study, fads and fashions reflect the issues of the times. Look at what happened in engineering after the Russians put Sputnik into orbit and to journalism after Woodward and Bernstein sent Nixon into exile. These fields surged, then declined, and surged again. The field of business administration is a remarkable case of this flux. During the 1950s and 1960s, it was a very low-prestige major, along with physical education and agriculture; it was a fall-back position for those who had failed in pre-med or engineering. But there has been a steady growth in its attractiveness and influence. Five thousand MBAs graduated in 1960, and sixty-three thousand in 1983![15] Now students clamor to get into business programs, especially accounting and finance. Waiting lists for business school admission are long, and the academic requirements to get into both graduate and undergraduate programs are getting higher all the time.

University budgets respond to these demands, and resources are allocated to those departments and programs where the demand is greatest. In the years since World War II and until around 1970, most university departments shared in an expanding resource pie, thanks to the largesse of the state and federal governments. This growing pie relieved the pressure on university officials to make difficult priority decisions on academic programs. They passed the wealth around, and most departments could be reasonably comfortable with their share of it. Those days of wine and roses came to an end in the 1970s, when university administrators and faculties had to make hard choices about priorities. The costs of operation soared, citizens complained about paying for nonvocational frills, and funding bodies looked at educational budgets to achieve economies.

The effects of these educational policies on the character of the universities have been profound. One immediate consequence is that programs and departments with declining enrollments are being eliminated or sizably reduced. The public demand for economies in education is being met at the expense of liberal and fine-arts programs. The resources thus freed are being reallocated to those departments emphasizing practical and vocational programs, which are of the greatest utility to modern organizations. In simple terms, the vocationalization of education means the none-too-subtle transfer of funds away from fields that have no direct application to the modern organization into those fields that do.

Since the modern organization can only flourish in an education-intensive society, the apocalyptic cries of university administrators that penurious state legislatures and populist governors will cause the collapse of their universities are misdirected. Universities will not collapse because organizational America cannot exist without them. Modern organizations require an accessible and effective educational system, and those who understand this requirement most clearly are the professional people, who have been university trained.

Therefore, the importance of the university can only increase because it is now the last step in the formal educational system, where the final polish is applied to professional aspirants. However, business educators Lyman W. Porter and Lawrence E. McKibben argue that management education in the future must expand continuing education programs for practicing middle-level managers, if business schools are to keep intact their preeminent role in the development of the professional people.[16]

The university, however, must be more than a place where people learn skills. It must also indoctrinate professionals in how to think managerially all the time. In fact, the modern university's most important mission is to engineer a closeness of fit between managers' characters and the role requirements of the job. The vocationalization of higher education goes to the heart of this matter, and its two main characteristics are leadership and methodology.

Leadership. Leadership is the main ideological theme emphasized in the career training of the professionals. Although we do not equate management with leadership, nonetheless, the terms are synonymous in orthodox managerial training. The study of leadership is very safe because it holds out promises for advancement through the organizational hierarchy and because it excites the expectations of most students that they will eventually become leaders. In this way, the neophyte professionals come to covet top managerial positions and to concentrate their efforts on obtaining them.

But there is a far more important reason for the emphasis on the vocation of leadership. Such training ensures that the professionals who aspire to top management positions are aware of the immense burdens associated with them. When such managers make decisions, the professionals will understand how they are made and will identify with the leaders' need for compliance from subordinates.

The reverse of leadership is "followership," and it should be asked why a similar emphasis is not given to that subject in training the professional people. It is, but it is subsumed under leadership. Management students are taught that they must always be obedient to managerial instructions, as a part of the process of becoming leaders themselves. Followership is a condition to be escaped from as soon as possible. Few of the MBAs we have taught believed they would be followers for very long.

But no matter what they may think, virtually all professionals will spend their careers being obedient to someone else. Why, then, is the emphasis always on leadership and leadership needs? The answer opens a Pandora's box. If professionals understand that they will be followers throughout their careers, they will ask questions about the rights of followers, instead of focusing on the needs of leaders. In other words, they will begin to think of themselves as democratic citizens, who have the moral obligation to question their rulers. This was anathema to Chester I. Barnard, who wrote: "The attitude fostered by democratic processes certainly weakens authority, and diminishes the probability to unquestioned obedience."[17]

For that reason, all management programs continue to stress leadership, and say nothing about followership. Prestige attaches to leadership. To suggest that there is a vocation for followership is unthinkable, and yet it is the calling of the true citizen in a democratic society.

Methodology. The methodology of managerial education is rooted in operational analysis, which, according to P. W. Bridgman, is that a "concept is synonymous with the corresponding set of operations,"[18] that measure it. This definition has two implications for vocational training in management. First, in order for a concept to have meaning in Bridgman's terms, it must be associated with a set of empirical measurements. For instance, the concept of personality does not exist apart from the tests that measure it. Personality becomes what personality tests say it is. Second, any questions associated with final causes—such as ascertaining the grounds of values—are meaningless due to the absence of empirical operations to measure them. To the extent that some measures are devised, as has been done in studies of ethics and values, they will become what the empirical yardsticks measure.

The vocational education of professional people mainly involves concepts to which operational analysis can be applied. The empirical orientation is dominant in all of the disciplines in administration, with the effect of making their contents measurable. This is evident in accounting, finance, marketing, urban development, and social welfare, among others. However, the truly critical change in management education is the application of empirical methods to the study of attitudes and culture. From the time that Herbert Simon published his influential book, *Administrative Behavior*,[19] it is axiomatic that no managerial technique can be certified as acceptable unless it has been empirically verified. Therefore, it is necessary to reduce as many human attitudes and behaviors as possible to sets of testable operations. The triumph of operational analysis is clearly demonstrated by examining the curricula of any major schools of business and public administration or the contents of the major professional journals in management. However, the development of professionals is not merely training in leadership and research. It is socialization in an orthodoxy about the worthiness of obedience and the superiority of empirically verifiable knowledge.

Credo 6: We Believe in the Sovereignty of Management

This credo is a summation and reaffirmation of the other beliefs in *credo in unam ordinationem*, especially Credos 2 and 4, concerning managerial escalation and homogenization. However, there is an important difference between this credo and those. Credo 6 states a political principle in which management always has sovereign power over technical specialties and personal preferences. Belief in this principle is of the utmost importance, because in the clamor and distractions of day-to-day operations, it is easy to forget that the organization does not revolve around individuals or technologies.

What does it revolve around? The organizational imperative! And that imperative legitimizes the power, status, and perquisites of the significant people and the professional people who hope to succeed them. They are the defenders of the sovereignty of management.

Credo 6 is addressed to any internal conflicts that might arise over the primacy of management authority and the exercise of managerial power. Dissidents cannot break that rule, nor can they rebel. Therefore, they must adapt to it or leave. Because the human embodiments of the sovereignty are the significant people, they are the focal point for organizational power. The professional people, like the courtiers in a feudal court, will become familiar with the practices, processes, and language of the powerful. In time, they will come to identify and cooperate with the significant people. In Cleveland's words, by such cooperation "employees will increasingly be professional people who think of themselves . . . as part of management."[20]

On Full Lunch Buckets

But, like the loyalty of courtiers, the loyalty of the professional people is conditional upon their self-interest. Porter and McKibben have commented on the fickleness of loyalty among business school graduates of recent vintage. They quoted from *Time* magagzine: "They [MBAs] tend to be more loyal to their personal careers than to any company."[21] We might add that their fickleness also applies to their loyalty to their bosses.

This is a telling observation, since if one word could capture the master virtue desired by the managerial elite of its professional subordinates it would have to be "loyalty." "Loyalty to the organization! Loyalty to us!" In some sense this is what *credo in unam ordinationem* is all about—loyalty upward. If we projected this creed back to the Dark Ages, it could easily be mistaken for a feudal oath.

We are not the first to ascribe feudalistic attributes to modern organizations.[22] Expectations of employee fidelity are the blood and bone of human-resource management. And as we have shown, management will go to great lengths to instill it, through a combination of belief and the application of behavioral science techniques. But if we probe the feudal origins of loyalty, we will find that it entailed a quid pro quo. The lords' minions gave their loyalties in exchange for protection from the barbarians and for grants of social and economic privileges.

The modern version of the feudal contract is this: If the professional people are loyal and obedient, they should expect certain reciprocal benefits, such as secure employment, modest advancement, a comfortable standard of living, and respect for their specialized contributions to the organization. Throughout the 1950s, it seemed as though this contract was honored by both parties, creating, as William H. Whyte, Jr. observed, overweening paternalistic organizations on the one hand, and loyal "organization men" on the other hand.[23] This was not a happy outcome, in Whyte's opinion, but it came close to the spirit that had inspired early feudalism. It continues in modern Japan to serve as a model of enlightened management for other nations, including America.

Fractures in this cozy arrangement started to appear in the 1960s and the 1970s. However, as Veblen noted, as long as the engineers (his equivalent to our professional people) could hear the rattle of a full lunch bucket they would be loyal. And loyal they were, generally, until the 1980s when the fissure widened between the interests of the professionals and the interests of higher levels of corporate management. The lunch bucket of many professionals stopped rattling.

This happened when, as Veblen put it, "the corporation financier . . . ceased to be a captain of industry and [became] a lieutenant of finance."[24] These lieutenants now play the game of mergers, acquisitions, and leveraged buyouts with a vengeance, showing little concern for the quid pro quo toward the professional people that made corporate feudalism in the 1950s work. In these games, many professional people were not protected and they lost their jobs. Therefore, if the professionals cannot rely upon their leaders for protection, why should they live up to their part of the bargain? Corporate "out-placement," humor training,[25] imagization programs,[26] and stress management will not make loyalty an ardent virtue in the breasts of the professionals.

It became obvious in the final years of the 1980s that the traditional organizational beliefs and roles of the professional people were under severe strain. The *credo in unam ordinationem* was always an ideal type, just as religious values and the Founding Values are ideal types. But the moral defalcation of too many of our public and private leaders in those years produced a cynicism among many professional people, at two levels. First, they began to realize that the credo was always an instrument of control, rather than a set of moral principles worthy of commitment. Second, and more wrenchingly, they began to realize that even if the tenets of the credo were applied with honor and integrity, they still would not be morally satisfying.

Notes

1. Thorstein Veblen, *The Engineers and the Price System* (New York: Harcourt, Brace and World, 1963), 82.
2. Thompson, *Organizations in Action* (see chap. 5, n. 9).
3. Barnard, *Functions of the Executive* (see chap. 1, n. 14), 215. Emphasis in original.
4. John Kenneth Galbraith and Nicole Salinger, *Almost Everyone's Guide to Economics* (Boston: Houghton Mifflin, 1978), 24.
5. James D. Mooney and Alan C. Reiley, *Onward Industry* (New York: Harper & Bros., 1931). Subsequently revised, and published as James D. Mooney, *The Principles of Organization* (New York: Harper & Bros., 1947). "Classical" organization theorists like Mooney and Reiley realized that staff support people, with the authority of expert knowledge, might exert undue influence on operating line executives with their general authority. So that this conflict of authorities would not disrupt coordination by violating the "unity of command" principle, Mooney and Reiley reasserted in unequivocal terms the structural supremacy of line authority over staff authority.
6. For example, see Melville Dalton, "Conflicts between Staff and Line Managerial Officers," *American Sociological Review* 15 (June 1950), 342–351.
7. Drucker, *The Practice of Management* (see chap. 1, n. 4), chapter 26.
8. See Daniel Bell, "Introduction," in Veblen, *Engineers and the Price System*, 21–26.
9. Lest this appear to be just another attack on humanistic psychology, let us make it quite clear that our objection is to its misuse as a technique of control. A similar concern is expressed throughout the fine book by Nisbet, *Twilight of Authority* (see chap. 1, n. 5).
10. Some of the issues concerning participation are discussed in Hart, "Theories of Government" (see chap. 6, n. 25), 603–621.
11. Sheldon S. Wolin, "Political Theory as a Vocation," *American Political Science Review*, 63 (Dec. 1969), 1081.
12. Cleveland, *The Future Executive* (see chap. 2, n. 19), 25. Emphasis in the original.
13. Scott, "Executive Development" (see chap. 7, n. 10), 191–203.
14. Alan Bloom, *The Closing of the American Mind* (New York: Simon and Schuster, 1987).
15. Fred M. Hechinger, "About Education," *New York Times*, 27 Apr. 1988, 25.
16. Lyman W. Porter and Lawrence E. McKibben, *Management Education and Development: Drift or Thrust into the 21st Century* (New York: McGraw-Hill, 1988).
17. Chester I. Barnard, excerpt from draft of notes on "The Requirements of Leadership in Democratic Societies," manuscript, Barnard Collection, Archives of the Baker Library, Harvard University, carton 1.
18. P. W. Bridgman, *The Logic of Modern Physics* (New York: Macmillan, 1927, 1960), 5.
19. Simon, *Administrative Behavior* (see chap. 7, n. 2). Mitchell and Scott have observed that one of Simon's major contributions in this book was to urge administration to use the behavioral sciences to validate administrative concepts. Mitchell and Scott, "The Barnard/Simon Contribution" (see chap. 3, n. 15).

20. Cleveland, *The Future Executive*, 46.
21. Porter and McKibben, *Management Education and Development*, 98–99.
22. For example, see Antony Jay, *Management and Machiavelli* (New York: Holt, Rinehart and Winston, 1967).
23. Whyte, *The Organization Man* (see chap. 1, n. 13).
24. Veblen, *Engineers and the Price System*.
25. Glen Collins, "How Punch Lines Bolster the Bottom Line," *New York Times*, 30 Apr. 1988, 17 and 19.
26. Morgan, *Images of Organization* (see chap. 7, n. 7).

9

The Significant People

The fit survive, and fitness means, not formal competence—there probably is no such thing for top executive positions—but conformity with the criteria of those who have already succeeded. To be compatible with the top men is to act like them, to look like them, to think like them: to be fond of and for them—or at least to display oneself to them in such a way as to create that impression.

—C. Wright Mills, *The Power Elite*

The Significant Job

The way to understand how a society functions is to ask the questions: who governs? why do the governed obey the governors? All nations elevate some individuals above the mass of the people. For centuries, Western societies have been ruled by kings, prelates, and generals. Sometimes they have even been led by statesmen, philosophers, and saints. While most nations have adopted more authoritarian forms of government, American history is a record of the success of democracy. But as our history has unfolded, the nature of the governing elite has changed. In organizational America, the new power elite is a direct outgrowth of the modern organization. While it may seem that our great public and private institutions often run themselves, of course they do not. At the apex of the ruling hierarchy are the top managing executives charged with making the cardinal decisions for their organizations. This last group has the ruling power in organizational America. They are the significant people.

These individuals, however, must not be considered equivalent with the jobs they occupy, since—in the theory of modern organizations—the jobs are always more important than their occupants. Significant jobs are those formal role positions at the command center of primary information networks within modern organizations, where the duties are almost entirely managerial, where the performance of the job provides its own ethical justification, and where grand strategy decisions are made that have both internal and external consequences for the organization. The significant job has five major characteristics.

Characteristic 1: The Highest Authority

Significant jobs give incumbents the highest authority in organizations. Even with that grant of authority, however, people in such jobs are not free to do what they will, for they are transient, while their jobs are permanent. As we have argued all along, one of the most important characteristics of the modern organization is the elevation of the function over the individual who performs the function. Even though the significant people can order other people about, and their perquisites are gaudy, they know as well as any lesser employee that they are, by design, dispensable. The significant job is more important to the modern organization than the significant person. Consequently, top managers are as confined to the expectations of their roles as are generals, cardinals, or university presidents. By the time individuals rise to the significant jobs, they have had years of service to organizations, and they know intuitively what the role requirements are. They can be trusted to do what people in their positions are supposed to do: keep their organizations healthy and ward off threats. Thus, the specific requirements of their authority do not have to be spelled out in detail. This gives the significant people a considerable amount of tactical leeway.

Characteristic 2: The Focal Point

Significant jobs are the focal point of all important information networks within organizations. Unlike the professional people, who receive only partial information, the occupants of significant jobs receive all of the information necessary for a complete overview of the organization, thus enabling them to design grand strategies. For instance, Barnard maintained that the information received by those at the apex was qualitatively different, because much of it pertained to the mission of the organization. This permitted those on top to issue "authoritative communications" to guide the enterprise in achieving its general purpose.[1] The monopolization of such information allowed the centralization of power at the top.

The classic example of the significant job at an information hub is that of the director of the Office of Management and Budget (OMB). This office is responsible for preparing the federal budget, so it is the one place where all information about the federal executive is gathered on a regular basis. It also prepares the president's legislative proposals to Congress, which makes the director privy to the president's plans. It is no wonder, then, that presidents try to appoint people they can trust to that position.

Characteristic 3: Purely Managerial

Significant jobs are purely managerial, because the occupants are responsible for coordinating all of the specializations in modern organizations. While this requires some delegation of authority to the professional people, the ultimate responsibility for coordination remains in the significant job. Accountability for performance exists informally in the coalition of top managers and formally in the rarified atmospheres of corporate boards.

Characteristic 4: Ethically Justified

Significant jobs provide their own ethical justification. When individuals assume significant jobs, they understand that society will suffer greatly if their organizations fail. Therefore, their actions taken to keep their organizations healthy can be ethically justified in terms of the national welfare. When Eisenhower's choice for secretary of defense, Charles Wilson, the head of General Motors, stated that "what is good for General Motors is good for America; what is good for America is good for General Motors," he captured that ethical justification of the significant job. He articulated the fact that the destiny of America is wrapped up with its large organizations. In the 1980s, the head of Chrysler, Lee Iaccoca, went public with that same message. The actions of organizational maintenance required of the significant people represent the epitome of morality, as they have learned it.

Characteristic 5: Nationally Influential

Occupants of the significant jobs make grand strategy decisions that affect the national welfare. Decisions to acquire or merge, to establish or close a military installation, to compete for government contracts, to deregulate an industry, or to enter a new market have national consequences. For instance, if a large corporation decides to relocate its headquarters from Seattle to Wichita, or to shift its manufacturing operations from the San Francisco Bay area to Taiwan, the interdependent network of organizations interacting with it will be heavily influenced.

Given this vital strategic responsibility, is it surprising that the significant people come to believe that they are the trustees of the national welfare? No one else participates in such high policy making. Consequently, we must look more closely at these guardians of the modern organization: these "men of systems."

These Men of Systems

The moral philosopher, Adam Smith, described a particular breed of governmental official who believed they could plan the complexities of human affairs to their specifications, and execute that plan. He called them the "men of system" and his description is applicable to the significant people, in both public and private organizations:

> The man of system, on the contrary, is apt to be very wise in his own conceit; and is often so enamored with the supposed beauty of his own ideal plan of government that he cannot suffer the smallest deviation from any part of it. He goes on to establish it completely and in all its parts, without any regard either to the great interests, or to the strong prejudices which may oppose it. He seems to imagine that he can arrange the different members of a great society with as much ease as the hand arranges the different pieces upon a chess-board. He does not consider that the pieces upon the chess-board have no other principle of motion besides that which the hand impresses upon them; but that, in the great chess-board of human society, every single piece has a principle of motion of its own, altogether different from that which the legislature might chuse [sic] to impress upon it.[2]

The new men of system, the significant people, are so sure of the worth of their ends that they do not question their right to implement their plans through the national managerial system: a network of people connected by their significant jobs in government, corporations, private philanthropic foundations, and exclusive universities. The control of the nation by this elite presents a problem for Americans, who believe they live in an open society. The great majority of the significant people are never elected by the citizens, nor are many even publicly known. Their decisions, and the processes they use to make them, are hidden from view. The eminent British author C. P. Snow has summed this up succinctly: "One of the most bizarre features of any advanced industrial society in our time is that the cardinal choices have to be made by a handful of men, in secret."[3] The dominant motive of the significant people is to preserve the institutional status quo, because it is the foundation of their power to rule America.

This elite was identified around the turn of the century. Then, it was thought to have been composed chiefly of the heads of giant financial and industrial organizations. Woodrow Wilson observed in a speech before the American Bar Association in 1910 that:

> We have witnessed in modern business the submergence of the individual within the organization, and yet the increase to an extraordinary degree of the power of the individual—of the individual who happens to control the organization. . . . There are men here and there with whom the whole choice lies. . . . There are men whose . . . power overtops whole communities.[4]

The membership of this elite now includes both public and private executives, and its acquisition of power was a unique event because it happened openly and quietly.[5]

The enormous successes of the national managerial system, particularly its corporate component, seem to confirm the legitimacy of this elite. Because of those successes, many influential people advocate management extension and escalation. Peter Drucker, for example, argued for a managerial rule superior to the sovereignty of the nation-state.[6] This is very heady stuff.

Drucker's vision of a worldwide managerial leadership did not necessarily imply collusion to bring it about. Wilson, in his speech to the Bar Association, did not accuse top corporate leaders of joining in a conspiratorial power grab. However, there has been no shortage of such allegations from those of the Left. Many of them argue that a consciously integrated, corporate managerial network exists. Over the years it has been termed "the finance capitalists," "the power elite," "the planning system," and the Trilateral Commission.[7] The Right has not been silent on this issue either. Its representatives fear that "socialist planning" by the government is a coordinated attempt to wreck the free-enterprise system.[8] They cite expanding regulatory agencies, welfare programs, and the bias toward organized labor as examples of concerted government policy to limit the freedom of choice of businesses.

The quarrel between the Left and the Right reflects disagreement over such issues as: whether the intentions of the managerial elite are benevolent or malevolent, whether centralization of power is the result of conspiracies or of natural organizational forces, and whether governmental executives or private managers have better foresight into the public interest. So vigorous has been this debate that the point of agreement between the two sides seems to have been forgotten: a national managerial system exists, and the thrust in the twentieth century has been toward the extension of managerial power.

Significantly, progressivists, such as Woodrow Wilson, recognized the existence of a managerial elite, but had trouble interpreting what this new breed of corporate managers meant to America.[9] Herbert Hoover, first as secretary of commerce under Harding and Coolidge and then as president, expressed a clearer vision. He imagined an "associative state" in which America's major institutions were linked in loose cooperative associations, guided by the moral authority of elite "scientific" managers in the private sector.[10] Later, writers, following Hoover's lead, acknowledged without hesitation that a managerial elite had emerged as the dominant class in America. Elton Mayo and Chester I. Barnard were notable among those who heralded its arrival, as the dynamic alternative to the Left-Right controversy over the relative merits of socialism or of capitalism.[11] They held that the primary goal of the managerial elite was to make organizations more effective by efficient use of resources. So long as managers helped the nation prosper, their legitimacy to rule would be unquestioned. The old issues, which divided the Left and Right, would be replaced by a new reality of a managerially controlled interdependent organizational network pouring out an abundance of material goods and services.

That assessment of the impact of managerialism on America has been persuasive. Managerialism has brought prosperity to the Republic, especially after World War II. It seems odd that, after years of informed commentary on the subject by people of all ideological shadings, anyone should doubt the existence of a managerial elite. But doubt it they do, even though there is convincing research demonstrating the intricate connections among the significant people as they interact in business, government, social, philanthropic, educational, and cultural organizations.[12]

Furthermore, the significant people, the "van of the vanguard," are united by mutual experiences, some of which they share with the professional people. For instance:

1. They share a common literature—books, journals, and newspapers—which maintains managerial orthodoxy.
2. They have a common technical language, both verbal and quantitative, learned as part of the socializing process in major schools of management and continuously reinforced by their personal associations with other elites.
3. They legitimatize their actions by appealing to the common methodologies of empirical validation and orthodox theory building.

However, the significant job unites them in ways unique to it. For instance:

1. They regularly attend elite interjurisdictional conferences involving people from the private and the public sectors (such as the Business Roundtable and the Commonwealth Club). More importantly, they are in each other's company on multiple corporate boards, boards of university trustees, museums, charitable associations, social clubs, and so on.
2. They control sophisticated communication systems that link them to one another.
3. They control the mass media, which allows them to project favorable images when it serves them to do so.

This partial list reinforces the argument that there is an elite world view, which transcends jurisdictional boundaries, shared by the significant people. Its orthodoxy is not the equivalent of conventional liberalism or conservatism, since it can include either of them without damaging the power base of the national managerial system. So, while short-term organizational tactics often differ, and competition does exist, the significant people seldom consciously pursue contradictory strategic aims. Thus, top government and private executives make strategic choices for the growth and survival of the entire inter-dependent system, because they understand that the destinies of all major organizations are inextricably linked.

Who Are the Men of System?

The significant people are not the mythic great captains of our industrial tradition. They are, for the most part, well-connected, intelligent, education-ally credentialed people who have risen slowly through the managerial ranks of their organizations. Their social origins are relatively democratic, in the sense that the majority of them are drawn from the American economic middle class. Mabel Newcomer's study of the big-business executive shows that the democratization of the significant people has been a trend since 1900. Around 45 percent of the top managers of big business came from the wealthy group in 1900, whereas this group accounted for less than 10 percent in 1964.[13] The gap was filled almost entirely by people from the middle-income class. Those rising to the significant jobs from the ranks of the poor show a slight increase over the sixty-four years of the Newcomer study, but it is not as dramatic.

The main instrument for the accession of the significant people to power has been education. Again, the Newcomer report makes this clear. Over 90 percent of the top managers surveyed had some college education; about 75 percent of them had college degrees.[14] Qualitatively, the most useful type of college education for vertical mobility is the vocational education discussed in chapter 8, because it equips people with the necessary technical and mana-gerial skills for organizational access and advancement. Therefore, the route to the significant jobs in organizational America lies through education that is not only specialized but, more important, managerial in character. The man-agerial aspect of formal education molds the incipient attitudes of students into the orthodox shape required by the management credo.

A 1986 *Fortune* 500 survey, using Newcomer's study as a model, con-firmed that many of her findings were still valid.[15] Chief among them were the social and economic origins of CEOs (largely middle class) and the importance of education to corporate mobility (26 percent had BAs, 31 per-cent MBAs, and 12 percent PhDs). The *Fortune* survey included some in-teresting additional demographic information. The vast majority of CEOs professed mainline Protestant religious beliefs, and close to 80 percent of them were Republicans. Mentioned in this *Fortune* 500 report is the number of women CEOs: two! There was no mention of racial minorities in the *Fortune* data base.

It also takes many years for CEOs to rise to the top, and frequently this long service is spent within one organization. Table 9.1 summarizes some data

TABLE 9.1
Tenure of Chief Executive Officers: 1977 and 1987

Year	CEOs avg. age	Tenure/Firm	Tenure/CEO	% of years as a CEO
1977	56.76 years	24.18 years	7.67 years	32%
1987	56.35 years	23.45 years	8.43 years	36%

Source: *Forbes*, 29 May 1978 and *Forbes*, 30 May 1987.

pertaining to CEOs' mobility, derived from the *Forbes* ranking of the major U.S. corporations for 1977 and 1987. The data show that the average age of the CEOs is about fifty-six years (the 1986 *Fortune* survey put it closer to fifty-eight). Their average length of service was around twenty-four years and they spent an average of about eight years as CEO. This suggests that there is very little interfirm mobility among the CEOs as a group, since they spend nearly 40 percent of their lives with the same corporation. Also, vertical mobility within these corporations is slow, since the percentages of years spent as a CEO to total employment were 32 percent in 1977 and 36 percent in 1987.

In addition to years of service, the choice of an executive career field seems to have an influence on whether people reach the top slots in their organizations. Table 9.2 compares *Forbes* data, for 1977 and 1987, on the fields of CEOs' during their careers. One noticeable change was the increase in the

TABLE 9.2
CEO Career Fields: 1977 and 1987

Career field	1977	%	1987	%
Administration	134	17%	121	15%
Banking	74	9	147	18
Finance	152	19	115	14
Insurance	15	2	25	3
Investment	6	1	21	3
Journalism	2	1	6	1
Legal	96	12	55	7
Marketing	59	7	60	8
Operations	51	6	93	12
Retailing	12	2	27	3
Sales	43	5	23	3
Technical	73	9	107	13
Founder	42	5	*	
Production[+]	38	5	*	
Totals	797	100%	800	100%

Source: *Forbes*, 29 May 1978 and *Forbes*, 30 May 1987.
*not reported.
+ Production was probably lumped together with operations for 1987.

numbers of CEOs with finance-related backgrounds: banking, finance, insurance, investment. The total number for 1977 was 247 (31 percent) compared to 308 (38 percent) in 1987. Another change was the 4 percent increase in CEOs with technical specialization, and the 5 percent decrease in CEOs with legal backgrounds. The other major areas of business activity—operations/production and marketing/distribution—showed virtually no change between 1977 and 1987.

Meeting all of these statistical criteria, however, does not guarantee promotions to the significant job. More is required, as Barnard observed:

> Perhaps often and certainly occasionally men cannot be promoted or selected, or even must be relieved, because they cannot function, because they "do not fit," where there is no question of formal competence. This question of "fitness" involves such matters as education, experience, age, sex, personal distinctions, prestige, race, nationality, faith, politics, sectional antecedents; and such very specific personal traits as manners, speech, personal appearance, etc.[16]

Hardly anyone, let alone a distinguished member of the elite managerial establishment, has written as candidly as Barnard about what it takes to become a significant person. Organizational loyalty and management competence do not, by themselves, qualify individuals for this rank. They must have the "right stuff" as well. Barnard identified many of the personal attributes upon which the selections are made.

A composite portrait of the significant person can be drawn. The average significant person is a white, middle-class Protestant male with a college education. He is about fifty-six years old; most likely he graduated from a university; he may have spent a few years in entry-level jobs that proved false starts, but by the time he was thirty he was working for the company that now employs him; and he practiced in one of the four traditional areas of business (administration, finance, marketing/distribution, and operations/production). Additionally, during those long years he was evaluated for his closeness of fit to the standards of the informal executive organization.

There is little reason to suppose that these patterns will change significantly, except that more white women may hold significant jobs in the future. We believe that the prognosis for blacks attaining significant jobs in the private sector does not look good. Consequently, if young people are very ambitious and want significant jobs, they should convert to a major Protestant faith, join the Republican party, obtain an MBA degree, adjust their gender and race, settle with one organization before turning thirty, practice a traditional area of business, and plan on staying with the same company for the best years of their lives.

During their rise to the top, most of the significant people become very conservative in their attitudes about how organizations should be managed and what the organizational world is like. They come to see it in terms of products patented, tax returns processed, bank loans given, companies acquired, and annual bottom-line profits made. This narrowing of perception creates individuals who have a very parochial outlook on life. This was confirmed in a study of chief executive officers by C. Spencer Clark, himself the CEO of a large corporation.[17] He measured the extent of the cosmopolitan versus parochial outlook of these people and found the majority to be parochial in their worldview. In spite of their obvious intelligence, their perspectives became synonymous with those of the companies they led. Like villagers in the Middle Ages, they seldom wandered farther than the sound of the bells in their parish church.

It is not at all strange that leadership in organizational America is as it is. Given our priorities, it could hardly be otherwise. We have democratized economic opportunity, and, as a consequence, America is mainly composed of a vast economic middle class devoted to materialistic tastes. We have attached great utility to education because it is the chief means through which the individual can secure employment and can be certified as a candidate for organizational advancement. We have made the organizational imperative the value foundation of America and entrusted our personal destinies to large organizations. We have said that we want reasonable people to run these organizations, and we have made the significant job the potential prize for such behavior. We have gotten the leadership we asked for: expert, prudent, well-intentioned managers. They made America a stunning success until 1973, when the OPEC cartel exposed certain inherent weaknesses in their leadership.

Crisis at the Organizational Apex

It has become evident that the significant people tend to be conservative, parochial, materialistic, unphilosophical individuals, driven by an ethic of personal advantage. While these flaws were not debilitating for the nation in the years of growth after World War II, the problems that surfaced after 1973 made them catastrophic. Two particular manifestations of those flaws have produced a confidence gap between the leaders and the led, as the sociologists Seymour Lipset and William Schneider report.[18] They are the demonstrable incapacity to manage complexity and dishonorable stewardship.

The Demonstrated Incapacity to Manage Complexity.

To someone living in Seattle, a place that is still barely more than a collection of fishing villages surrounding an airplane factory, a visit to any other major American city gives the impression that that city is totally out of control. This impression is perhaps strongest in Washington, D.C., the civic heart of the nation. We once stayed in an expensive hotel there and in the evening decided to walk to a nearby restaurant. The doorman stopped us, warning of indescribable dangers to those afoot, for all was anarchy on the streets.

In contrast, when we visited some major government agencies, all was sane and orderly inside the guarded buildings. People went about their jobs with an air of security and a spirit of competence. The order within the buildings was as far removed from the disorder outside as Parliament was from Bedlam. The same contrast existed when we visited corporate buildings. Obviously, the order within cannot be translated into order outside.

The inabilities of the significant people, in both the public and the private sectors, to make our cities safe is only one example demonstrating a very important fact: The significant people are simply ordinary people who are overmatched by the problems they must solve. They are unable to fit all of the complexities of human interaction into organizationally rational plans that they can enforce. They are defeated by the incomprehensible complexities of interorganizational dependencies.

The significant people know that they now must extend their planning to *networks of organizations*. They understand that other organizations are among the most important entities in their environment. This expansion of the elite perspective shifts their responsibility from the confines of their own organizations to the multitude of organizations that surround them. But ordinary human beings cannot effectively manage these enormously complex networks of interdependency.[19] As a result, the leadership of the significant people, based upon their skill and vision, has been called into question.

The significant people, as a class, are no more expert or visionary than any other intelligent, well-educated group of people who could do significant jobs. Thus, the burden of their assumption that they are the leaders of the nation must be shifted from their claims to expert skill and foresight to the demonstration of "moral rectitude that the . . . elite is more ethical, trustworthy, honorable, and accountable in its use of privilege than another hypothetical group."[20]

The Default of Stewardship.

Stewardship, as we defined it in chapter 3, entails honorable conduct in the management of other people's property. But it is broader than that. It also includes a respect for the people's moral sensibilities. Those responsibilities require a constant demonstration of trustworthiness in economic and personal conduct.

The evidence of moral decay among too many American leaders—in the public, private, educational, and religious institutions—in the 1980s belies such a demonstration. The decline in public confidence in these leaders has been more affected by their dishonor than it has by their incompetence and lack of vision. There is little need to document here all of the media accounts of managerial rip-offs and frauds that have fed the public with a steady diet of outrageous leadership behavior. Two quotations from *Time* magazine sum things up.[21]

> White collar scams abound: insider trading, money laundering, greenmail, greed combined with technology has made stealing more tempting than ever. Result: What began as the decade of the entrepreneur is becoming the age of the pinstriped outlaw.
>
> A relentless procession of forlorn faces assaults the nation's moral equanimity, characters linked in the public mind not by any connection between their diverse dubious deeds but by the fact that each in his or her own way has somehow seemed to betray the public trust.

From the evidence of moral decay at the apex, the public has apparently concluded that leaders are primarily interested in themselves, and in making as much money as possible. This lack of discipline in the use of privilege has seriously compromised the leadership's legitimacy, so much so that Lipset and Schneider concluded that the public confidence "appears to be based in large part on variations in the perceived ethical standards of those involved in each institution."[22] The elite has brought public distrust upon itself, if not by direct participation in corrupt practices, then by fostering organizational cultures in which the immoral and the illegal are encouraged and rewarded.

To conclude, the point of the two sections above is to establish that the inability to solve the problems of organizational complexity and the widespread demonstration of dishonorable stewardship are responsible for the crisis of legitimacy at the apex. That crisis is threatening the American status quo, which includes incumbent leaders, institutional structures, and the justifications for the exercise of power.

The Circulation of the Elite

This situation has made relevant again the observations of the Italian sociologist Vilfredo Pareto.[23] He identified certain key concepts about the leadership of modern organizations, of which the "circulation of the elite" was of central importance.

Pareto described history as a graveyard of elites and believed that the circulation of the elite was the catalyst of social renewal. He argued that the changing balances of power implied in the fall of an old leadership and in the rise of a new one to take its place was what preserved social order and equilibrium. The failure of an elite to rule effectively resulted from its unwillingness or its inability to adapt itself to new values required by changing times. People in the lower classes, who are more often in touch with these emerging values, circulate to leadership positions. The old elite is retired.

The nation has had one such circulation, when the business leaders of nineteenth-century America were replaced by the professional managers early in the twentieth century. It was a quiet, nonviolent transition, but that is not always the case. Elites often try to resist their unseating, with consequent social turmoil. The present state of affairs in organizational America—distilling into the crisis of legitimacy at the apex—portends another circulation of the elite. This has created the possibilities of three alternative futures, with no guarantee that this transition will be peaceful.

Three Alternative Futures

The first possibility is revolution in the classic sense of the word. The existing elite might be eradicated by being deprived of their wealth, power, and prestige through the destruction of the institutions they control. This future seems most unlikely, since Americans do not have a tradition of revolution. Our tendency has been to detach the legitimacy of the institutions from the legitimacy of their leadership, and then peaceably remove the incumbents from office. However, America is not immune to revolution. There is nothing written in the Book of the Ages that says we will never experience such turmoil. But the probabilities are low.

The second possible future is the restoration of public trust in the moral character and the managerial competence of its leaders. At one level, it will require the demonstration that they have the competence to solve the problems of organizational complexity. But, more significant, it will require that the elite undergo an ethical conversion, which includes their accountability to their constituencies for their stewardship. Not all leaders are bereft of ethics, but they must make their commitments more obvious to the public.

This brings us to the third alternative future, which seems to us the most probable. That alternative is moral drift. The serious problems in our organizational environment will attract the concerted attention of managers, who will try to meet the demand to keep their organizations alive. While they may not be able to solve those problems, at least the effort will be made.

What is of greater concern is the moral drift, for nothing destroys a society (short of all-out war) more thoroughly than moral bankruptcy. We have been very critical of American leaders, because we believe that power brings with it heightened moral obligation. But the public must bear a significant amount of blame for moral decay.

For instance, Americans may simply lower their expectations of honor in their leaders in exchange for material security. In fact, one way to interpret the confidence polls is to say that they reflect a persistent and lasting decline in the public's expectations of elite honor. Americans may believe that what really makes a difference in their personal lives is not management honor, but management power. Therefore, if Americans receive enough of the resource pie to satisfy their material well-being and their sense of security, they might continue to support the faltering managerial elite. Abuses of power and corruption will be tolerated in exchange for goods and services.

The prospect of drift does not mean stagnation. Drift implies movement toward some altered condition, and that condition will probably be totalitarianism. That will mean the death of the American dream that we brought into being with the inception of the Republic. Senator Inouye caught the essence of this when he was quoted at the close of one of the Iran-Contra hearings in 1987: "If the American people find this acceptable in the 200th anniversary of the Constitution, then God help the Republic."

Notes

1. Barnard, *Functions of the Executive* (see chap. 1, n. 14), 165–166.
2. Adam Smith, *The Theory of Moral Sentiments*, ed. D. D. Raphael and A. L. Macfie (Indianapolis: Liberty Classics [1759, 1790], 1982), VI.ii.2.16., 233–234.
3. C. P. Snow, *Science and Government* (New York: Mentor), 9.
4. Reprinted in William Z. Ripley, *Main Street and Wall Street* (Boston: Little, Brown, and Company, 1927), 3–4.
5. This has been described in: Alfred D. Chandler, *The Visible Hand: The Managerial Revolution in American Business* (Cambridge: Harvard University Press, 1977).
6. Peter F. Drucker, *The Age of Discontinuity* (New York: Harper & Row, 1969), 91–101; and *Managing in Troubled Times* (New York: Harper & Row, 1980), 109.
7. Thorstein Veblen, *The Theory of Business Enterprise* (New York: Mentor, 1958 [1904]); C. Wright Mills, *The Power Elite* (New York: Oxford University Press, 1957); John Kenneth Galbraith, *The New Industrial State* (Boston: Houghton Mifflin Company, 3rd ed., 1978); and Laurence H. Shoup, *The Carter Presidency and Beyond* (Palo Alto: Ramparts Press, 1980).
8. Ludwig von Mises, *Planned Chaos* (Irvington-on-Hudson: The Foundation for Economic Education, 1947); F. A. von Hayek, *Collectivist Economic Planning* (London: George Routledge & Sons, 1935); Milton Friedman, *Capitalism and Freedom* (Chicago: University of Chicago Press, 1962).
9. The place of managers who had "power without property" in America was pondered by Berle and Means, *Modern Corporation and Private Property* (see chap. 4, n. 13).
10. See Ellis W. Hawley, *The Great War and the Search for a Modern Order, A History of The American People and Their Institutions, 1917–1933* (New York: St. Martin's Press, 1979).
11. Mayo, *Human Problems* (see chap. 4, n. 91); Barnard, *Functions of the Executive*.
12. See, for example, Michael Useem, "The Social Organization of the American Business Elite and Participation of Corporate Directors in the Governance of

American Institutions," *American Sociological Review*, 44 (Aug. 1979), 553–572; and Gwen Moore, "The Structure of a National Elite Network," *American Sociological Review*, 44 (Oct. 1979), 673–692.

13. Mabel Newcomer, "The Big Business Executive," *Scientific American Special Report* (1965), 6.
14. Newcomer, "The Big Business Executive," 11.
15. Maggie McComas, "Atop the Fortune 500: A Survey of CEOs," *Fortune* (28 April 1986), 26–31. For a similar, earlier survey, see Charles G. Burck, "A Group Profile of the Fortune 500 Chief Executives," *Fortune* (May 1976), 172–177, 308, 311, and 312. The main point of interest in comparing these two surveys, done ten years apart, is how little changed are the salient characteristics in the demographic profiles of CEOs.
16. Barnard, *Functions of the Executive*, 244.
17. C. Spencer Clark, "Corporate Responsibilities and Management Perception" (Seattle: University of Washington, doctoral dissertation, 1975). See also his article "Management's Perception of Corporate Responsibility," *Journal of Contemporary Business* 4 (Summer 1975), 15–30.
18. Seymour Martin Lipset and William Schneider, *The Confidence Gap* (New York, The Free Press, 1983). See also the review of this book by Theodore J. Lowi, *New York Times Book Review* (10 April 1983), 7, 28–29. Lowi criticized the authors for their conclusion that the confidence gap is the fault of a misinformed, wrong-headed American public. He suggests instead that it reflects a healthy, mature distrust by the people of their leadership—the price of vigilance necessary to preserve liberty, 29.
19. In a review article, Mitchell and Scott analyzed the research on organizational effectiveness. They found no studies persuasively demonstrated the relationship between organizational performance and managerial expertise or vision. The inability to draw convincing conclusions about the relationship between organizational performance and managerial traits results from the problems of interdependency and complexity. Terence R. Mitchell and William G. Scott, "Leadership Failures, the Distrusting Public, and Prospects of the Administrative State," *Public Administration Review*, 47 (November–December 1987), 445–452.
20. Ibid., 448
21. *Time* (25 May 1987), 14 and 22.
22. Lipset and Schneider, *The Confidence Gap*, 79.
23. Vilfredo Pareto, *The Mind and Society*, trans. and ed. by A. Livingston (New York: Harcourt, Brace, 1935). The framework of his social theory included five concepts: the social system, equilibrium, residues and derivations, language as the medium for expressing residues and derivations, and the circulation of the elite. These concepts were used to interpret the results of the famous Hawthorne studies in human relations. See F. J. Roethlisberger and William J. Dickson, *Management and the Worker* (Cambridge: Harvard University Press, 1939). Elton Mayo was the only influential management scholar to make much of the concept of the circulation of the elite. See Mayo, *Human Problems of an Industrial Civilization*, 167–180. In his biography, Trahair noted that Mayo believed that the circulation of the elite in America had been interrupted, preventing capable people from the lower ranks from moving into positions of leadership. Richard C. S. Trahair, *The Humanist Temper* (New Brunswick, N.J.: Transaction Books, 1984), 260.

10

The Probable Future

*Perhaps societies are governed in their on-
ward march by laws of which we are ignorant.
Do we know whether it is their destiny to avoid
the mortal errors which beset them? Or whether
they are not led into them by the same dyna-
mism which carried them to their prime?
Whether their seasons of blossom and fruitful-
ness are not achieved at the cost of a destruction of the forms in which their strength was
stored?*

—Bertrand de Jouvenel, *On Power*

The Moral Drift into Totalitarian America

Time and circumstance invariably lead all nations into periods wherein they
must make profound alterations or perish. New conditions and new attitudes
put so much pressure upon established values and institutions that fundamental changes become necessary. Sometimes these changes rip societies to shreds,
and completely new political forms rise from the ruins. Other times, the result
of change is an amalgam of elements of the old institutions fused with elements of the new. This synthesis alters institutions so that they are both
sufficiently familiar to keep the society functioning, yet modern enough to
respond to contemporary demands.

America is in one of these historic periods. It will probably not be violent,
but it will result in drastic value changes in our society. Some anticipate them
with blind optimism, for they believe in a benevolent American dialectic, in
which the forces of history will inevitably combine to produce an even better
nation. We believe such faith is dangerous, for there is no guaranteed utopia
waiting for us.

But if there is no inevitable millennium, there is a probable destination, to
which we have alluded in the last chapter. People will continue to support the
organizational status quo as long as it delivers material benefits to them.

When the people grow fearful, in the face of crises, they will seek security in organizations that will become increasingly centralized, despotic, and intrusive on their personal freedom. This they will do even in the absence of demonstrable management honor, competence, and vision. As George Reedy, former press secretary to President Lyndon Johnson, correctly observed: "A society confronted with insoluble problems usually turns to its organs of repression."[1]

The United States has heard the clamor for authoritarian rule from the earliest days of the Republic. After the American Revolution, the accumulation of crises produced constant demands to establish everything from a monarchy to a military dictatorship. Had it not been for the courage of the most influential political leaders of that age, our democratic institutions would never have been established, let alone survived.

It did not end there, of course, for the pressures for authoritarianism have surged and declined throughout our history: the repression of dissent by the federal government in the North during the Civil War, the unjust treatment of the Japanese-Americans during World War II, and the witch hunts of the McCarthy era are but a few examples. Americans have often looked to the illusory security of state power in times of national crisis—real or imagined. But, in the past, the power was wielded in fairly traditional ways. However, in the larger and more complex problems of the future, power will be used in a different way: it will be used in support of the national managerial system, to preserve the network of modern organizations.

It is appropriate that the chapter begins with a quotation from Bertrand de Jouvenel. As clearly as anyone, he reminds us that power is counterpoised to such things as "rights," "liberty," and "dignity," since power is almost always used to abridge the rights of people. Granted, on some occasions, as in the use of federal power to guarantee the rights of black Americans, it can be applied for just ends. But, mostly, power erodes the rights of the people. It must be stated emphatically once again that the great danger we face is a *moral* danger—that the battle is against those who would suppress the Founding Values in the name of organizational health.

Behind the dramatic ebb and flow of our history, a truly epic moral force has been gathering momentum: the modern organization. Its presence was felt before the Civil War, but its influence began to accelerate in the late nineteenth century, with industrialization and urbanization. By World War I we were well on our way to an organizational society.[2] A few protested this shift in values, but the great majority did not really comprehend what was happening.[3] After World War I, the changes in our value system were obscured as we entered a tumultuous half-century of booms and busts, of hot and cold wars. The withering away of the Founding Values was scarcely noticed until, by the mid-1970s, the values of the organizational imperative had more or less replaced them. Inherent in the organizational imperative is the need to eradicate any contradictory values. The transition to a fully organized society is not quite complete, however, for even now there is still a lingering loyalty to the Founding Values. It has been this residue of commitment to these values of our past that has prevented the complete domination by the modern organization.

The danger lies not in the obvious incivilities of our contemporary society, since this is only a transitional stage out of which we must move. Organizational America is like a franchise motel: it is only a place to lay over before continuing the journey to another destination. The precariousness of our age has come about because the maintenance and stability of the modern organization has taken precedence over the realization of the values that energized this country in the first place. The question is whether we continue our moral drift into a future given over totally to the organizational imperative's values, or whether we change course and reassert the Founding Values in ways that are appropriate for our times.

The most probable answer to this question lies in a basic fact about social change: no society changes all its values and institutions at once. Successful change depends upon the durability of some essential institution within the society: the army, the church, or something else. The fate of a society during a transitional period is often determined by its most enduring institution.

The most perdurable institution in America is the modern organization, and it will likely remain so throughout the years ahead. Because of its permanence, it will provide continuity in the midst of the inevitable changes that face us, and it will be the dominant force in shaping our future. The odds favor the triumph of the organizational imperative, if for no other reason than that it has the inertia of material success going for it. It is our belief, and our fear, that the great waltz of history will end in a totalitarian America that is the logical culmination of the organizational imperative, unimpeded by any residue of the values that this nation has held in esteem for two centuries.

The word "totalitarian" immediately summons up images of a grim Orwellian state, governed by manifestos enforced by jackbooted thugs. Indeed, most of the familiar totalitarian regimes have displayed those characteristics. But it is a mistake to be distracted by the authoritarian trappings and an even greater mistake to dismiss totalitarianism as just another form of dictatorship, with which the world is so familiar.

Only a few scholars have correctly analyzed the totalitarian potentials in America.[4] But, then, totalitarianism is a comparatively recent phenomenon and the only modern form of government, because its base of power is rooted in the modern technology of human control.[5] A number of authors have argued that technology is essential to totalitarianism, but that interpretation is incomplete. The fact is that technology is meaningless without the modern organization, which links it to human attitudes, culture, and behavior. Without the organization, technology is as useless as humming machines on an empty, Dali-esque plain. By confining all human behavior within the rules of technically advanced organizations, it is possible to obtain total control over the people. Thus, the modern organization is the essential feature of totalitarianism, because it is the primary means for control.

But totalitarianism is not necessarily an inevitable American destination. An awareness of our national jeopardy has been growing. Interestingly, many of those most aware of our predicament are part of the national managerial system. But those managers who recognize the totalitarian threat are not able to address it. In fact, they must work to strengthen the control of the organization over the individual. They are confronted with immediate organizational problems: hostile mergers and acquisitions, slackening productivity, increasing interorganizational complexity, worsening product quality and design, growing worldwide competition, political uncertainty, and reluctant employees. These are the day-to-day problems of operating managers, and the conventional way to solve them is by strengthening managerial control. Most managers shrug off the great sweep of events external to their organizations and go with the flow. They drift with events and concentrate on making their own places within the organizations more secure.

So, in spite of some members of the managerial elite who see the problems, most are content to drift, albeit while making their organizations more efficient. The response of these "efficient drifters" is a modern version of what was called "muddling through" in the 1950s. Efficient drifters want management practice to be more psychologically sophisticated, they want the organizational environment to be more humane, they want organizations to pursue good ends, and they emphasize the need for managers to be adept at handling contingencies. However, those committed to efficient drifting believe that before everything else (with the possible exception of self-preservation) must come the maintenance of the organization.

Compare modern organizations to a raft—a very modern, comfortable raft—that the managerial crew understands because they built it. The raft is drifting pleasantly downriver, presumably headed for a happy, if unspecified, destination. Suddenly, rapids are spotted some distance ahead, and both passengers and crew grow uneasy, sensing trouble. They could not only lose control, they could even lose the raft! Something must be done in a hurry. Under the circumstances, the only thing that appears reasonable to the efficient drifters is to keep on doing what they have been doing, only better. So, plans are formulated, equipment is secured, the crew is given emergency assignments, and the passengers are calmed. It is almost as if these routine emergency activities have a magic effect when performed with dispatch and faith. Passengers and managers are confident that they will ride out the rapids in safety, because surely nothing untoward can happen to such well-organized, well-intentioned, nice people.

Alternatives to toughing it out in the rapids are not considered for a variety of reasons: the current is too strong for backing up, the shores on either side are considered too dangerous to risk beaching, and the raft is too familiar and too valuable to abandon; besides, all of their skills and training have been committed to rafting. Options to the predetermined drift downriver are simply unthinkable. Perhaps the raft *can* survive, but at a terrible cost. The danger the efficient drifters have barely perceived is that if the raft is not to founder, and if both passengers and crew are not to drown, it will most certainly require autocratic leadership and unquestioning obedience to orders. Rough water does not allow for democratic procedures, and it certainly does not permit any freedom or much dignity. What it requires is strenuous rowing. If the turbulence is short-lived, the reasoning goes, then the people can return to a more pleasant and democratic way of rafting. Unfortunately, the dangers stretch out far ahead, and, once committed to the cause of saving life, limb, and the raft, it is extremely doubtful that the leaders would voluntarily surrender their positions of absolute authority. Nor would the rest of the people on the raft want them to!

If our society's destiny is left to the efficient drifters, we will surely be deposited onto a totalitarian shore. The efficient drifters are unwilling to alter the organizational imperative and want to preserve the national managerial system intact. As it now stands, the efficient drifters are in control, and the major responsibility for the preservation of the established order is with them.

This totalitarian prospect offers, at best, an orderly life in troubled times. Most probably it will consign Americans to lives that will be unfulfilled, bleak, atomistic, homogeneous, and sterile almost beyond our present comprehension. At worst, it could pitch us into a garrison state. Hitler and Stalin are dead, but the voices of conscience still warn us of the horrors of human life in twentieth-century totalitarian societies.

Granted, our traditions and circumstances are different from those of the countries that have become totalitarian. Nonetheless, we are in the process of developing our own version of total control. Its peculiar characteristics have been described throughout this book, but the fact that we are Americanizing totalitarianism should certainly not be reassuring. The "niceness" built into modern organizations is preferable to concentration camps and mass executions. Nevertheless, the single goal of totalitarianism, whatever its window dressing, is the complete control of all individuals' lives by a ruling elite.

The tragic irony of our present situation is that we have the institutions that would allow individuals to realize their full potential. Our magnificent, albeit flawed, institutions of government, commerce, education, law, and religion can provide us with security, employment, consumer goods, learning, justice, liberty, and spiritual relief. We have the technology to free us from labor, giving us the possibility of work. We have the leisure time to permit individual intellectual and aesthetic development. We have communication systems to keep us informed and entertained. We have the productive capacity to provide everyone with reasonable economic well-being. Finally, we have the scientific and engineering capabilities to enable us to solve the confounding problems of energy, food, pollution, and the like. Most important, we are the beneficiaries of the original American Revolution, which established the "unalienable" rights of the individual over those of any despotic system of power. In short, all the necessary elements are present to enable us to achieve the dreams of the founders of the Republic.

With all of our exalted ideals, our successful institutions, and our promising opportunities, what has gone wrong? It is a moral failure. As we have tried to make clear, the successes of our organizations have led us to concentrate on the problems of their maintenance and health, with a corresponding neglect of the moral character of the individual.

Who Will Challenge the Organizational Imperative?

There is a historical impression that an existing order must originate from one of two sources: the governing elite or the masses. Regarding the former, Mikhail Gorbachev, the Secretary General of the USSR, wrote: "revolution from above" means that "profound and essentially revolutionary changes [are] implemented on the initiative of the authorities themselves but necessitated by objective changes in the situation and in social moods."[6] A post–World War II German historian compiled a list of the changes that Bismark wrought on Germany in the nineteenth century, which was also reform from above.[7] Most of the arguments in favor of reforms from below, directed against entrenched privilege, were inspired by the Enlightenment. Some of them resulted in constitutional governments and democratic societies. The American Revolution was the most successful example of reform from below.

The problem with such bipolar thinking about reform is that it does not describe our American situation. Reform always involves both leaders and the people. The problem is: with whom does it *start*? The answer is that reform comes from a serendipitous combination of leaders and the people. Thus, the issue for organizational America is: what happy combination of people, events, and circumstances would lead to a successful challenge of the organizational imperative and its managerial elite?

Why Reform Will Not Come from the Significant People

The significant people could reform organizational America if they desired, but they will not. They are the great beneficiaries of the privileges that come from maintaining the status quo. If it were just a matter of the material comforts that come from wealth, then there might be more reason for optimism that they would institute the necessary reforms, for many persons of great wealth have devoted themselves to social improvement. The significant people are conservatives, but theirs is a conservatism that is rooted in the possession and use of power more than it is rooted in money. They receive unending deference, they are excused from the monotonies of ordinary life, they have security and golden parachutes, and at their level in the organizational hierarchy, power makes all value issues simple.

Significant people are always surrounded by ranks of professionals who alter reality for them so that they will not be plagued by the incivilities of ordinary life. While rudeness, mediocrity, and boredom are the rule for the average citizen, such is not the case for the significant people. They believe that the continuous courtesy and praise they garner from their subordinates is their due. When criticism is necessary, it is usually given in a decorous manner. When they talk, others listen. When they tell jokes, others laugh. Lesser managers and other supplicants imitate their manners and their dress. The majority must listen, laugh, and imitate.

Homage always distorts reality. The regimen Plato required for those who would be philosopher-kings was spartan in the extreme. He knew what the distortions of deference could do to one's ability to rule. In the American experience, George Reedy described the skewing of reality that occurs when the most significant person among significant people, the president, has all power at his disposal.[8] David Halberstam discussed how General Westmoreland's staff in Vietnam altered intelligence and battle reports to fit his preconception of how the war *should* be going.[9] Indeed, it takes extraordinary persons not to believe in the false realities generously provided by their staffs.

In spite of all the support, significant people sometimes fail to do their jobs well, or they get caught breaking laws. But even when these lapses receive widespread publicity, the significant people are protected. Very few are banished permanently to tract homes, let alone forced onto the welfare rolls or into jail. If they go astray, they get a slap on the wrist or a sabbatical for twelve to eighteen months in a minimum security federal prison or they retire to elegant sulking in Grosse Pointe or San Clemente. The significant people have the most financially secure lives imaginable. It is almost as if there were a "Benevolent Protective Association of Significant People." Obviously, these are the perquisites of power that no sane person would want to jeopardize by ill-advised attempts at institutional reform.

But the main cause for the conservatism of the significant people is careerism. It is an institutional tenure system that travels under the labels of "seniority" policies for civil employees and "promotion from within" policies for corporate employees. The net effect of these policies, as we have seen, is that managers are steeped in the values of their organization for many years before they advance to significant jobs. As Richard A. Gabriel and Paul L. Savage wrote about the military: "The higher one's military status, the less one's tendency to perceive differences between the ideal military ethic and the way it operates in practice. Clearly, higher ranks perceive *less* of what is 'wrong' with the Army than lower ranks!"[10] The data in chapter 9 on the tenure of CEOs in corporations give some insight into the practical consequences of these policies on managerial careers: people must be prepared to spend the best part of their lives with one organization in order to aspire to its top slot.

There are many explanations for this phenomenon, but the critical one is that organizations need at their head people of demonstrated loyalty and reliability. Writing about "organizational personality," Chester I. Barnard noted: "those who have a strong attachment to an organization . . . are likely to have a code or codes [of ethics] derived from it if their connection has existed long."[11] Thus, extending Barnard, careerism ensures that the personal priorities of the significant people are compatible with the needs of their organizations.

In summing up, the most important reason why reform will not come from the significant people is because it is in their interest to preserve their power. This great power allows the significant people to dwell, as Machiavelli reasoned, beyond the zone of good and evil. In an interview, a white male business executive was asked why more women were not CEOs of major American corporations. His candid answer was, effectively: We have the power and they don't. Why would we want to give it up? His answer probably would have been the same if he was asked about any other ethnic, social, or religious group in America that did not have access to the significant job. So, it seems reasonably clear that the significant people will not be inspired to make reforms that could erode their power base.

Why Reform Will Not Come from the Insignificant People

One of the persistent and poignant myths in the radical tradition is that of an enraged people rising up in righteousness to shatter the old tyrannies and create a new utopia. There is a beauty to this vision of a revolution from below, but it is largely a fantasy. While the people running rampant can indeed shatter an ancient regime, they very seldom create and maintain the utopias of which they dream, as Bertrand de Jouvenel so convincingly argued.[12] The masses are powerful, and they have been mobilized too often for any sane elite to take them for granted. The people are slow to anger, but once their anger is set in motion they are implacable. However, in a society as technically advanced as ours, the masses do not have the organizational expertise to make and maintain the necessary reforms. They can destroy the status quo, but it is doubtful that they can build a better nation.

Marx clearly understood the need for organizational ability if revolution is to succeed. He wrote of the proletariat rising and ending the great historical dialectic in pure communism. But, in order for that day to come, the masses had to be made aware of their plight and had to be organized for effective political action. Since they could not do it themselves, the critical role of organization was assigned to the middle-class intellectuals. In fact, Lenin urged that the new Soviet leadership learn by studying Frederick W. Taylor's scientific management. [13]

The insignificant people in organizational America are very, very far from the repressed proletariat of Marxian theory, as the bourgeois radicals of the late 1960s found to their chagrin. But, they are the majority in America, and latent power is still theirs. However, they are also the beneficiaries of employment in modern organizations. As such, they are constantly told of their good fortune in having a job and being able to consume an unending flow of consumer products. They are constantly bombarded with intensive advertising propaganda to tell them how well-off they are. They are trained to accept accelerating consumption as the inevitable way of their lives. In their heyday, the media evangelists Jim and Tammy Bakker raised consumption to theology: "When things start hoppin' I go shoppin'." Thus, people are admonished at all times not to mess around with the horn of plenty, because such actions will obliterate their jobs and their consumption potential. This is not a context from which militant masses, bent upon reform, are likely to arise.

The Practicability of Reform by the Professional People

The professional people are the custodians of the modern organization. Without them, it cannot function. In an everyday sense, the professionals are more critical to the modern organization than the significant people, for they know how to do the basic jobs that the significant people either do not know or have forgotten how to do.

A parallel can be drawn here if it is not pushed too far. Marx believed that the control of industrial societies would eventually fall into the hands of the proletariat, for they knew how to run the machines of the society. These were skills that the owners did not have. Consequently, the power of reform would accrue to those who operated the equipment that made an industrial society possible. In organizational America, the essential equipment is the modern organization, and it is the professionals who make it work. It stretches the Marxian parallel a bit out of shape, but the argument might just be made that the professionals are "the new proletariat," in the sense of having those technical skills upon which the health of the modern organization is predicated.

However, we are pessimistic that the professional people will recognize their historical potential and seize their opportunity to challenge the organizational imperative and reform modern organizations. Thorstein Veblen, at his cynical best, introduced "A Memorandum on a Practicable Soviet of Technicians" as follows:

> It is the purpose of the memorandum to show, in an objective way, that under existing circumstances there need be no fear, and no hope, of an effectual revolutionary overturn in America, such as would unsettle the established order. Notoriously, no move of this nature has been made hitherto, nor is there evidence that anything of the kind has been contemplated by the technicians. They still are consistently loyal, with something more than a hired-man's loyalty, to the established order of commercial profit and absentee ownership. [Modern readers should substitute "organizational imperative" for "commercial profit and absentee ownership."][14]

Veblen's assessment of the revolutionary potential of the technicians applies to the professionals. Their reform potential is virtually nil. The professionals are not likely to become the spiritual and intellectual leaders of a reform movement. The professional people are trained to look upward to leaders for cues to action and to avoid thinking about problems not assigned to them. Closely related to this is the fact that through the organizational imperative the professionals are conditioned to accept their own dispensability, which encourages an attitude of powerlessness to create change.

Nevertheless, some professionals have enough hubris to think they can influence the great organizations, but they believe that they cannot create important reforms until they occupy the significant jobs themselves. So they serve their time, get their tickets punched, and wait for the day when they will be elevated to the significant job. But herein lies the trap. In the process of striving, they become what they do. They turn into human extensions of the organizational imperative, and its institutional conservatism smothers their dreams. After twenty-six years in the organizational deep freeze, awaiting the top job, the best they can hope for is that the next generation of upwardly mobile professionals will somehow be able to fulfill their youthful dreams of reform.

All of the above not withstanding, the professional people could challenge the organizational imperative, for at least four reasons. First, many of them are still young enough, both in years and in the organization, that they are receptive to new ideas. The ideas of radically modifying the organization may not be well understood by these people, but they are not necessarily anathema to them. The professional people are not exactly champing at the bit to reform organizations now, but they are at least open to new ideas.

Second, the professional people practice specializations that cut across the jurisdictional boundaries of organizations. They are unified by common managerial techniques and language. These are preconditions for effective political action, which can be used either for reform or for the preservation of the status quo.

Third, the professional people understand organizational structure and behavior, so they know the critical places in organizations where reforms are most likely to be effective. They know how to generate the behaviors required for organizational change, and they know how to organize and coordinate masses of people for effective action.

Fourth, and most important, the professionals are correctly situated for creating basic organizational and social reform. Gorbachev wrote that the "distinctive feature and strength of perestroika [is] that it is simultaneously a revolution 'from above' and 'from below.' "[15] This clearly focuses restructuring on the center, where these vectors converge. The domain of the professional people is where the Soviets want to decentralize authority and to increase the power of local decision-makers. The Soviet Union has much farther to go in this respect than the United States or even Yugoslavia. Nevertheless, from the standpoint of organizational principle, what is true in the Soviet Union is true also in America. The center of organization is the strategic leverage point for reform, and the professional people are in it. But the issue is not just one of organizational principle, it is one of the commitment of the people's hearts and minds as well: it is a matter of moral choice.

To Have and Have Not

The title of Ernest Hemingway's novel about the Depression summarizes the motives underlying the professional people's decision to reform the organizational imperative. Whether they expect "to have or have not" in organizational America will heavily influence their moral commitment to change organizations. Although there may be in us all a submerged and ill-defined moral sense that the organizational imperative offends the right, the good, and the decent, this sense can only be triggered into revolutionary action by the realization of a fundamental disjunction between one's expectations and one's concrete, objective circumstances. Few professional people see such a sundering in their lives; most expect "to have"; and the majority of them misunderstand the realities about their place in the organizational firmament. The main reality is that most of them will never be significant people. They will probably remain in similar professional jobs until they retire. Given this perspective, their attitudes toward careerism must change. They need to realize that the satisfaction of employment comes not from the prospects of advancement, but from the performance of work, having friends on the job, and *the reform of organizations*. Being content with doing the same job expertly within a better organization should not be considered a sign of a defective character. Rather, it should be esteemed and rewarded as a worthy life goal. Professionals should not think of themselves as upwardly mobile careerists but as relatively stable specialists.

A change in attitude toward careerism implies a parallel change in attitude about the organization. It is very difficult to identify with a modern organization, especially if one's aspirations for the highest jobs within that organization are unrealistic. Therefore, the professional people must identify with the subunits of the organization, departments or project teams, where they apply their skills in enclaves with others having similar qualifications. Such reidentification demands a major refocusing, since it is completely inconsistent with the belief in the ubiquity of management. It is within the subunits that the possibilities of work satisfaction, friendship, and reform are to be found. As a corollary reality, professionals must reconcile themselves to the fact that they will mainly be followers for as long as they are employed by a modern organization—with all of the moral obligations that followership entails.

Consequently, professionals must face the reality that they cannot alone, as isolated specialists, bring about needed organizational reform. This speaks to their obligation to build associations representing specializations *based upon the principles of voluntarism*, described in chapter 4, to challenge the conservatism of the significant people. This type of action, however, may require the greatest attitudinal change of all, because it demands the rejection of organizational paternalism. Thus, the professional people in organizations need to *think* of themselves more as independent contractors than as loyal employees.

The final and hardest reality for the professional people is economics. We touched on the subject in chapter 8 in terms of rattling lunch boxes, but we raise it again because people respond passionately to changes in their financial condition. Professionals were once regarded and, indeed, they regarded themselves, as the secure apparatchiki of modern organizations. In the language of economics, they were a "semifixed cost"—part of the administrative overhead. As such, they were economic light-years removed from the insignificant people, who were considered "variable costs."

In this era of leveraged buyouts, when organizational leanness is a dominant management image, it is fairly clear that the professional people are no longer as favored in the administrative overhead as they previously were. They are becoming variable costs and less secure in the process. Their terrible prospect is, of course, loss of job and loss of the status that goes with it. They could sink into the ranks of the insignificant people. Although this might be an awful comedown, they would at least be working. The truly horrible specter is that they might drop out of the economic mainstream entirely and join the invisible people.

So, it appears that in the constellation of roles that compose organizational America, the professional people are, potentially, the stars of reform. But their commitment to reform depends on how they will interpret and act on their economic, social, and organizational self-interest. If large numbers of America's cadre of professionals in organizations find themselves economically, psychologically, and spiritually dispossessed, they could be the most potent force for reform. Such is unlikely, however, and we are not too hopeful that reform will come from the professional quarter. Therefore, we must go beyond the nominal boundaries that define the institutional matrix of modern organizations and seek other sources and principles for reform.

Notes

1. George E. Reedy, *The Twilight of the Presidency* (New York: World, 1970), 190.
2. It would be burdensome to cite the most relevant literature about the rise of the new value system of the modern organization. However, the following three books are excellent, even though there are areas of disagreement. Chandler, *The Visible Hand* (see chap. 9, n. 5); Paul Boyer, *Urban Masses and Moral Order: 1820–1920* (Cambridge: Harvard University Press, 1978); James Willard Hurst, *The Legitimacy of the Business Corporation in the United States: 1780–1970* (Charlottesville: The University Press of Virginia, 1970).
3. Of particular interest are the observations about the "Progressives" and the "Status Revolution" in Richard Hofstadter, *The Age of Reform: From Bryan to F.D.R.* (New York: Vintage, 1955), especially chapter 4, "The Status Revolution and Progressive Leaders."
4. One of the most perceptive analyses is Nisbet, *Twilight of Authority* (see chap. 1, n. 5). See, also, Jacques Ellul, *The Political Illusion*, trans. K. Kellen (New York: Knopf, 1967).
5. The literature about totalitarianism is vast. The classic works are by Arendt, *The Origins of Totalitarianism* (see chap. 7, n. 9), and Ellul, *The Technological Society* (see chap. 2, n. 12).
6. Gorbachev, *Perestroika* (see chap. 6, n. 24), 55.
7. Han Kohn, ed., *German History: Some New German Views* (London: George Allen & Unwin Ltd., 1954), especially 65–93.
8. Reedy, *Twilight of the Presidency*.
9. Halberstam, *The Best and the Brightest* (see chap. 4, n. 4), 544–545.
10. Gabriel and Savage, *Crisis in Command* (see chap. 3, n. 10), 90.
11. Barnard, *Functions of the Executive* (see chap. 1, n. 14), 270.
12. Bertrand de Jouvenel, *On Power*, trans. J. F. Huntington (Boston: Beacon Press, 1962), especially chapter 14.

13. Nikolai Lenin, "Scientific Management and the Dictatorship of the Proletariate" in John R. Commons, ed., *Trade Unionism and Labor Problems* (Boston: Ginn, 1921), 179–198.
14. Veblen, *Engineers and the Price System* (see chap. 8, n. 1), 132.
15. Gorbachev, *Perestroika*, 57.

11

The Organizations of the Individual Imperative

> *It was easier to understand their hold on the college, I thought, when one saw their considerate good-nature, right in the middle of their politics. No one could run such a society for long without a degree of trust. That trust most of the college had come to place in them. They were politicians, they loved power, at many points they played the game only just within the rules. But they set themselves limits and did not cross them. They kept their word. And in human beings, particularly with the young, they were uneasy unless they behaved in a fashion that was scrupulous and just.*
>
> —C. P. Snow, *The Masters*

The Inconclusive Victory of Organizational Imperative

The last chapter concluded with the pessimistic forecast that American leaders were so obsessed with their personal advantages, short-range organizational goals and internal organizational efficiencies that they were allowing our nation to drift free in the current of the organizational imperative. Because its logic ends in totalitarianism, that will be our inevitable destination unless our circumstances are dramatically altered. We had reached this conclusion at the end of the 1970s and, while we still believe that it is correct, America does not *seem* appreciably closer to totalitarianism now than it was then. But, then, we have not been hit by a precipitative geopolitical explosion, an epic depression, or a global environmental disaster, any of which would have provided the raison d'être for the regimentation of the nation.

So, the logic of the organizational imperative still aims America at a totalitarian future: we have not escaped the rapids, we may not have reached them yet. The drift into the rapids has been slowed, for three reasons, none of which included any heightened leadership awareness of the dangers ahead. The first, and most important, reason is that our historic constitutional freedoms and institutions are still intact. Granted, American politics still seem to confirm H. L. Mencken's assessment that "the primary business of the man in politics . . . is the snatching and safeguarding of his job."[1] Nevertheless, our institutions—a functioning two-party system, the checks and balances of government, dual sovereignty, and redress through a court system—have slowed the totalitarian drift.

The second reason is that the organizational imperative does not work all that well. Blessedly, many Americans have refused to play their roles in our organizational society according to the scripts written for them. The techniques of mass domination have not fully produced pliant and obedient insignificant people who are accepting of their personal insignificance in the face of imperious organizational needs. Fewer professional people are loyal to their organizations and leaders. The significant people have demonstrated their inability to manage complexity. Even more, they have offended the public trust by allowing a morality of personal advantage to override their stewardship responsibilities. Finally, the invisible people refuse to stay invisible, and their agonies continue to offend the sense of decency and fair play still held by most Americans.

Finally, the organizational imperative is stalled because it is morally "unnatural."[2] It does not take into account the innate needs of individuals for moral autonomy and individual expression, which are essential to "the pursuit of happiness," correctly understood. As an ethical system, the organizational imperative appeals to nothing morally positive within the individual. Although it promises—on its own terms—security, order, and the possibility of "satisficing"[3] hedonic desires, it discourages personal moral growth, expressions of social conscience, and individual creativity. In short, the organizational imperative is morally bankrupt.

Nonetheless, it is still the dominant value force in modern America. The organizational imperative is the basis of both educational curricula and administration, from grade school to graduate school. It is the centerpiece of the moral orthodoxy of contemporary management, which means that it provides the justification for virtually all management decisions in all sectors. It provides the lingua franca of the articles and books used to train managers and to improve organizational performance. Finally, the reputations of most management scholars and practitioners are based upon their expertise in the applications of the organizational imperative. They are the defenders of the faith.[4] Though disputed it may be, the organizational imperative is still deeply entrenched in American life, and our leaders persist in planning our future in its terms. Unless we rebel, we will continue to follow a lie.

This is deeply disturbing, especially now. Just as the approach of a new year triggers the need for an assessment of one's life—followed by resolutions—so the approach of a new century prompts some nations to serious soul-searching. Most dramatically, in the late 1980s, Mikhail Gorbachev openly attacked some of the ills of the Soviet society.[5] His assessments were surprisingly candid and accurate. His proposed restructuring—including glasnost, decentralization, and a limited free market —might open Soviet society in ways unseen in its entire history. While there is much that we can learn from Gorbachev's assault on the rigidities of his country's system, it must not be overlooked that *his prescriptions fall, for the most part, within the parameters of the Soviet version of the organizational imperative.*

And therein lies the fruitlessness of almost all of the proposals for reform in America, whether from politicians, business leaders, or public servants. They call for reform through an intensification of the techniques of the status quo, with which they are so familiar. In their defense of casuistry, two scholars relate the story of a handicapped young woman, who was unable to live on her Social-Security payments. To augment her income, she devised a telephone answering service that allowed her to maintain a subsistence living. When the agents of the Social Security found out, they not only cut her payments, they demanded some money be repaid. Before anything could be done, the young woman killed herself. The TV reporter concluded his report on the case by saying: "There should be a *rule* to prevent this kind of thing from happening."[6]

The story illustrates our point. It was a rigid adherence to the rules that had destroyed the young woman, so—according to the precepts of the organizational imperative—it would require further rules to prevent such things from occurring. Yet the true answer lies in having administrators govern by compassion, decency, and a sense of honor. But that requires the abandonment of the organizational imperative, and that is unthinkable.

Put another way, our leaders ask us to intensify our devotions to the organizational imperative, which might buy us some time, but in the end it will be our ruin. The organizational imperative is destructive of any hope that we might have for a future of individual freedom. Lincoln, in his famed "We cannot escape history" message to Congress of 1 December 1862, admonished the nation to escape from the tyranny of the "usual" way of doing things:

> The dogmas of the quiet past are inadequate to the stormy present. The occasion is piled high with difficulty, and we must rise with the occasion. As our case is new, so we must think anew, and act anew. *We must disenthrall ourselves.*[7]

Our revolution must begin, in Lincoln's term, by "disenthralling" ourselves—of refusing to live in servitude to the organizational imperative. Our revolution must transcend the hegemony of the organizational imperative and *bring a renaissance of the Founding Values*. We must recover them, for they are slipping away, and then use them as they were intended: as the moral foundation for every institution in American society.

The Individual Imperative

The ethical system of the organizational imperative leads to a malignant collectivism. The corrective is an ethical individualism,[8] based upon the Founding Values. Thus, we must state clearly that we rest our prescriptions upon the moral validity of the Founding Values, which bespeak a transcendent moral truth. These values, that are embedded in the enabling documents of the nation, are the foundation of our political and legal systems. This makes them the foundation of all other American institutions.

Just as we summarized the values of the modern organization under the title of the organizational imperative, so also—in a parallel construction—we summarize our understanding of the Founding Values under the title of the "individual imperative." The primary proposition of the individual imperative is: *All individuals have the natural right to actualize the potentials of their unique selves throughout the stages of their lives.*[9] The secondary proposition follows: *The primary justification of any organization is the extent to which it promotes the actualization of those individual potentials.*

These propositions entail the belief that all individuals have an innate human nature that impels them toward the actualization of a unique self: moral, intellectual, and aesthetic. To deny that imperative—regardless of the cause—is to alienate the individual.[10] That governments can block such actualization is apparent, and one might argue that the American Revolution was fought for just such a reason. But it is also certain that *any* organization can do the same thing and that that is the curse of the organizational imperative.

The second proposition of the individual imperative was made clear by James Madison in a very revealing, but often misinterpreted, passage in the most famous of *The Federalist Papers*, the Tenth. The purpose of that editorial was to argue for the proliferation of groups as a protection for democracy. But in a single sentence, he caught the essence of democracy. Writing about property, he observed:

> The diversity in the faculties of men from which the rights of property originate, is not less an insuperable obstacle to a uniformity of interests. The protection of these *faculties* is the first object of government.[11]

Note that he argued that the protection of the "faculties," rather than the protection of property, was the primary object of government. The theme was repeated, in different ways by different individuals, throughout the founding years. It is the sounding theme of pluralism, that there was a sanctity to each individual's life and that it was the purpose of government to foster individual freedom.

As with the organizational imperative, there are four corollaries that follow from the individual imperative. First, all individuals have the civic obligation to realize their full potentials, otherwise they diminish self. When self is diminished, the life of every individual in the community is, correspondingly, diminished. Second, all individuals have the civic obligation to promote human diversity, since pluralism is an essential precondition of self-actualization. Third, all individuals have the civic obligation to reject all forms of human instrumentalism: individuals are ends in themselves, not instruments for attaining other goals.[12] Finally, all individuals have the civic obligation to dissent when any individual, institution or organization abridges the Founding Values.

Given this vision of the organizational imperative, it is necessary to consider the sort of reformed organization within which it would flourish. Our thoughts about organizational reform start with an examination of the two values essential to the Republic: the value of the individual and the value of the community. This can best be introduced through the use of an exemplary story.

Community and the Individual Imperative

The British scientist-novelist, C. P. Snow, wrote eleven novels in his monumental "Strangers and Brothers" series. In the gem of this series, *The Masters*, the central character, Lewis Eliot, recounts the events leading to the election of the new headmaster—or "Master"—of a small college in Cambridge University, in 1937. Some of the fourteen faculty members (or "masters") are men of great acclaim; others are known only to the small circle of the college. Some are arrogant, others are humble, and their ages range from the mid-twenties to the late-seventies.

The thirteen masters in residence learn, to their sorrow, that their Master is dying. They immediately recognize the need to agree in advance upon a new Master, so that the college may avoid the ambiguities of interrupted leadership. Although there are political divisions and alliances, envies, disagreements, ambitions, and intrigues, the key to the novel is the binding sentiment among the masters in the college: a strong sense of personal honor and a mutual collegial respect.

This respect is emphasized by their essential trust that the vote of each master for the new Master will be made on the basis of their judgment of the ultimate good of the college, and not in the self-interest of any individual voter. Their mutual regard, as well as their self-respect, was sorely tried at times, since the masters differed greatly in their personalities, professional creeds, and personal ambitions. As one of them commented, "I always think that the danger with any group of men like a college is that we tend to get on each other's nerves."[13] However, each master's tolerance countered his irritation, such that his personal integrity was preserved and the *community* of scholars was maintained.

In the end, Paul Jago—who most wanted to be the Master, and who had sacrificed academic recognition to serve in college offices—learned that he was not to be the new Master. For Jago, the status of the position would have validated his decision to be a college man, rather than an acclaimed scholar. But the real problem was that he "longed for the trappings, titles, ornaments, and show of power,"[14] and these ambitions were fatal to his candidacy. A bare majority of his colleagues voted against him, not to deny him the prize, but to advance the cause of the community. In doing so they exercised a "tough love," because their rejection was (with one or two exceptions) of a man they liked and cared for. They understood the pain the decision would cause him and had the grace to partake of that pain themselves.

The story of the election was illustrative of, among other things, the exercise of an honorable discipline by the members of an intimate community. Most practiced the self-centered and ferocious discipline of scholarship, for the sake of scholarship and their personal reputations. But they also loved the community of which they were a part, and they could use that same discipline to advance the welfare of their community. But, they were aware at all times of the cost of destroying the dreams and the self-regard of one of their own kind. The point of Snow's novel is to demonstrate the fragile, but essential, dialectic between respect for individual diversity and the tough love required by community well-being. Overall, this balance depended upon the trust among all members that their colleagues would do what was right to advance their community's interests as well as their own. In short, the fulfillment of obligation among equals is both the greatest test and the most noble expression of civic morality.

Perhaps the moral issues are best summarized in an exchange among some of the masters, including the narrator, Lewis Eliot. Nightingale, in frustration, expresses the wish that the oldest men should be disfranchised. Brown disagrees:

> "No," said Brown. "If we cut them off at sixty-five or seventy, and didn't let them vote after that, we should lose more than we gained."
>
> "What do you mean?"
>
> "I think I mean this: a college is a society of men, and we have to take the rough with the smooth."
>
> "If you try to make it too efficient," I said, "you'll suddenly find that you haven't a college at all."[15]

Brown's reference to the college as "a society of men" has prescriptive implications over and above the simple description, and it is to these that Eliot alludes. The significant ideal in human life is that we exist together as a "society of individuals," with all that such a term implies: a strong sense of individuality as well as of community, the "rough with the smooth," and the understanding that it cannot be efficiently managed. The beliefs must exist within the individual and be the object of free moral choice. They are best summarized in the tension between the needs of the individual and the needs of the society.

The Dialectic between the Individual and the Society

One of the most important debates of the eighteenth century was whether society was natural to, or destructive of, the individual.[16] Those like Thomas Hobbes believed the individual would always be at war with society. In modern times, no one has stated that dismal proposition more effectively than Sigmund Freud.[17] But the Founders were of a happier frame of mind, for they believed both that individuals were intended for society and that nature had equipped them with the necessary attitudes to prosper there.[18] But nature did not provide for an automatic harmony between individuals and society. People had to seek it by constantly engaging in moral discourse about the needs of society versus the needs of individuals. This was the classic form of the dialectic that the Founders endorsed. The dialectic can be seen in our constitutional history and the ongoing debate over the relationship between liberty and justice.

On the one hand, we usually cluster the needs of the individual under the rubric "liberty" (or "freedom"), which pertains to the individual's freedom of choice.[19] The needs of society, on the other hand, are usually clustered— and less successfully—under the rubric of "justice," which pertains to the guarantee of fairness in society. To amplify on the concept of the dialectic, the individual imperative rests upon free choice among real alternatives, whether individual or social. Thus, Norton defines liberty:

> To live freely the life that is one's own requires perennial knowledge of alternatives, and knowledge of these alternatives as live options such that the free man can at any moment choose to do, not what he will do, but one of several different things.[20]

Following that definition, justice—"the paramount virtue of society"—is defined by Norton as:

> Justice, in the first instance, subsists in principles for the allocation of goods and responsibilities within a social grouping. . . . [The] foundation of justice is the

presupposition of the unique, irreplaceable, potential worth of every person, and forms of sociality that neglect or contradict this presupposition . . . deal justice a mortal blow at the outset.[21]

Thus, in the ideal conception, liberty and justice support and nourish each other. However, in daily human affairs there is a tension between the two that has had a persistent and vitalizing effect on American life.

We would ask the readers to apply these two definitions to the story in *The Masters*, cited above. We can see both principles were present in the college, and believed in by all of the masters. But the election caused them to weigh one against the other. The key element in the novel was the dialectic among the masters, as they attempted to resolve the problem of who should lead them.

Although liberty and justice are desirable principles in their own right, the greatest good comes from their dialectical interplay. The fear is not so much that liberty *or* justice will be extinguished, but that the American dialectic will end—which will lead to the elimination of both of them. In America, both conceptions are now distorted in fundamental ways, to meet the needs of the organizational imperative. It has insidiously twisted the meaning of liberty, into greed-driven personal advantage, and justice; into despotic, rule-defined, managerial paternalism.

As we suggested in the first chapter, the end of the dialectic is the end of America. This realization makes our project in the rest of this chapter clear. It is to sketch, in broad outline, the agenda for moral discourse about modern organizations that will help keep the dialectic alive. This agenda is predicated on the natural right, derived as Norton argues from genetic human reality, that all individuals should be permitted to realize their full potentials at every stage of their lives. Organizations must be designed and led with this moral truth in mind.

The Organizations of the Individual Imperative

The direction that moral discourse will take is unpredictable, but the direction it should take is evident. That discourse requires the personal commitment to a better future—a future in which organizations celebrate the moral, intellectual, and aesthetic integrity of each individual and promote the enhancement of such integrity. In other words, we suggest the reformulation of modern organizations based upon the values of the individual imperative.[22]

Immediately, the defenders of the management orthodoxy will reject such a proposition, citing the ultimate criterion in modern society: the bottom line. They will argue that such a change will automatically cut into productivity and profits. But this is not the real issue. The driving force behind managerialism is not productivity or profit, but power. Thus, what we are confronted with is purely a power issue: the defenders of the organizational imperative see such change as threatening their perquisites, status, financial well-being, and power. For our part, we argue for the revolution: the design of new organizations — rooted in the Founding Values — and basing their success on the confidence that freeing people from the constraints of the organizational imperative will unleash undreamed-of productivity. To that end, we have chosen four conditions that are critical in organizational life: limitation of size, social enclaves, organizational governance, and moral discourse in management.

The Individual and Organizational Size

"Organizational size" is an overworked subject in economics and management: nearly everyone decries large organizations but accepts them for the supposed efficiencies that come from centralization and large scale. But this criticism is deceptive because the treatment of size in these fields has been instrumental and market related, pertaining to optimization and structural design. Barren to the discourse, in management and economics, is the moral issue: that smaller social units, rather than larger ones, are more conducive for the enhancement of people. This is not to say that rich sources of commentary on this subject are missing, just that we must look beyond the orthodox management and economic literature for them.

Let us consider two modern views on the morality of the limitation of organizational size.[23] First, shown in figure 11.1, is the formulation offered by economist Kenneth Boulding.[24] The economist in Boulding creeps into

Figure 11.1

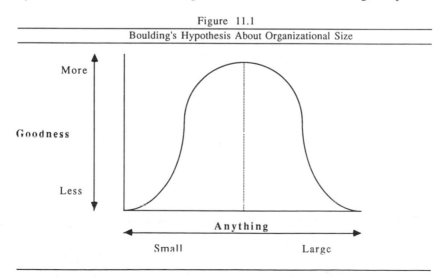

Boulding's Hypothesis About Organizational Size

More

Goodness

Less

Anything

Small   Large

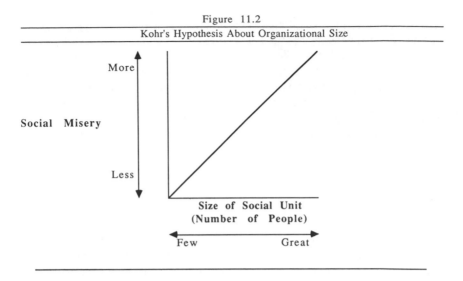

Figure 11.2

Kohr's Hypothesis About Organizational Size

this illustration, but Boulding the philosopher is more important. His axes are drawn along moral dimensions: too much or too little of anything on either side of a certain point reduces its goodness.

The moral question Boulding raises is the necessity for limitation in size in order to achieve an essential and appropriate proportionality in human life. Proportion holds in all things, not only size. For instance, on the low side of courage is cowardice and on its high side, foolhardiness. Without a sense of proportionality, people are led to excesses in one direction or the other. The point is that the practice of virtue in organizations is either furthered or impeded by the organization's size.

Second, Leopold Kohr treats the morality of the limitation of organizational size differently, based upon a most dyspeptic assumption about human nature.[25] For him, the main cause of social misery is essentially evil people in social aggregates that are too large, as shown in figure 11.2

In arguing for small-cell units, Kohr does not expect human nature to be magically transformed from evil to good, or human behavior from vice to virtue—since human nature is rotten to the core! But those same evil people, in small social containers, create less misery than they do in large social containers. For example, a war between Liechtenstein and Württemberg would create less *net* social misery than a war between Germany and France.

What then do these views of size limitation suggest for the organizations of the individual imperative? They raise the issue of the scale of anything that bears on the humane and pleasing: buildings, cities, universities, or whatever. Yet, in all of the many aspects of organizational scale, numbers of people surface as the critical variable. *This is because limitation of the size of social units is connected to moral discourse.* The intimacy permitted by small groups is related to the development of community, as the election in *The Masters* so clearly demonstrates. It, in turn, is an essential component of individual moral development and moral autonomy.

The primary question on proportionality and size in modern organizations is the possibility of achieving autonomous work groups that become local communities within large organizations. In the business world, Japanese quality circles are models of sorts, but their purpose is to enhance productivity. Our conception of community is far less instrumental, as we discuss next.

Social Enclaves and Moral Obligation

The notion of "social enclaves" within organizations implies the existence of a relatively independent unit within a larger unit. For instance, the college in *The Masters* was contained within Cambridge University. While it had a great deal of independence, it was still a part of the larger whole. In this sense, it was an enclave. The moral issue raised by social enclaves is the presence or absence of diversity in modern life. The public administration scholar A. G. Ramos takes the position that market-driven, managerial societies suppress diversity because of the unilateral reinforcement of instrumental values and behaviors.[26] The possibilities for people to have a wide range of substantive experiences in social enclaves, other than the market driven type, are reduced.

Reform of this condition is based upon Ramos's principle of delimitation, which is similar to the principle of subsidiarity. It takes as given that in good societies larger social units leave to smaller ones the activities that they (the smaller) can best perform. The assumption is that delimitation increases the opportunity of richness and diversity of human experiences. This principle emphasizes positive values such as self-help, local self-government, community building, group and individual creativity, and, most important, the function that intermediate institutions perform in buffering the individual and small groups from importunities imposed by the overwhelming power of large government and private corporations. These values enhance people because diversity makes individual moral choice possible.

Enclavization resembles pluralism, countervailing power, and decentralization. However, those parallels are insufficient, since enclavization is concerned with the substantive and moral aspects of the individual's place in a community. With respect to modern organizations, they imply the intentional restructuring of work units to achieve more humane values. Enclaves are not sought with the good of the organization in mind: they are desired because they morally enhance individuals through substantive experiences with work, friendship, permanence, and obligation.

Work, Friendship, and Permanence

Enclaves are places where people work instead of labor—where they transcend the modern job and find the possibilities of individual expression. We argued, in chapters 6 and 8, that work is the act of imprinting that which is unique about self upon something in the world. It is within the enclaves of the organization that individuals will find the leeway to give expression to themselves in their creations. Thus, priority must be given to the reduction of standardization and homogenization throughout every part of the organization, and particularly within the enclaves. This is not a task totally of job enlargement or enrichment, for it requires employee education and self-knowledge.

However, there is a condition of organizational homogenization that must be eliminated within the enclaves, and that is the standardization of relationships. We have not dealt with this aspect of self-knowledge yet, and it is well to do so now. Self-knowledge necessitates friendship, and it is a critical feature of the social enclaves. Norton defines friendship as a " 'congeniality' that obtains between persons who are alike in loving the good, but different in respect to the particular good each loves."[27]

Friends have true concern for each other's welfare. And although this concern is expressed in different ways on many levels, the least appreciated is the substantive part that friendship has in the refinement of each individual's uniqueness. Recall the metaphor of the diamond cutter in chapter 6. The cutter's responsibility is to strike the stone so that its full potential is realized. So it is with friends: one helps the other to realize uniqueness. This process is extraordinarily personal, intimate, and intense—and it cannot occur unless individuals associate regularly in community-like enclaves.

This raises another point: enclaves must have some degree of permanence. But permanent social enclaves are in direct confrontation with the organizational pressures of careerism and mobility. They have caused Americans to have many acquaintances but few friends. The impermanence of individual lives due to organizational mobility and careerism is not conducive to friendships that have refining qualities. There is a pathos involved in the quest of so many individuals to return to their roots. Our national character has made us like the wandering Odysseus, never at home even in his own organization. More permanence would lend continuity to an individual's life narrative.

Thus, the subject of intentional enclaves that are designed to promote the interrelated conditions of work, friendship, and permanence must be an essential part of the moral discourse that will bring into being the organizations of the individual imperative.

Moral Obligation

Moral obligation intensifies when free people associate in formal organizations and social enclaves. For leaders, such obligation requires them to be accountable to their followers. For the followers, it demands their informed and voluntary consent to obey leadership commands. Both accountability and voluntary consent are based, ideally, upon a civil intelligence—held in common by the leaders and the led—through which they subordinate personal and institutional interests to the general welfare of the community. This allows, as political scientist Robert Pranger wrote, "large numbers of persons [to] participate on an equal footing in making important . . . decisions thus perfecting their own development as well as their community's."[28] Again, we refer the reader to the example of the masters, who struggled with all of their aspirations to advance the cause of their community.

This ideal conception of moral obligation requires leader accountability to their constituencies for the single reason that they have *power*. The relationship of the leaders and the led to the exercise of power is the foundation of political philosophy, for there is something primal in that relationship. But in modern organizations, where managers accrue very real power, there is literally nothing in the promotion and incumbency processes to ensure that the "better sort"[29] of person acquires power, nor is there guidance on the moral or ethical entailments of the possession of power. Nearly all of us have had the experience of watching a friend or acquaintance, with no forewarning, turn from friend Jekyll to managerial Hyde upon promotion and the attainment of power.

The implication this has for accountability is that formal organizational assessment procedures must be expanded, from merely assessing performance to evaluating the way leaders handle power, at all levels, and on a regular basis. Hence, any realistic approach to leader accountability should include frequent, formal, multiple, and accessible evaluations.[30] These procedures have to be coupled with organizational governance mechanisms that permit removal or rotation of leaders who are determined by their constituencies to be wanting in skill or moral character. Thus, a necessary aspect of the organizations of the individual imperative must include means that ensure the prompt and orderly circulation of an inept or immoral elite.

This issue has been understood, if not perfectly practiced, in democratic societies. However, it is far from being either appreciated or acted upon for controlling the administrative elites, who often run public and private organizations as if they were Persian satrapies. Such leaders are not to be endured, for they are an affront to the Founding Values.

The obligation of followers to consent voluntarily to a leader's authority means that they must, at the same time, harbor an inherent suspicion of the powerful. Even if the better sort get the powerful offices, they can be corrupted. The Founders understood the myriad pitfalls of power, and they checked it and balanced it at every turn. But the control of power also requires a major commitment on the part of the followers.

Consequently, voluntary consent implies the moral duty of an individual to take action when confronted by injustices resulting from the wrong headed, or unjust, exercise of power. John Rawls suggested two ethical guidelines: conscientious refusal, which obligates individuals to reject offensive values but also requires them to know why their values are preferable, and civil disobedience, which obligates individuals to risk involvement in order to change that which is offensive.[31] The possibilities for discourse about these two guidelines are immense, but one subject—moral courage—seems to be a particularly salient matter relative to the obligations of followers. Of this there can be no doubt: the ethical imperatives that Rawls proposes require moral courage. Such courage must stem from the individual's love of justice and a sense for the welfare of the community. It has two components: reason and passion. They correspond to conscientious refusal and civil disobedience.

On the side of reason, knowledge is the cognitive component of moral courage. It implies a clear awareness of choice between right and wrong alternative values. Choice presumes freedom, in the sense that although one knows the values being acted upon, one is not bound by them. The individual is able to postulate reasonable alternative values after an informed, imaginative interaction with the objective world.

On the side of passion, heroism is the action component of moral courage. Considering the nature of our world, such acts of heroism are likely to be small, often private, lonely, unheralded, and regarded by many as naive and futile. Yet the small act may be the most heroic of all for these very reasons. It is based upon the passionate belief that an individual interacting with the world can change it in ways that are positive for a desirable future.

The virtue of moral courage in followers is shaped by intellectual honesty and by actions directed at righting wrongs. Virtue, however, is its own punishment in organizations, and most have figured this out. Therefore moral heroism is, in fact, the driving passion in the practice of Rawls's ethical imperatives—a passion Bishop Joseph Butler called resentment. He wrote, "resentment . . . is to be considered as a weapon, put into our hand by nature, against injury, injustice, and cruelty."[32] Arguing for this passion, Butler asked, "but is it cool reflection in the injured person, which for the most part, brings the offender to justice? Or is it not resentment and indignation against the injury and the author of it." Thus, if the use of power has contributed to the demeaning of others' lives, and if there are followers who resent these injustices and injuries, then it is obligatory that they withdraw their voluntary consent to leadership.

The obligations of leaders and followers implies hierarchy, and our discussion so far has been couched in those terms. However, Snow's novel requires us to ask another, nonhierarchial, question: What are the moral obligations that people, as equals, have to one another? Answers to this question are often made in terms of collegiality, professional courtesy, sorority, fraternity, or the brotherhood of combat. They have qualitative and substantive meanings for social enclaves; people in enclaves trust each other, appreciate and support the diversity of individual members, and exercise tough love if an occasion warrants, as Snow so poignantly demonstrated.

Organizational Governance and Justice

America has been described as a sea of freedom filled with islands of despotism. This metaphor implies a disparity between the rights and liberties enjoyed by Americans as citizens versus those denied them as employees of organizations. If such a disparity exists, and we believe that it does, then moral discourse must address this issue: if the Founding Values are true and our national life is predicated upon them, then should not all organizations be governed by them?[33] To simplify, let us refer to this as "the federal model."

The Federal Model

The federal model is a decentralized organizational governance system that parallels, in some respects, the way that our Republic is governed. Thus, organizational federalism would require the separation of governance powers, a system of checks and balances among the functional units, and some form of shared sovereignty among the enclaves within the larger governing unit. Obviously, none of this fits the prescriptions of orthodox management theory and practice, and so it is anathema to mainstream American organizations. But, to paraphrase "Engine Charlie" Wilson: if federalism is good enough for America, why isn't it good enough for General Motors?

Chester I. Barnard was aware of the features of federalism, and, although he supported them for governing the Republic, he specifically rejected them for organizational governance.[34] His reasons were based on a belief that organizations required "authoritative communication" from an elite of managerial experts. Federalism, in Barnard's view (actually he called it democracy), would thwart the application of managerial knowledge and skills to organizations. Therefore, Barnard implicitly endorsed an autocratic approach, where all the governance functions were concentrated in the executive, and where the balance of power was overwhelmingly vested in centralized management authority; management sovereignty had to be absolute. Orthodox management, at present, does not deviate from this principle.

But what can be said about unorthodox management governance? It is evident that the realpolitik of organizations sometimes override standard theory and practice. For example, the management scholar Henry Mintzberg described an organizational design that he called the "professional bureaucracy."[35] It is a form of organization that seems best suited to complex organizations that require employees to have high-order skills and experience. Such organizations are designed around modules of expertise that resemble social enclaves. They are exemplified by universities, law and public accounting firms, general hospitals, social-work agencies, and school systems.

Organizations such as these employ relatively independent professionals with extensive training and socialization in the practice of their occupation. Given the nature of their work, they need considerable autonomy and discretion. Furthermore, the important values that influence professional practice originate from outside of the employing organization in the associations to which the professionals belong: for example, the American Bar Association, the American Medical Association, etc. Professional bureaucracies having these characteristics seem to be suitable for full-scale application of federalism, and there is some indication that the more effectively performing professional bureaucracies are managed by federal principles.[36]

The comparative freedom of the professional in federalized organizations is no doubt good for them and good for their employers as well. The problem is that the federal model does not extend to employees who are lesser qualified and who lack the support of professional associations. Can federal principles be applied to them? The answer is yes, and some sense of this can be had by understanding the nature of the due process systems that are essential for guaranteeing to all employees the rights and freedoms that they enjoy as citizens.

Due Process in Organizations

Systems of due process, commonly called procedural and substantive due process, are mechanisms of governance that implement corrective and distributive justice. Procedural due process provides the means for redressing grievances if an employee believes that his or her rights have been abridged. Substantive due process focuses on employee interests and is concerned with distributive justice in the allocation of organizational resources. These forms of due process are analogous, respectively, to the judicial and legislative functions of government.

A great deal has been written about the theory and practice of due process in organizations.[37] Many companies report having Management Initiated Grievance Systems (MIGS) for settling employee disputes over rights. There are also uncounted numbers of employee participation schemes that to some degree involve employees in resource allocation decisions. However, all of these programs, plans, and techniques do not add up to real protection of employee rights and interests. Ninety-nine percent of all MIGS do not have the final step of the procedure heard and decided by an outside arbitrator. Thus, these judicial systems are not independent of management's executive authority and are, in effect, captive management personnel practices.

Furthermore, management does not permit employees to participate in substantive due process activities with anything like a grant of power that is necessary to make it meaningful in negotiating their interests. Management's executive authority dominates the legislative action.

In contemplating a desirable future, two modest suggestions come to mind with regard to due process. First, procedural due process has to be an independent judicial function that includes other representatives besides managers on the hearing boards. It also must have impartial, third-party arbitration as a final and binding step in the procedure. Second, substantive due process demands equalization of power among those who divide the resource pie. Some view West Germany's codetermination laws as a way to achieve power equalization. Others see unions as the answer to equalized negotiating power. In certain instances both approaches could be helpful.

However, cooperative employee ownership of organizations seems to be a more effective approach to power equalization. Few things in America equalize power as effectively as property, unless it is a Colt revolver.[38] As things stand now, the absentee owners of American corporations are unable to intervene in behalf of their employees' interests even if they wanted to reallocate resources for the sake of justice.

In conclusion, the prospective costs of due process systems that really make a difference in protecting employees seem to be very high in terms of money, lost management sovereignty, and organizational effectiveness measured strictly by efficiency standards. However, the potential benefits are great if different standards than these are used, such as enhanced citizen virtue, managerial fairness, and humane organizations. The issue that organization governance poses for our deliberation in moral discourse is the trade-off between these costs and benefits. The masters were aware of this trade-off and consciously opted for the benefits over the costs.

Moral Discourse in Management

Throughout this book, and particularly in this chapter, we have called attention to many issues that should be raised in forums for moral discourse.

We have not, however, discoursed on moral discourse itself. In order to avoid the impression that moral discourse is a deus ex machina we have conjured up to sidestep difficult or awkward problems, we must conclude our book by discussing its principles.

Moral discourse must be engaged in by honorable people who seek to know, to believe in, and to act upon moral truth. These people are the intellectuals, and philosopher Barnard Henri L'Evy placed them in categories: the metaphysicists, because they consider the ontological possibility of revolution; the artists, because they, in affirming life, also affirm civilization; and the moral philosophers, because they offer the alternative of "a morality of courage and duty confronting the dismal cowardice of submission to facts."[39] They need to employ the great instruments of intellect, from reason to passion, to contest with one another in a moral dialectic. The discourse should include both the issues of truth and the issues of application, for, as Adam Smith wrote: "The most sublime speculation of the contemplative philosopher can scarce compensate the neglect of the smallest active duty."[40]

Although intellectuals must lead the way, any normal person can engage in such discourse, and for them to do so would enhance their moral character. Certainly the Founders hoped that the citizens of this nation would so occupy themselves. But, since there are no morally neutral acts, there are some upon whom the obligation for moral discourse about affairs in management *should* weigh more heavily. These are the people who hold power—that is, people whose ideas, decisions, and actions significantly affect the lives of others. Because our book is about organizations, we point to the extraordinary obligation of management theorists and practitioners to engage in reasoned moral discourse.

However, we must enlarge our conception of "reason." Managerial reason, unfortunately, is at a far remove from that form of reasoning advocated by the Founding Fathers of this nation. It is limited almost exclusively to the resolution of organizational problems, which does not get managers any closer to a knowledge of, and faith in, the Founding Values. The limitations of orthodox managerial reasoning became apparent in the latter 1980s, when America was rocked with a seemingly unending series of ethical scandals. Business leaders, many of whom were truly concerned, went hunting for "ethicists" to speak with them about how to straighten things out. But what was wanted was not moral discourse; rather, they wanted "ten hands-on principles that we can apply." Ethics was seen as just another problem that would yield to good management procedures.

The Founders wrote and spoke about reason in many forms, from the validation of empirical results to the intuitive confirmation of an individual's natural rights. We chose to use reason in the latter manner and would agree with Jefferson, about whom the historian Adrienne Koch wrote:

Jefferson retained his fundamental thesis about the opposition between two theories of society (one founded on force, bolstered by privilege, and administered by power-thirsty functionaries and orders independent of the will of the people; the other founded on *reason* and justice, marked by faith in natural rights, governed by deputies of the people, chosen by them and dependent upon their will).[41]

In this sense, moral reasoning is much more than problem solving. It is the essential precondition for individual moral autonomy, for it exposes the full range of moral choice. Moral reasoning has substantive and qualitative properties. From this perspective, reason informs the actions that individuals take in search of a life that has liberty, justice, community, and proportion. Reason can discriminate qualitatively among competing values, and, in this respect, its glory is that it can cut through superficialities to moral truth and thus be faithful to itself. Of all the aspects of the individual imperative, moral reasoning is first, for it validates the moral premises upon which the imperative rests.

For that reason, we argue that the only way to untrack the organizational imperative is through a moral reasoning that will lead us to the renaissance of the Founding Values. Such reasoning must be an integral part of the curriculum in all schools of management, whether public or private. At the minimum, the work of the great moral philosophers must be taught: from Hobbes, Locke, Rousseau, Hume, and Smith, to Jefferson, Adams, Madison, and Wilson. But even those who are well instructed in these classical works can still have vile moral characters. The real test of management is not just in its formal instruction in moral philosophy, or puzzle solving in cases on ethics. Rather, the measure is the commitment that a school of management has to the obligation to add positively to the good moral character of its students.

Thus, students must be persuaded to understand that every management decision—whether involving policy or personnel—requires significant moral consideration. This is particularly necessary when the matter of promotion comes up, for we cannot allow for the "vertical invasion of the barbarians." Moral autonomy has no meaning in a rule-dominated, command environment.

The nurture of a commitment to the individual imperative will be difficult, but what better way can we use our time? If the pursuit of honor, decency, gentleness, and loveliness does not seem a worthy life goal, then we are lost before we start. Jefferson understood that the way would be slow, but such was the only course for a free people. He described his feelings to Reverend Charles Clay, in 1790, arguing for patience:

The ground of liberty is to be gained by inches [so] we must be contented to secure what we can get, from time to time, and eternally press forward for what is yet to get.[42]

For those, like ourselves, who write most ardently about the "original intent," it is fatal to forget that in all its interpretations, the freedom of the individual was paramount. Time seems to be working against us now, and the possibilities of the twenty-first century look dim for a free American nation. Nonetheless, our belief in the Founding Values leaves us no other alternative but to try for their renaissance, brought about through moral discourse and the application of the principles of right in all organizations. If we do manage to achieve that rebirth of the Founding Values, then the future takes on a bright aspect, and we will pioneer a new path into a lovely and gentle future.

Notes

1. H. L. Mencken, "Bayard vs. Lionheart" (26 July 1920), in H. L. Mencken, *On Politics: A Carnival of Buncombe*, ed. M. Moos (New York: Vintage, 1956), 18.
2. For a superb defense of the validity of innate moral nature, see J. Budziszewski, *The Resurrection of Nature: Political Theory and the Human Character* (Ithaca: Cornell University Press, 1986).
3. We take the word from Simon, who wrote: "While economic man maximizes — selects the best alternative from among all those available to him; his cousin, whom we shall call administrative man, satisfices — looks for a course of action that is satisfactory or 'good enough.'" So much for any exalted notion of "happiness," for Simon defines administrative theory as "peculiarly the theory of intended and bounded rationality — or the behavior of human beings who *satisfice* because they have not the wits to *maximize*." Simon, *Administrative Behavior*, 2nd ed. (New York: Free Press, 1957), pp. xxiv, xxv.
4. They are the defenders of the old paradigm, as described by Thomas S. Kuhn, *The Structure of Scientific Revolutions* (Chicago: University of Chicago Press, 1962).
5. Gorbachev, *Peristroika* (see chap. 6, n. 24) 22–23.
6. Albert R. Jonsen and Stephen Toulmin, *The Abuse of Casuistry: A History of Moral Reasoning* (Berkeley: University of California Press, 1988), 9. Emphasis in original.
7. Carl Sandburg, *Abraham Lincoln: The War Years — I* (New York: Scribner's, 1939), 3: 621. Emphasis added.
8. Note the essays in Kolenda, ed., *Organizations and Ethical Individualism* (see chap. 1, n. 11).
9. We use the term "actualize," rather than "realize," in the manner suggested in Norton, *Personal Destinies* (see chap. 1, n. 11), especially chapter 1, "The Ethical Priority of Self-Actualization," 3–41.
10. Thus, the adjective "unalienable," attached to the word rights, needs to be taken seriously. For a brief discussion, see the rather uneven book by Garry Wills, *Inventing America: Jefferson's Declaration of Independence* (Garden City, N.Y.: Doubleday, 1978), especially chapter 16, " . . . inalienable rights . . . ," 229–239.
11. James Madison, "Federalist No. 10" in *The Federalist*, ed. J. E. Cook (Middletown, Conn: Wesleyan University Press, 1961), 58. Emphasis added.
12. "The first principle of the doctrine of virtue is: act according to a maxim of *ends* which it can be a universal law for everyone to have — According to this principle man is an end, to himself as well as to others. And it is not enough that he has no title to use either himself or others merely as means (since according to this he can still be indifferent to them): it is in itself his duty to make man as such his end."

Immanuel Kant, *The Doctrine of Virtue: Part II of The Metaphysics of Morals*, trans. M. J. Gregor (Philadelphia: University of Pennsylvania Press, 1964), 55–56.

13. C. P. Snow, *The Masters* (New York: Scribner's, 1951), 200; in the three-volume collection C.P. Snow, *Strangers and Brothers* (New York, Scribners, 1972).

14. Ibid., 54.

15. Ibid., 36.

16. This section is based on Scott, "Management Governance Theories" (see chap. 6, n. 26), 277–298.

17. "This contention holds that what we call our civilization is largely responsible for our misery, and that we should be much happier if we gave it up and returned to primitive conditions. . . . It was discovered that a person becomes neurotic because he cannot tolerate the amount of frustration which society imposes on him in the service of its cultural ideals, and it was inferred from this that the abolition or reduction of those demands would result in a return to possibilities of happiness." Sigmund Freud, *Civilization and Its Discontents*, trans. J. Strachey (New York: Norton [1931], 1961), 33, 34.

18. Most of them would have agreed with Adam Smith, who wrote: "It is thus that man, who can subsist only in society, was fitted by nature to that situation for which he was made." Smith, *Theory of Moral Sentiments* (see chap. 9, n. 2), II.ii.3.1., 85.

19. For a brilliant discussion of the ramifications of positive and negative liberty, see Isaiah Berlin, "Two Concepts of Liberty" in his classic book *Four Essays on Liberty* (Oxford: Oxford University Press, 1969), 118–172.

20. Norton, *Personal Destinies*, 26.

21. Ibid., 310.

22. This section is based in part on William G. Scott, "Organizational Revolution: An End to Managerial Orthodoxy," *Administration and Society*, 17 (Aug. 1985), 149–170.

23. Note, for instance, the relevant sections on the size and quality of the population in an ideal state in Book 7, "Political Ideals and Educational Principles," in *The Politics of Aristotle*, trans. E. Barker (New York: Oxford University Press, 1958), and the discussion in E. Barker, *The Political Thought of Plato and Aristotle* (New York: Dover [1947], 1952), 406–422.

24. Kenneth Boulding, *From Abundance to Scarcity: The Hammond Lectures* (Columbus: Ohio State University Press, 1978).

25. Leopold Kohr, *The Breakdown of Nations* (New York: Dutton, 1978).

26. Ramos, *New Science of Organizations* (see chap. 5, n. 5).

27. Norton, *Personal Destinies*, 306–307.

28. Robert J. Pranger, *The Eclipse of Citizenship* (New York: Holt, Rinehart and Winston, 1968), 54.

29. The notion of the "better sort" of person is taken from the splendid book by Pincoffs, *Quandaries and Virtues* (see chap. 1, n. 11), especially part 3, "Education for Good Character."

30. L. W. Fry, W. G. Scott, T. R. Mitchell, and P. L. Nemetz, "Who Evaluates the Evaluators?" (Paper presented at the Annual Meeting of the Academy of Management, Anaheim, California, 1988.)

31. John Rawls, *A Theory of Justice* (Cambridge: Harvard University Press, 1973).

32. Bishop Joseph Butler, *The Works of Joseph Butler*, ed. W. E. Gladstone (Oxford: Clarendon Press, 1977).

33. This section is based on Scott, "Management Governance Theories."
34. Barnard, *Functions of the Executive* (see chap. 1, n. 14), especially 279–280 and 222–223.
35. Mintzberg, *Structure in Fives* (see chap. 4, n. 22).
36. Fry et al., "Who Evaluates the Evaluators?"
37. For an unusual and informative approach, see E. Allan Lind and Tom R. Tyler, *The Social Psychology of Procedural Justice* (New York: Plenum Press, 1988).
38. This is not just a quip. See the comments about the importance of citizen militias in achieving democracy in Western society, in Pocock, *The Machiavellian Moment* (see chap. 4, n. 2).
39. Barnard Henri L'Evy, *Barbarism with a Human Face* (New York: Harper and Row, 1979), 194-195.
40. Smith, *Theory of Moral Sentiments*, VI.ii.3.6., 237.
41. Adrienne Koch, *The Philosophy of Thomas Jefferson* (Gloucester, Mass: Peter Smith [1943], 1957), 139. Emphasis added.
42. Thomas Jefferson to the Reverend Charles Clay, 27 January 1790, as quoted in Koch, *Jefferson*, 188.

Epilogue:
The Requisite Conditions for a Worthy
Life—A Dialogue

The corporate boardroom on the seventy-fifth floor of the Union Center Building in Seattle has a commanding view of Puget Sound. The northern islands and cliffs, the western Olympic mountain range, and the flat southern tidelands can be seen through the three large picture windows that form the west wall of the room. When the days are clear and bright, which is seldom in the Pacific Northwest, these landmarks are set against a background of incomparably blue sky and water. The vista from the room at night is no less entrancing. The string of lights on the waterfront, the luminous ferryboats crossing Elliot Bay to Bremerton, the glow of the Space Needle, and the sparkling homes on Queen Anne Hill blend into an urban scene that many visitors regard as one of the more beautiful in the world.

The boardroom harmonizes with the attractiveness and diversity of the surrounding country. It is open, bright, and finished in woods native to Washington's forests. The decorations, which are used sparingly, are reminders of the state's maritime tradition. A large oil painting of a magnificent sailing vessel hangs on one wall. Some antique nautical instruments and Northwest Indian artifacts are arranged tastefully on the other walls.

Notably absent is the usual massive conference table for the board of directors. Casually arranged modern, Scandinavian-style chairs and low tables are used instead. This furniture is subtly oriented toward a medium-size desk, which is occupied by the board chairman during regular meetings of the corporate directors. At other times the room serves as a gathering place for higher-level executives to relax, entertain a few guests, or hold small, informal meetings.

Although it departs from tradition, the boardroom still reflects the dignity and authority of individuals who hold power. The room suggests that the corporation's executives are mindful of the environment, that they have not forgotten the early inhabitants and industries that made the area great, and that they are comfortably informal in the conduct of their affairs. Thus, the boardroom blends physically and socially with its place and time. However, its understated elegance also suggests that those who sit there are aware of

181

their preeminent influence in this region of the nation. In a somewhat similar manner, it fits its members just as the communal room fit the masters in C. P. Snow's novel.

One late evening last February, an anomalous presence appeared in the empty, half-lighted room. Seated on one of the scattered chairs under the painting of the ship, dressed in disheveled clothes in the fashion of the nineteenth century, was the ghost of the Russian novelist Fyodor Dostoevsky. He had come to converse about individual freedom, as a condition of the worthy life, with history's most famous management theorist, Chester I. Barnard.

Dostoevsky did not wait long, for Barnard was already materializing in the leather chair behind the desk. "Typical," thought Dostoevsky, "he just assumes the boss's chair is his!" But he also knew that Barnard was a genuine rarity among American business executives. He had read extensively in philosophy and social theory, was acquainted with many leading American intellectuals during the 1930s, 1940s, and 1950s, and he wrote thoughtfully and influentially about management.

But it is not clear what had prompted this meeting between Barnard and Dostoevsky. How could they have much in common? Barnard had been president of an AT&T operating company and, later, president of the Rockefeller Foundation. Dostoevsky, on the other hand, was a prominent—albeit somewhat disreputable—novelist and mystic in another country and century. Had they discovered they were both men of action? Had they learned that they had similar philosophical interests? Had they realized that they both had a knack for prophecy? Maybe it was just the sheer pleasure of one first-rate intellect engaging another in moral discourse.

Whatever the reasons, they had anticipated the debate with pleasure, as only those of an earlier generation could understand. What could be more pleasant than to meet in this delightful room, enjoy the lovely nighttime views, and discuss the conditions necessary for a worthy life? They had eternity at their disposal. Being uninvolved in daily affairs, they could deal with the subject with a detached objectivity denied them during their lives.

Feeling comfortable and at home behind the desk, Barnard greeted Dostoevsky. "Welcome, sir, and let me say how much I admire your book *The Brothers Karamazov*. It has many virtues, but, like so many others, I've always been impressed by the parable of the Grand Inquisitor. This is one of your most profound pieces of writing, particularly because it gets right to the heart of the relationship between freedom and worthy living."

"Thank you, but I'm not sure your admiration of it alone is appropriate, Mr. Barnard. In some ways, *The Brothers* built upon *The Possessed*, which I wrote eight years earlier."

"Ah. You mean that the views expressed by the Grand Inquisitor were an extension of the utopian philosophy of your earlier character Shigalev?"

In spite of his fame, Dostoevsky was impressed. Not many Americans had much tolerance for the lugubrious wanderings of Russian authors. "You are correct. My purpose in both books was to denounce utopians of all kinds and to demonstrate that their atheistic programs for social reform would ultimately lead the people away from worthy lives and into nihilism. *The Brothers Karamazov* was a refinement of that idea, but its essential elements are contained in *The Possessed*."

"I remember that prediction. What do you think now?"

"The followers of Shigalev and the Grand Inquisitor are dominating the twentieth century, just as I said they would. They won by blood and violence in Russia. In America, they will win by exploiting the indifference of the people. Either way, the Shigalevists will triumph exactly as I predicted."

"As I recall," said Barnard, "Shigalev discovered a paradoxical system. He started with unlimited human freedom and ended with unlimited despotism."

"That was the key to his ideas. However, Shigalev was getting at a very important point about leadership."

"Oh, yes! Shigalev's thought was that, for men to find happiness and live worthily, humanity had to be divided into unequal parts, where one-tenth has dominion over nine-tenths."

"Quite right," replied Dostoevsky.

"You seem critical of this inequality. My feeling is that leadership and inequality go hand in hand. This isn't necessarily bad, since a worthy life is seldom found in a choice between absolute freedom or absolute despotism. Most people have had to settle for a compromise, maybe tilting in one direction, but never entirely."

"The direction of the tilt *is* what is important. It is the stuff of prophecy."

"Well, what is the direction that will lead to worthiness?" asked Barnard.

"If man does not seek self-worth in the freedom of Christ, he will seek it in earthly comforts and follow those who are able to provide them, despite the consequences."

"So, the result of not following Christ is, in your thinking, unlimited despotism."

"That is my opinion. And see how correct my prophecy has been for the twentieth century."

"It has and it hasn't," Barnard observed. "There were and are despotic regimes; but there also were victories for the secular democratic nations in the West during this century."

"You are missing my point. In order to be victorious, these democracies had to become like the nations they were opposing. And while some freedoms were restored after the various wars, these freedoms were never fully returned to the people."

"That's hardly an original observation, Dostoevsky!"

"Perhaps I put it too simply, Barnard. War merely accelerates the despotic trend in democratic nations. With or without it, even those nations with a tradition of freedom will eventually succumb to this trend."

"By other means than turning away from God, as you claim?"

"By embracing the only other alternative that humans have: a mixture of secular humanitarianism and materialism."

"Therefore, people will surrender their freedoms to the despotic one-tenth because they give them material comforts. Beyond this you see no option?"

"You have the gist of it. A worthy life is now defined in America by comfort, security and possessions. The rules to achieve them are laid down by the leadership elite, and the American people are trained from childhood to obey the rules. In fact, it is hard to find a more rule-dominated people than your American progeny. And, if unthinking obedience to rules, in search of material comfort, isn't a definition of nonfreedom, I don't know what is."

"You are not exactly brimming with optimism tonight, are you, Dostoevsky? I don't agree with your assessment of things, but, as a matter of curiosity, who are these despots to whom you allude?"

"You won't like this, Barnard, but you were one of their forerunners. Your intellectual friends at Harvard, your executive position with the telephone company, and your book contributed to the fulfillment of my prophecy. I see you as a utopian, much like the Grand Inquisitor. You gave management a reductivist set of ethical rules to follow, but you never encouraged the examination of the value premises upon which those rules were based."

"Nonsense! You seem to forget that I've read *The Brothers Karamazov*. There are no parallels in our work. American executives are generally rather ordinary citizens I tried to help do a better job. I don't see any connection between that and the vicious methods of repression used by the Grand Inquisitor."

"Come now, Barnard, there is no need to get overwrought."

"But I am disturbed! The Grand Inquisitor was evil. Do you think that I am evil? Do you really believe that the generations of managers who have been influenced by my work are the spawn of the Grand Inquisitor? It is an unjust charge, Dostoevsky."

"Not so. I do not claim that evil was a conscious choice on your part, or on the part of the managers of modern organizations. But you have allowed evil to creep up upon you. The real tragedy is that you managers unwittingly drift into the ways of the Grand Inquisitor, because you refuse to consider the values upon which your managerial orthodoxy is based. But, since the subject disturbs you so, let's drop it for the moment. I would like you to explain a passage in your book."

"Can you quote it?" asked Barnard.

"Yes, because it is a memorable statement. Your words are, 'So among those who cooperate the things that are seen are moved by things unseen. Out of the void comes the spirit that shapes the ends of men.' Tell me, Barnard, what is the void? What is the spirit? What are the ends?"

"The meaning of that passage should be clear to anyone who has studied or practiced management. The void is a chaotic state existing before humans learned to cooperate in organized ways. It was the state of humanity that existed before the invention of organizations. Granted, organizations are merely artifacts that must be animated by the people in them. The quality of their performance is entirely the result of managerial leadership. And there is the 'spirit': a leadership that creates cooperation among people in organizations."

"That explains the void and the spirit of it, but what are the ends toward which all this activity is directed?"

"Ah, the ends," mused Barnard, who was now on familiar ground. "The ends are the clearest of all. Cooperation, created by enlightened managers, will bring the mutual satisfaction of individual and organizational needs. Managers create the requisite conditions for everyone to lead worthy lives. They are the moral force behind cooperation."

"Then, is it correct to say that managers are the real leaders of modern countries, not politicians, soldiers, capitalists, or scientists?"

"Yes! That was my prophecy, but I must admit that I borrowed a lot of it from Herbert Hoover."

Agitated, Dostoevsky rose from his chair, walked to the window, and stared abstractly at the black water of the Puget Sound below. "Yet, is it not also true that as managers are encouraging people to cooperate, they are also strengthening their organizations' control over them? And doesn't this deny individuals their freedom and enslave their souls? Your 'managerial society' seems exactly like the Grand Inquisitor's, except that it is not so crudely coercive. Remember that he said, 'Freedom and bread enough for all are inconceivable together.'"

"That is *not* what I had in mind. I wrote clearly in my book . . . "

"Barnard, none of your writing is clear!"

". . . that there was, in the late 1930s, a contest between those who held extreme views of vast regimentation and endless subordination with those who held equally extreme views of liberty and unrestricted self-will. The enlightened managerial way in America never led to one or the other of these absolutes. I wanted to show the dangers of extremism of all kinds; I also wanted to show that there are alternatives."

"Such as?"

"My way, and the way of all enlightened managers, is a way of moderation. Good managers are Aristotelians. They seek proportion; they have modest aspirations; they are ascetic; and, above all, they believe in the power of cooperation and science to find a rational path between ideological extremes.

Your Grand Inquisitor and Shigalev are monsters. They are pathological creations of malevolent societies. They want humans to be worthy, but only as they define the term. They will use means that are both cynical and oppressive. Americans would never stand for such leaders. In my estimation, you Russian intellectuals tend to overdramatize everything."

Dostoevsky turned from the window and started pacing in front of Barnard's desk. "Maybe there *is* a point that I missed in my passion for drama. The Grand Inquisitor and Shigalev believed that people could live worthily only by following their rules. These characters of mine were prophetic in more ways than I care to imagine. They were the prototypes for Lenin and Stalin. Considering what Russia was like, it didn't occur to me that there were any alternatives for my people: Christian freedom on the one hand or totalitarian repression on the other. After listening to you, I believe that there is a third alternative. However, it is difficult for me to describe."

"You've not been at a loss for words before. Try!"

"All right, and please try not to take what I say personally. Perhaps there is a condition in which people can be kept suspended, in limbo. Initially, leaders do not consciously seek or avoid this condition. Rather, it just happens. But, having happened, there is no excuse for the leaders not to be aware of what has happened. And, ever more, there is no excuse for the leaders not to take advantage of it."

"I simply don't understand what you're driving at, Dostoevsky."

"Please, hear me out. Suppose for a moment that repression does not take the form of killing dissidents, running concentration camps, or terrorizing citizens with the secret police. Suppose instead that the strategy is to anesthetize people with material comforts. Imagine, further, that the leaders convinced the people that these comforts are the sure indicators of worthiness. If they were successful, who could possibly object—especially if the leaders appear to be nice people? The results would be exactly the same—oppression. The people's sensitivities would be so dulled that they would not realize what was happening to them. They would be securely asleep. Then all could be managed according to the managerial dream of balance, moderation, reasonableness, and proportion without popular objection. Life might be drab and sterile, but it would be orderly and secure. In this light, Shigalev and the Grand Inquisitor *are* anachronistic. Their actions would inflame people. Your strategy of oppression is much more effective for modern times. Why, even Mikhail Gorbachev seems to be following your prescriptions."

"I must protest!" cried Barnard.

Dostoevsky interrupted. "It just occurs to me, my friend, that you have pulled a switch. You have objected to the brutal controls of the state described by Orwell in *1984*, but you have substituted the more subtle, pleasurable controls described by Huxley in *Brave New World*. How clever! Who could possibly object to control by niceness? But it is still total control."

"This is not true. I never wanted people to be oppressed any more than I wanted to have their development stifled."

"What you wanted isn't the issue. I suspect that your work has been misused as much as mine. Can you imagine me being cast in the role of a sympathetic prophet of Soviet socialism? Well, I have been! Since my words can't be purged, they are perverted. Such is the consequence of literary deconstructionism."

"You're not still feeling persecuted, are you, Dostoevsky? Besides, *my* message has not been twisted. I wrote nothing that was contrary to what decades of managers either before or after me have believed. In a sense, I merely codified what managers have held to be their true rights and duties."

Barnard and Dostoevsky talked through the night. At dawn, the shades were drawn. They decided to rest during the day and promised to return to their conversation at sundown. They met the next evening, refreshed and anxious to pick up where they had left off.

"Last evening, Chester—may I call you Chester?—you said that you tried to arrange management ideas in an orderly way. I think it is popular these days to say that you were making a 'paradigmatic statement,' so that future managers might be properly instructed in appropriate ways to act."

"That was what I was trying to do, although after thinking it over, I wasn't merely a codifier. I believe I made several valuable contributions to management knowledge. Incidentally, isn't 'paradigm' an awful word?"

"No worse than 'ideal benefactions.'"

"Touché, Fyodor."

"Let's get back to the subject. If you intended your book to be a guide for future managers, then my opinion is that it was a misdirected one. You made cooperative effort the measure of morality. But you went further. You required that managers persuade people that their worthiness was determined by the extent that their values were consistent with organizational values. I believe you said that this could be done by 'deliberate education of the young and propaganda for adults.' This does not seem to me to advance the cause of individual freedom."

Barnard began to fidget behind the desk, because Dostoevsky had struck a sensitive point. "When you take my words out of context, you can draw any inference you like. Let me try to explain more fully—it involves the whole issue of leadership. The reality of modern life, or life in any historical period, is that an elite must lead. Pareto saw this and thought that the circulation of the elite was the immutable historical force behind social change. I foresaw that the new elite circulating into modern industrial nations would come from a managerial class. I asked myself, 'What's better, to have this new elite impervious to their moral responsibilities, or to have enlightened leaders, sensitive to these responsibilities?' The question was rhetorical—the enlightened minority must instruct the majority in appropriate ethical behavior. The rules are derived from the morality of cooperation and organization. It's as simple as that. The rest follows like an exercise in Euclidean geometry."

"Your Euclidean metaphor is dangerous. His geometry works only when you accept his premises. But let's go along with *your* premises for a moment. Take, for example, your advice that managers appropriate the right to define the values for the 'nine-tenths.' This is pure Shigalevism, and it is the main a priori premise in your system. Once that premise is accepted—that the basis of organizational morality is cooperation—your system is as irrefutable as Shigalev's. It's the same as assuming that parallel lines never cross. Given that assumption, the rest of Euclid's geometry cannot be disproved. The difficulty with your view of managerial leadership is that you equate its moral responsibilities with maintaining cooperative systems. Since managers have the power to define the rules of cooperation, the freedom to make moral choices is eliminated. In this respect, you are no different from the utopian socialists, who figured that the conditions that led to worthy human lives required nothing more than the application of a few morally neutral rules of social geometry."

"What's wrong with making people's lives more comfortable and safe?" asked Barnard.

"Only that you Americans equate comfort and safety with freedom."

"That is not true, at least not entirely. There is much ambiguity in moral leadership. You credit my prescriptions for ethical behavior with more precision than I claimed for them. The few who make moral choices for the many have to suffer. I have no doubt that top managers suffer because they have the final responsibility for human welfare."

"The more you talk, the more you sound like the Grand Inquisitor . . . "

"Don't say any more; I know what's coming. You're going to quote your passage about the 'happy millions' and the 'ten thousand martyrs.'"

"It did occur to me," said Dostoevsky. "You must agree that the most notable totalitarian leaders of your twentieth century have borne me out. Lenin, Mao, and Hitler saw themselves as martyrs to their ideological causes. Regardless of them, you wrote about the complex nature of executive morality. Am I incorrect, or don't you imply that managers who shoulder this burden are martyring themselves for lesser humans who are not faced with such enormous dilemmas of moral choice?"

"I believe these people *are* martyrs in some ways. But theirs is not a self-conscious martyrdom, nor is it particularly dramatic. A martyr needs an audience to witness the magnitude of his sacrifice, and the managerial elite is not highly visible. The tragedy of their lives is made greater by their anonymity. This, Fyodor, is why I object to your accusation that I advised managers to usurp the right of defining values. Rather, they are forced by the irresistible logic of their circumstances to promulgate values based upon cooperative principles."

"So the matter of choice does not enter into the managerial calculus? Are their choices morally neutral and caused by organizational forces beyond their control?"

"It's more complicated than that. Fyodor, please try to see my point of view. Organizations thrive on appropriate human actions; they founder on inappropriate actions. There are no morally neutral acts, and, therefore, the success or failure of all cooperative endeavors depends upon the moral quality of what people do. Don't you see? There is nothing sinister in wanting people to cooperate more effectively."

"Oh, I can agree with that!"

Barnard pressed on, encouraged that he had finally gotten Dostoevsky to concur with something. "Managers are obligated more than nonmanagers to act morally in organizations. But the important thing is that all people act with a sense of commitment, obligated by their organizational roles."

Dostoevsky narrowed his eyes, giving Barnard an incredulous, ironic look.

"You're not following me, are you, Fyodor?"

Dostoevsky said nothing, but his expression made Barnard uneasy. So he hurried to explain further. "Your character the Grand Inquisitor is a perfect example of what I'm trying to get across to you. Wasn't he apart from his flock as well as a member of the flock at the same time? This situation is only paradoxical if we forget that the leaders and the led are engaged in a *mutual* effort to accomplish a goal that they couldn't alone. Wouldn't you agree?"

"Perhaps," admitted Dostoevsky.

Dostoevsky then asked, "Isn't it true that if people do different things in an organization, this will make them different? The Grand Inquisitor was different from the lesser members of his flock because he had the power of his position. He used it to increase his church's dominance over the flock. The Grand Inquisitor's sin—his personal tragedy if you prefer—was that he *knew* oppression was evil. Nevertheless, he took advantage of people's blind obedience and in return gave them comfort and security. He twisted this weakness to his advantage, and, as a result, his organization became so powerful that he could successfully challenge Christ when He returned a second time. Yes, the Grand Inquisitor had the knowledge of good and evil; and, with a full understanding of the consequences, he chose evil."

"Managers," replied Barnard, "have to make choices too; my concern was that they choose the good. The Grand Inquisitor believed that despotism was necessary for people to live worthy lives. However, I believe that my cooperative system fulfills the conditions better. It is the middle ground between unlimited freedom and unlimited despotism. In my philosophy, people and organizations can reach an accommodation where both can achieve their aims without damage to either. This is my idea of good, and it can be obtained if the managerial elite makes moderate and decent choices. Given these conditions, it is appropriate for leadership to be in the hands of a managerial class."

"Chester, Chester, Chester," sighed Dostoevsky, "your utopian conditions for achieving the good are impossible to meet; management is not the same thing as moral leadership."

"It is!"

"Not if you stop and think about it. Your ideal manager, if I understand correctly, is a decent, psychologically balanced, technically competent individual—right? How many managers in your country now fit this description?"

"Most of them—say, 90 percent."

"If this is the case, why aren't Americans more confident in their leadership? Why is there so much corruption in high places?"

"Probably because some managers still haven't mastered the skill of creating true cooperation among people, while a few others have been seduced by money and power."

"Nonsense! All that twaddle is good for is keeping human-relations consultants and ethicists employed."

"What are you suggesting, Fyodor?"

"Let's use Shigalev and the Grand Inquisitor as examples. Their actions were true to their ideals, and these ideals were selfless, in the sense that they were willing to sacrifice themselves for humanity. This is rather decent, don't you think?"

"Fyodor, you *are* a sophist!"

"On top of it, the Grand Inquisitor was a competent manager. The point is that Shigalev and the Grand Inquisitor were monstrous because their acts were based on perverse values. The reason Americans are not happy and confident, in spite of their material blessings, is because the people who lead them profess false values. Their good intentions will not provide the requisite conditions for others to lead worthy lives."

"Then what does it take, Fyodor, beyond repudiation of cooperation and organization?"

"I don't think that either can or should be repudiated. But I do believe that the moral virtues—such as beneficence, gratitude, veracity, and justice—can be practiced within organizations. I would argue that managers, and all people for that matter, sharpen their moral senses so that the virtues within them get in touch with the objective world outside of them. This is necessary for sound moral judgment and autonomous moral action."

"That's all quite noble, but how do you propose bringing about this sharpening of the moral senses?"

"Not by imposing rules on people, Chester, but rather by honing moral language through discourse, so that people can make informed moral choices."

"Can you give me an example?"

"What we are doing right now is an example of moral discourse. But, let me select another that is more pertinent to practical affairs—the rightness or wrongness of insider trading. One might say that it is right because it improves the efficiency of capital markets. This is not an insignificant argument, as it is derived from the virtue of beneficence. However, another might argue that it is wrong since it allows certain people to profit by privileged information. Again, an important argument, since it is based upon the virtue of justice."

"Your example indeed raises ethical problems, but I don't understand how it applies to people's moral senses."

"It is simple, Chester. Individuals alone could 'intuit' absolutely nothing from either one side of the argument or the other. My belief is that an individual's moral character can be improved only from discourse with others. It is not a matter of my buying your brand of ethics or your buying mine. It is more a case that wise conversation will hone our moral wit."

"This leaves you in a serious moral dilemma, Fyodor. Assume that you have two professors of moral philosophy who are both ardent Nazis. They can, as far as I can see, engage in moral discourse for days on end and all they will hone is their debating skills. At the end, they will still be Nazis. Perhaps you believe in a good Nazi character? However, I will leave you to struggle with that dilemma on your own time. Let me return to the matter of managers. Assume that I agree with you. Still, not everyone in management has the will or the wit to engage in such moral discourse."

"Sticking with the managerial argument, you are quite right, and that is why there must be an enclave of responsible and accountable intellectuals. They must have these conversations and then make them known to the population at large."

"So, Fyodor, you are now recommending a leadership by an intellectual elite. Why, are they less susceptible to corruption than the managerial class?"

"Because they do not have the power that comes from controlling vast resources, and because their deliberations—their words and ideas are public. They are not the final arbitrators of other people's choices. They merely ask the questions that set the tone for the public debate. It seems to me that this was the spirit behind *The Federalist Papers*."

"Not quite. The authors of those papers were not setting the tone for a debate, they were trying to win it! Be that as it may, I understand your general idea. So, let us assume that your enclave of moral philosophers convenes. Tell me, what is the first question that your group would—or should—ask?"

"What are the requisite conditions of a worthy life in modern organizations?"

Index

Academy of Management Review, 102
Administrative Behavior (Simon), 124
Alienation, 90–91
American Federation of Labor (A.F.L.), 57
American Revolution, 146, 150
Arendt, Hannah, 89
Attitudes, manipulation of, 98–101

Baritz, Loren, 25
Barnard, Chester I., 11, 21, 120, 123–124;
  criteria for promotion to significant jobs,
  137; on federalism, 173–174; on human
  motivation, 98–99, 101; on organiza-
  tional culture, 101–102; on organiza-
  tional morality, 33, 49; on organizational
  personality, 152; on professional jobs, 112;
  on worthy life, 182
Barzun, Jacques, 85, 87
Behavior, organizational, 30–33
Behavioral sciences, 83
Bendict, Ruth, 101
Bentham, Jeremy, 83
Boulding, Kenneth, 167–168
Brothers Karamazov, The (Dostoevsky), 182
Burnham, James, 21–22
Business administration, 122–124
Butler, Joseph, 172

Careerism, 151–152, 156
Carnegie, Andrew, 59
CEOs, 135–138
Clark, C. Spencer, 138
Cleveland, Harlan, 108, 119–120, 125
Community, 54–55, 163–165
Complexity, 138–139
Conformity, 51
Consensus, 39
Consumption, 72–74
Culture, organizational, 101–102

Delimitation, 169

Detroit, 14
Dewey, John, 7
Dispensibility, 52–54
Dostoevsky, Fyodor, 182
Drucker, Peter, 4, 115, 133
Due process, 174–175

Easton, David, 17
Education, vocational, 121–124
E. F. Hutton, 24
Eisenhower, Dwight D., 8
Elite, managerial, 5–6; circulation of, 140–
  141; mass support techniques, 78–80;
  shield of invisibility, 36–37. *See also* Sig-
  nificant people
Ellul, Jacques, 21–23, 28–29, 106, 107
Engineers and the Price System, The (Veb-
  len), 116
Environment, 15–17
Ergonomics, 99–100
Evil, 24
Exchange theory, 98–99
Expectations, 18–20
Expediency, 34–36
Externalism, 83–84

Factory, 90
Family of Men, The, 87, 89
Federalist Papers, 162
Federal model, 173–174
Forbes, 92, 136–137
Fortune 500, 92, 135–136
Founding Values, 5, 9, 24, 30, 47, 146–147,
  162–163, 165, 171–172, 176–178
Friendship, 170
Functional morality, 23–25
Fussell, Paul, 74
Future as History, The (Heilbroner), 15
Future Executive, The (Cleveland), 119–120

Gabriel, Richard, 29–30, 152

Galbraith, John Kenneth, 72–73, 114
Gompers, Samuel, 57
Gorbachev, Mikhail, 90, 150, 155, 161
Gulf Oil, 36–37

Halberstam, David, 151
Harvard Business Review, 121
Hawthorne studies, 100–101
Health, organizational, 33–34, 38
Heilbroner, Robert, 15, 28
Henderson, Lawrence, 100
Hierarchical obedience, 31
Hobbes, Thomas, 81
Hoover, Herbert, 133
House of Intellect, The (Barzun), 85
Human developmentalists, 117–118
Human Problems of an Industrial Civilization, The (Mayo), 48

Indispensability, 52–54
Individual imperative, 162; and community, 163–165; dialectic between individuals and society, 165–166; and governance and justice, 173–175; and moral discourse, 175–178; and organizational size, 167–169; organizations of, 166–167; and social enclaves, 169–173
Individualism, 27–28, 50–52, 84
Industrial psychology, 99–100
Information, 130
Inouye, Daniel, Sen., 142
In Search of Excellence (Peters & Waterman), 102
Insignificant people, 71, 152–153; strategies for mass domination of, 77–80, 77–93; tactics for mass domination of, 97–108
Integrative propaganda, 106–108
Intellect, 85–88
Intelligence, 85–86
Invisible people, 72, 74–75

Jefferson, Thomas, 176–177
Job, modern, 91–93
Job, professional, 111–113
Job, significant, 129–131
Jouvenel, Bertrand de, 146

Kant, Immanuel, 102–103
Keegan, John, 106
Kennedy, John F., 13–14, 45

Kittrie, Nicholas N., 59
Koch, Adrienne, 176–177
Kohr, Leopold, 168

Labor, 88–90
Language, manipulation of, 107–108
Lasch, Christopher, 9–10
Lasswell, Harold D., 77
Leadership, 14–15, 23–25, 29–30, 123–124
Legitimacy, 20–23, 30–31
Leisure time, 72–74
L'Evy, Barnard Henri, 176
Lewis, Sinclair, 66
Lincoln, Abraham, 161
Line management, 114
Lipset, Seymour Martin, 19, 138–140
Locke, John, 81
Loyalty, 125–126

Machiavelli, Niccolo, 46–47
McKibben, Lawrence E., 123, 125
Madison, James, 162
Malleability, human, 48–50
Management Initiated Grievance Systems (MIGS), 175
Management theory, 34–36
Managerial code, 113, 115–116
Managerial escalation, 118–119
Managerial Revolution, The (Burnham), 21
Managers, professional, 3–6
Manipulation, 97–104
Marx, Karl, 153
Maslow, Abraham, 117
Mass domination: and innate moral nature, 82–85; and insignificance, 80–82; integrative propaganda tactic, 106–108; and intellect, 85–88; manipulation tactics, 97–104; preemptive control tactic, 104–106; and "weenie syndrome," 77–80; and work, 88–93
Masters, The (Snow), 163–165, 166, 169
Mayo, Elton, 48–49, 100
Mencken, H. L., 160
Men of system, 132–138
Michels, Robert, 20–22
Milgram, Stanley, 51
Mill, John Stuart, 50
Mintzberg, Henry, 174
Modern job, 91–93
Moral discourse, 175–178

Moral drift, 141–142, 145–150
Moral intentionality, 6–8
Morality: failure of, 10–11; functional, 23–25; innate moral nature, 46–48, 82–85, 103
Moral obligation, 171–173
Motivation theories, 98–101
Munsterberg, Hugo, 100
Myths, 101

National managerial system, 3
Newcomer, Mabel, 135
New York Times, 19
Niebuhr, Reinhold, 2
Nisbet, Robert, 9
Nixon, Richard, 80
Norton, David, 11, 66, 165–166, 170

Obedience, 50–52; hierarchical, 31
Office, 90
Office of Management and Budget (OMB), 130–131
OPEC embargo, 14, 36
Operations analysis, 124
Organ, Dennis W., 51
Organizational determinism, 6–8
Organizational imperative, 3, 37–40, 159–162; reform of, 150–157; rules for behavior, 30–33; value changes under, 43–62; vulnerability of, 10–11
Organizational size, 167–169
Organization Man, The (Whyte), 11, 44
Orwell, George, 107

Pareto, Vilfredo, 140
Participatory management, 90–91
Pateman, Carole, 90–91
Paternalism, 58–60
Paton, Alan, 2
Permanence, 170
Peters, T. J., 102
Philosophers, 7
Planning, 56–57
Plato, 151
Platt, John, 29
Popper, Karl, 24
Porter, Lyman W., 123, 125
Possessed, The (Dostoevsky), 182–183
Poverty, 74–75
Power, 77, 146, 171, 175

Practicality, 18
Practice of Management, The (Drucker), 115
Pragmatism, 32–33
Pranger, Robert, 171
Preemptive control, 104–106
Production unit, 71
Professional people, 70–71; and loyalty, 116–126; as occupants of professional jobs, 111–113; and professional obligation, 113–116; and reform of organizations, 153–157
Propaganda, integrative, 106–108

Ramos, A. G., 169
Rationality, 31–32
Rawls, John, 172
Reagan, Ronald, 10
Reedy, George, 146, 151
Riesman, David, 50
Roles, organizational, 65–67; mega–roles, 67–70; off–the job, 72–74; on–the–job, 70–72; out–of–organization, 74–75

Salinger, Nicole, 114
Savage, Paul, 29–30, 152
Schaar, John, H., 30, 31
Schneider, William, 19, 138–140
Scott, William G., 120–121
Self–actualization, 117
Self–concept, 81–82
Self–sufficiency, 16
Significant people, 70–71, 150–152; crisis at organizational top, 138–141; men of system, 132–138; and moral drift, 141–142, 145–150; significant jobs, 129–131. *See also* Elite, managerial
Simmel, George, 65–66
Simon, Herbert, 33, 98–99, 101, 102, 124
Skinner, B. F., 84–85
Smith, Adam, 132, 176
Snow, C. P., 29, 132, 163–165, 173
Social enclaves, 169–173
Socially approved occupation, 72
Soviet Union, 155, 161
Specialization, 54–55
Spontaneity, 56–57
Standard of living, 16
Stewardship, 32, 139–140
Symbolism, 101

Tannenbaum, A. S., 91

Taylor, Frederick W., 35, 39
Technical code, 113, 116
Technology, 28–30, 73–74
Thayer, Frederick, 74
Thompson, James, 111
Time, 125, 140
Time crunch, 17
Tocqueville, Alexis de, 1, 50
Toffler, Alvin, 72
Torrey, E. Fuller, 59
Totalitarianism, 97, 147–150
Turner, Frederick Jackson, 52

Universal behavioral techniques, 3
Utility theory, 99

Value system, 27–28, 43–45, 146

Veblen, Thorstein, 111, 114, 116, 126, 154
Virtue, 24
Vocational education, 121–124
Voluntarism, 57–58, 156

Waldo, Dwight, 3
Watergate, 14, 80
Waterman, R. H., 102
"Weenie syndrome," 77–80
West Germany, 175
Whyte, William H. Jr., 11, 44, 126
Wicker, Tom, 74
Wilson, Charles, 131
Wilson, Woodrow, 132–133
Wolin, Sheldon S., 119
Work, 88–93, 170
Worthy life, 181–192